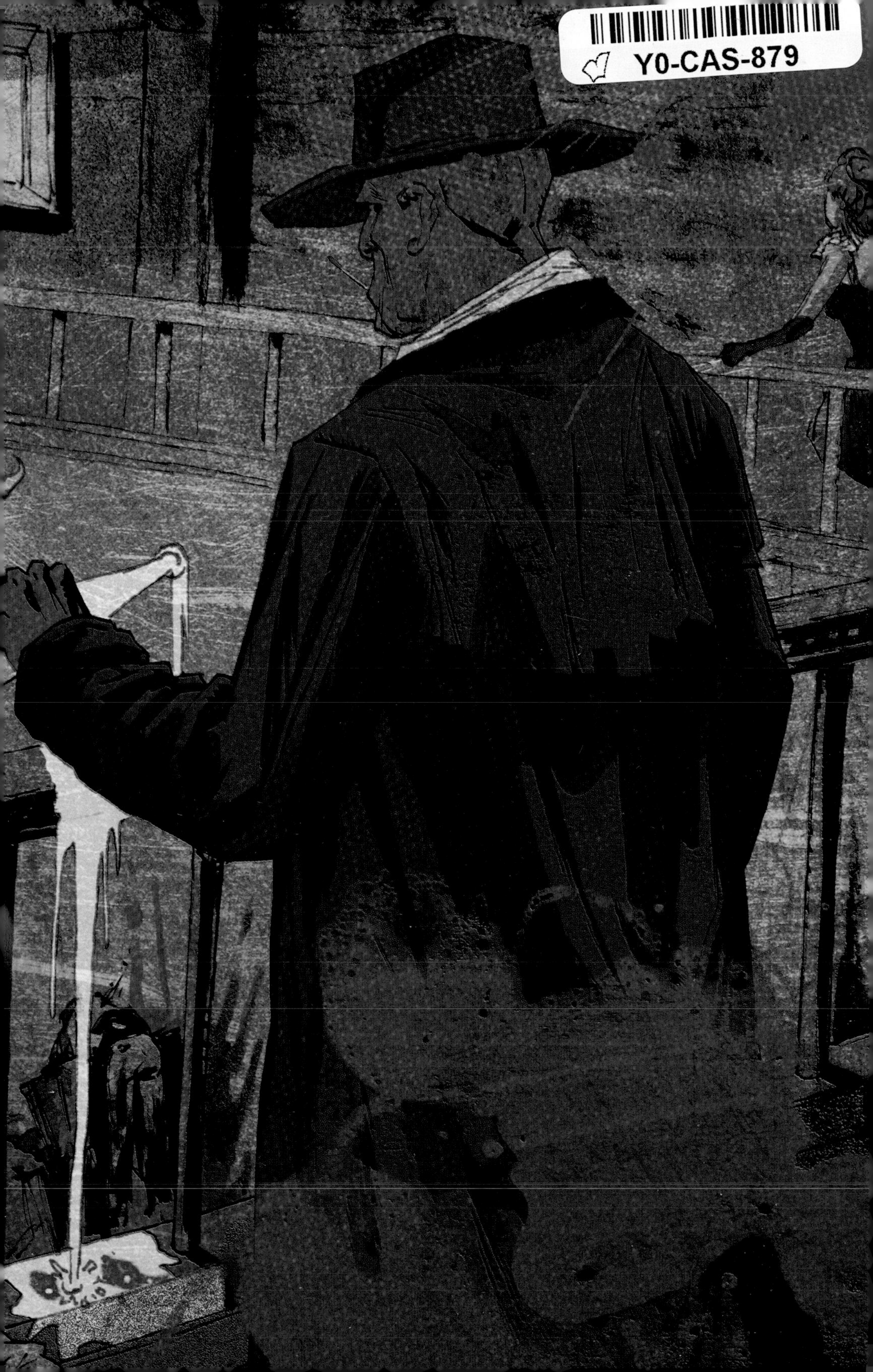

PALE HORSE

Ross Richie - Chief Executive Officer
Mark Waid - Chief Creative Officer
Matt Gagnon - Editor-in-Chief
Adam Fortier - VP-New Business
Wes Harris - VP-Publishing
Lance Kreiter - VP-Licensing & Merchandising
Chip Mosher - Marketing Director
Bryce Carlson - Managing Editor

Ian Brill - Editor
Dafna Pleban - Editor
Christopher Burns - Editor
Christopher Meyer - Editor
Shannon Watters - Assistant Editor
Eric Harburn - Assistant Editor
Adam Staffaroni - Assistant Editor

Neil Loughrie - Publishing Coordinator
Brian Latimer - Lead Graphic Designer
Erika Terriquez - Graphic Designer
Travis Beaty - Traffic Coordinator
Ivan Salazar - Marketing Assistant
Kate Hayden - Executive Assistant

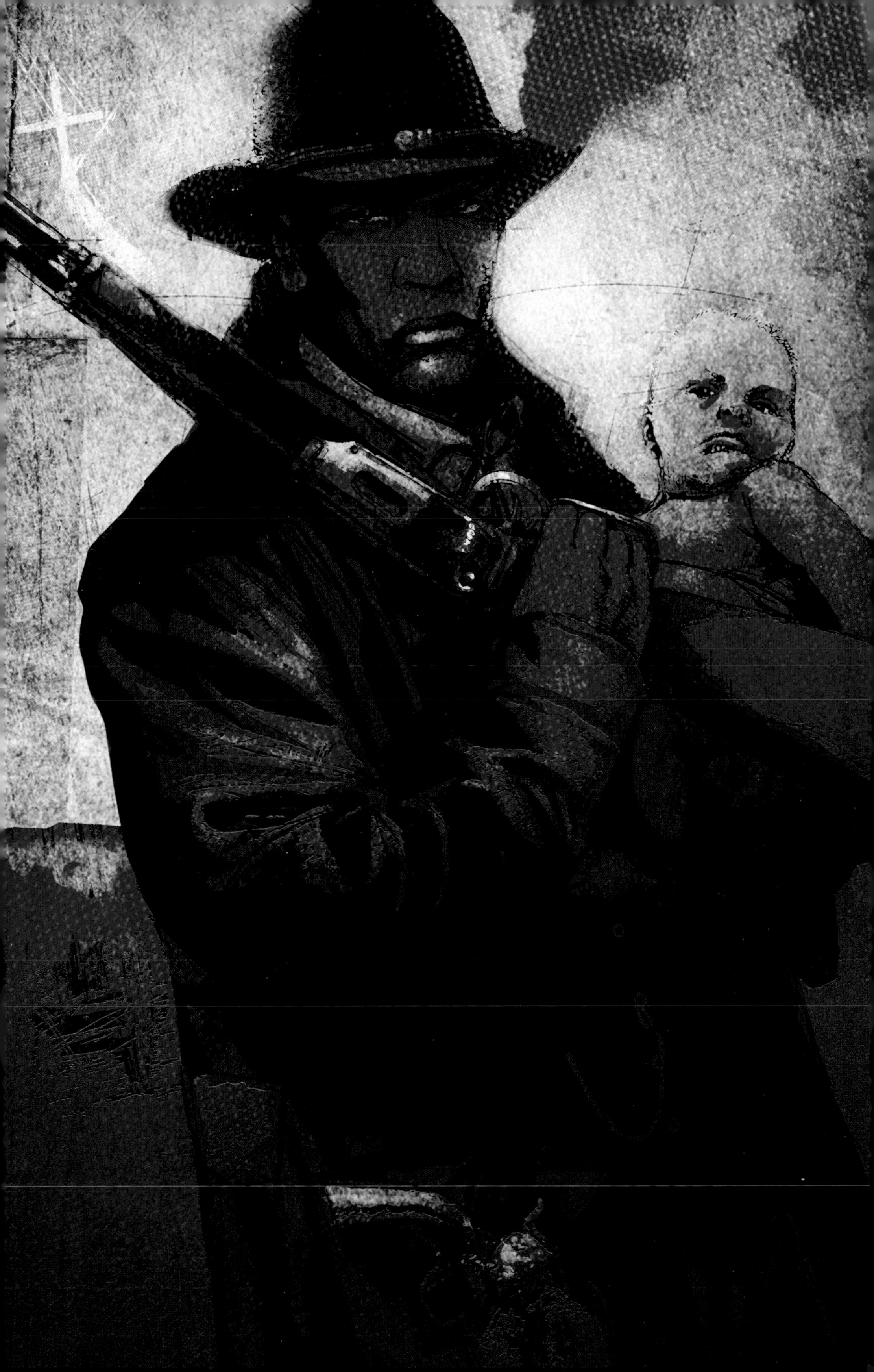

story by **ANDREW COSBY**
written by **MICHAEL ALAN NELSON**
drawn by **CHRISTIAN DIBARI**
colorist **ANDRES LOZANO**
assistant **JAVIER SUPPA**
letterer **JOHNNY LOWE**

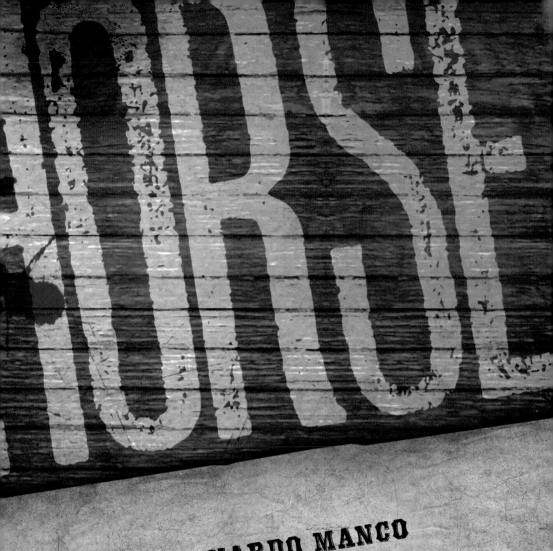

cover **LEONARDO MANCO**

colors by **NICK FILARDI**

editor **DAFNA PLEBAN**

trade designer **STEPHANIE GONZAGA**

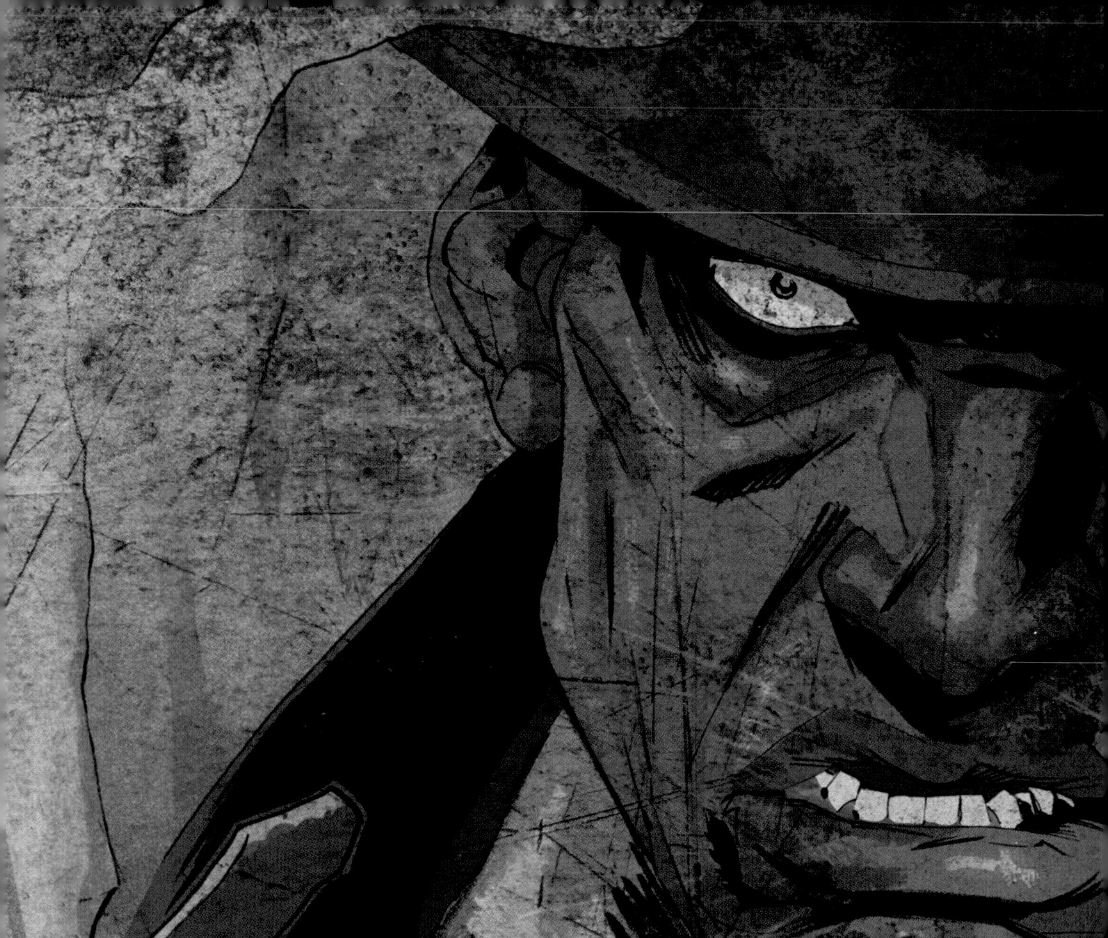

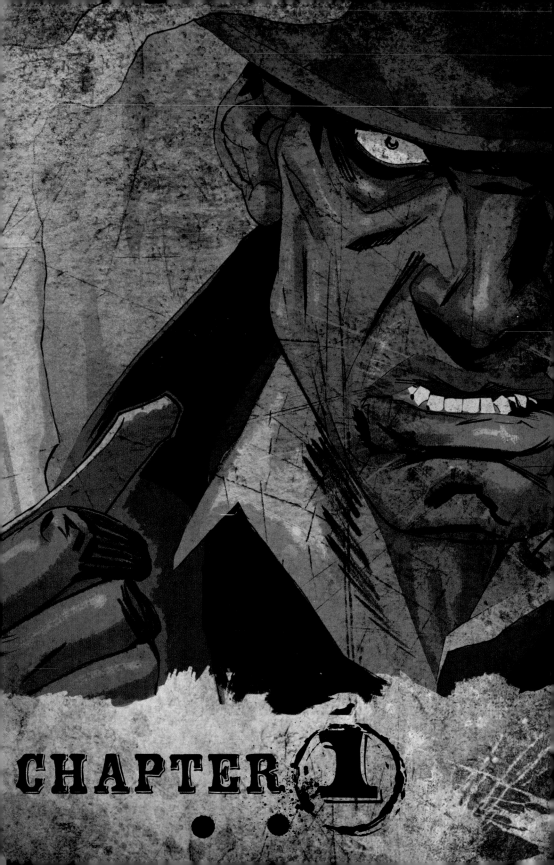

CHAPTER 1

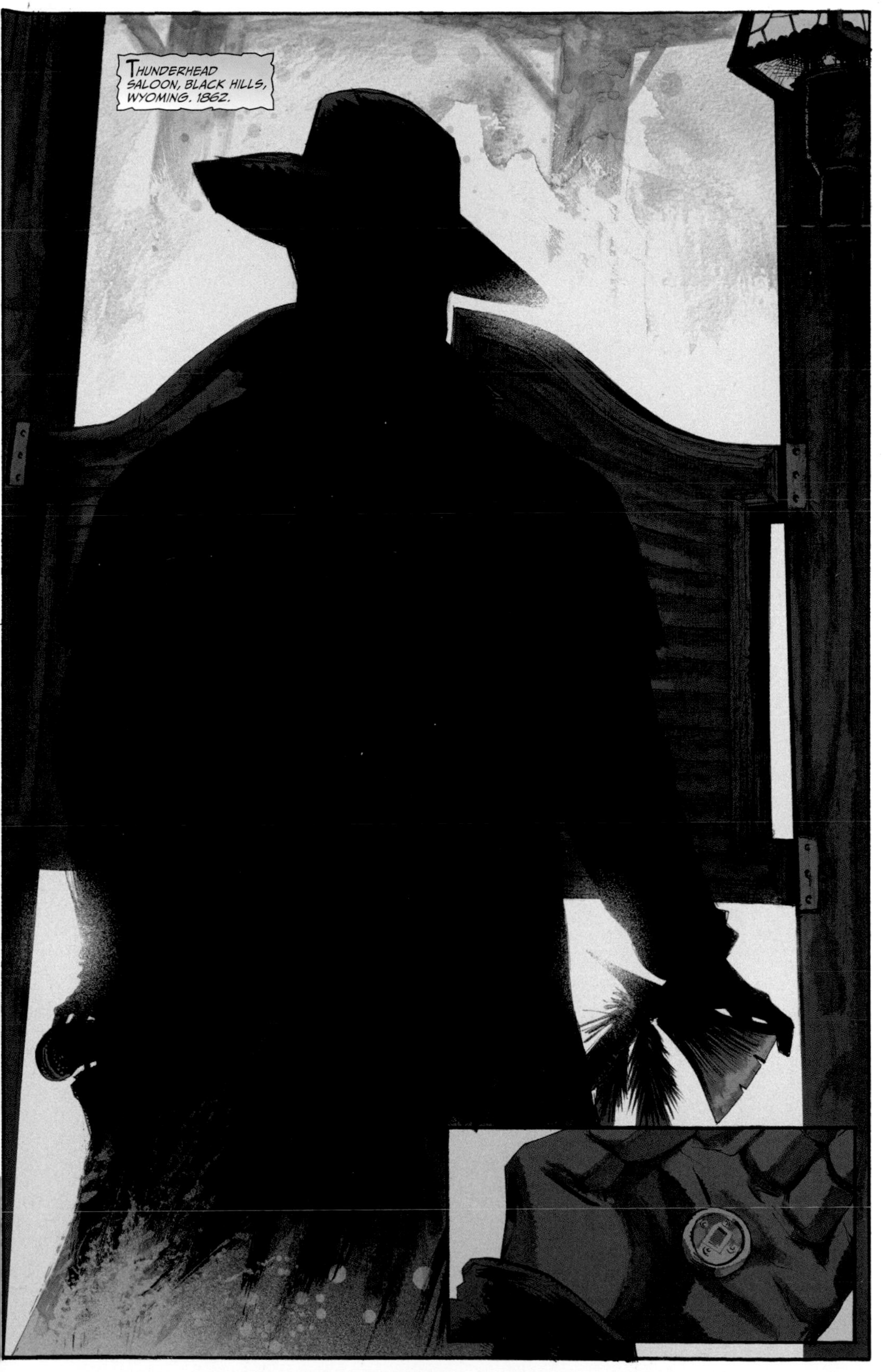
THUNDERHEAD SALOON, BLACK HILLS, WYOMING. 1862.

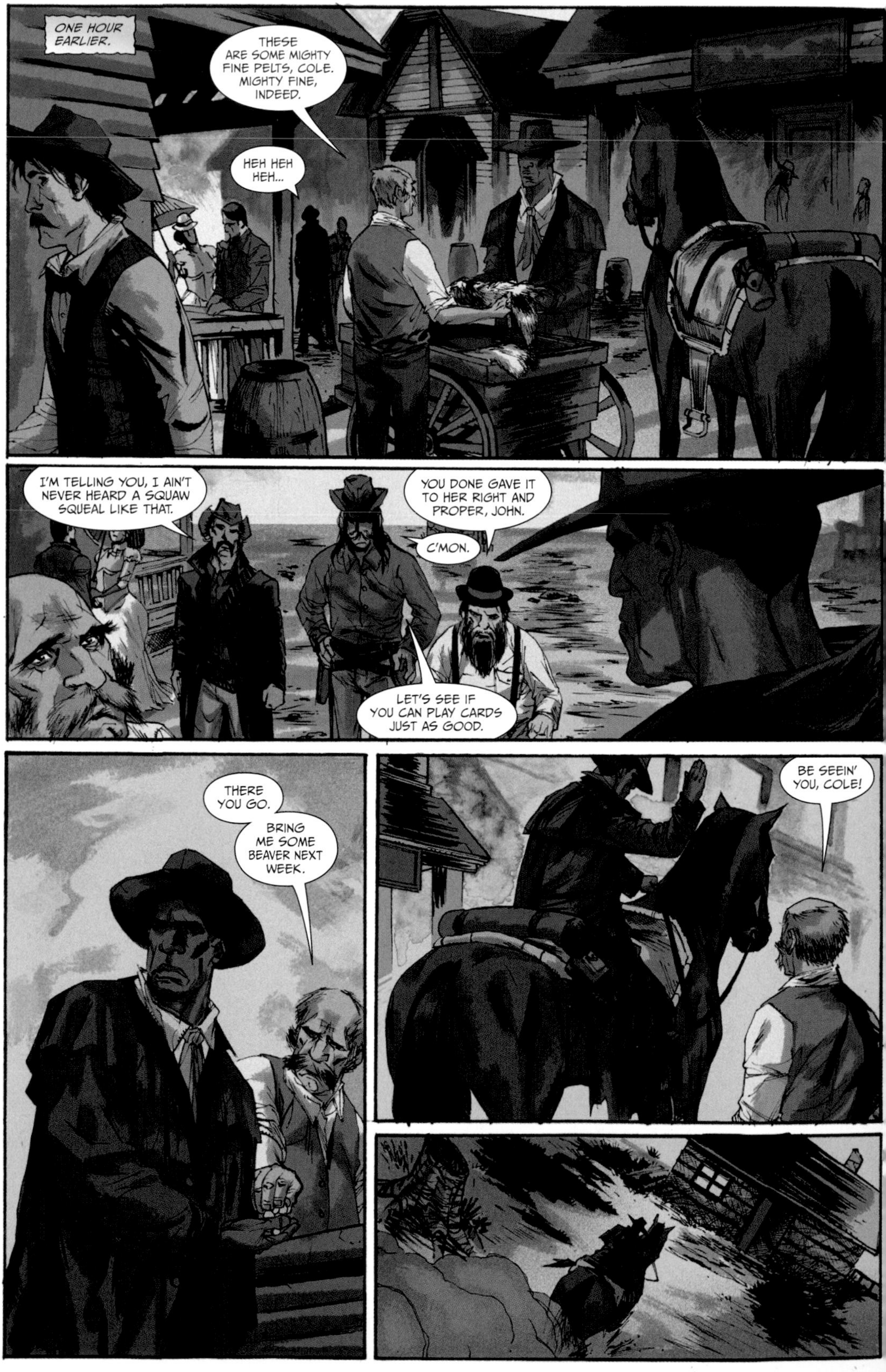
ONE HOUR EARLIER.
THESE ARE SOME MIGHTY FINE PELTS, COLE. MIGHTY FINE, INDEED.
HEH HEH HEH...
I'M TELLING YOU, I AIN'T NEVER HEARD A SQUAW SQUEAL LIKE THAT.
YOU DONE GAVE IT TO HER RIGHT AND PROPER, JOHN.
C'MON.
LET'S SEE IF YOU CAN PLAY CARDS JUST AS GOOD.
THERE YOU GO.
BRING ME SOME BEAVER NEXT WEEK.
BE SEEIN' YOU, COLE!

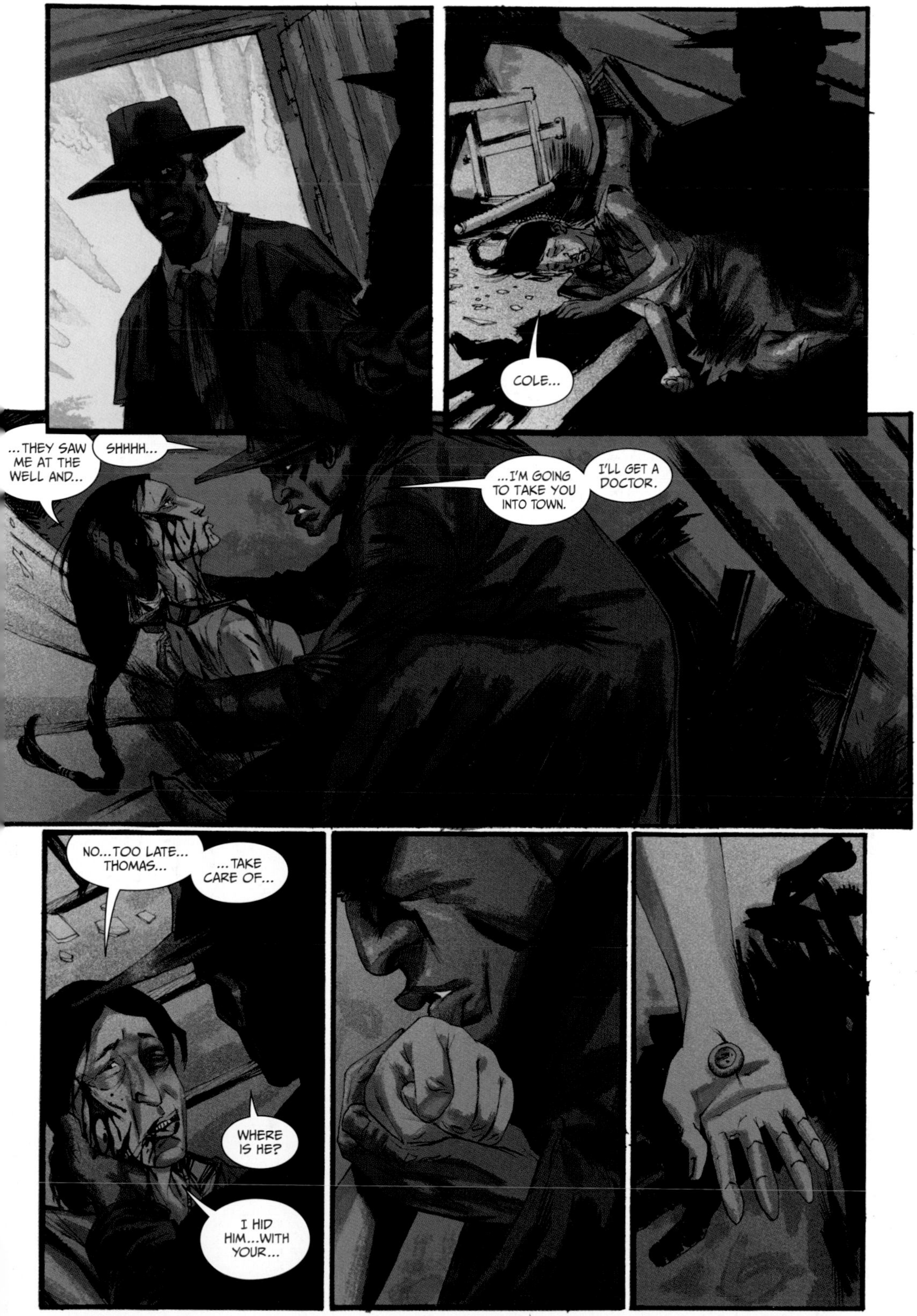
COLE...
...THEY SAW ME AT THE WELL AND...
SHHHH...
...I'M GOING TO TAKE YOU INTO TOWN.
I'LL GET A DOCTOR.
NO...TOO LATE... THOMAS...
...TAKE CARE OF...
WHERE IS HE?
I HID HIM...WITH YOUR...

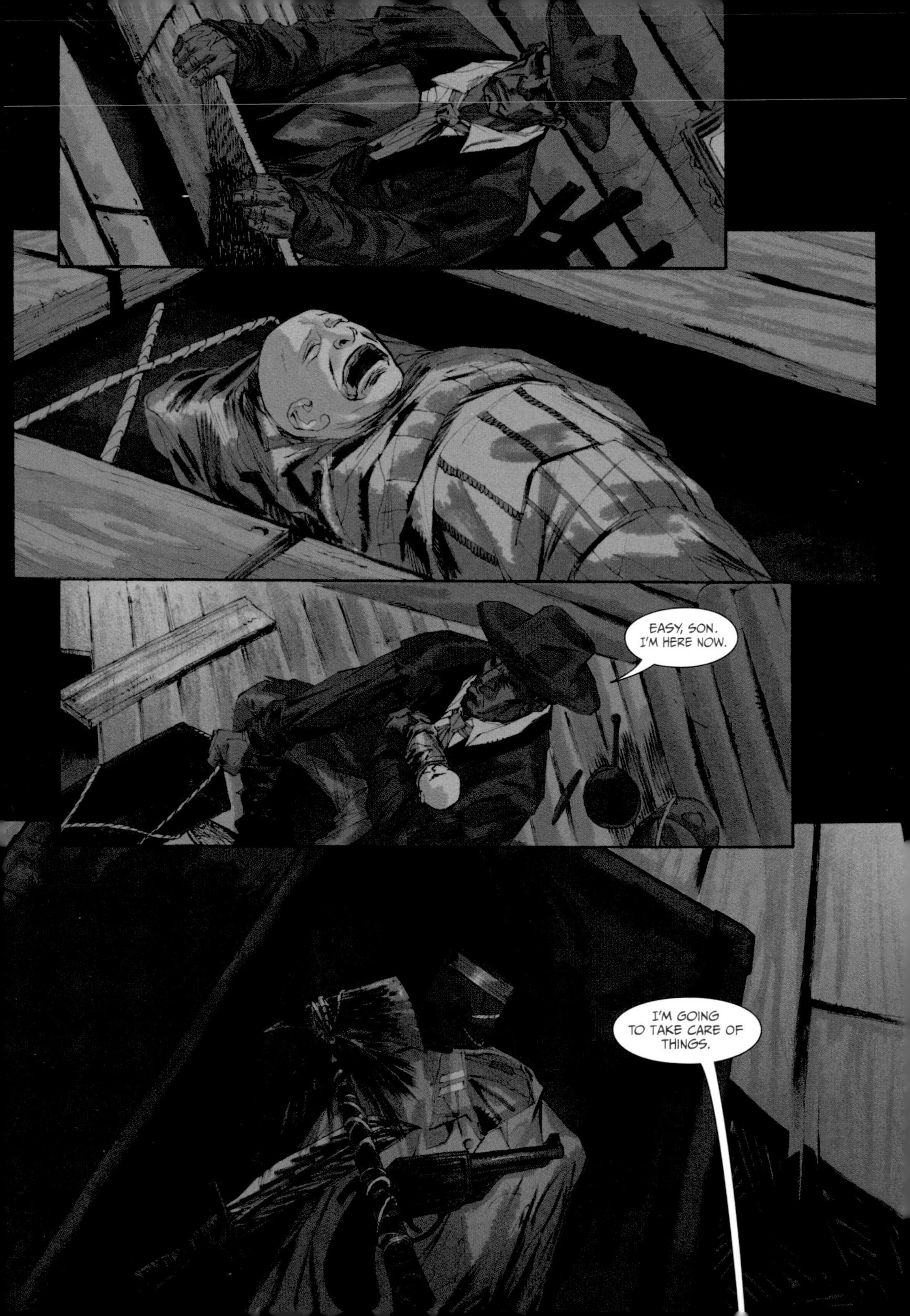
EASY, SON.
I'M HERE NOW.
I'M GOING
TO TAKE CARE OF
THINGS.

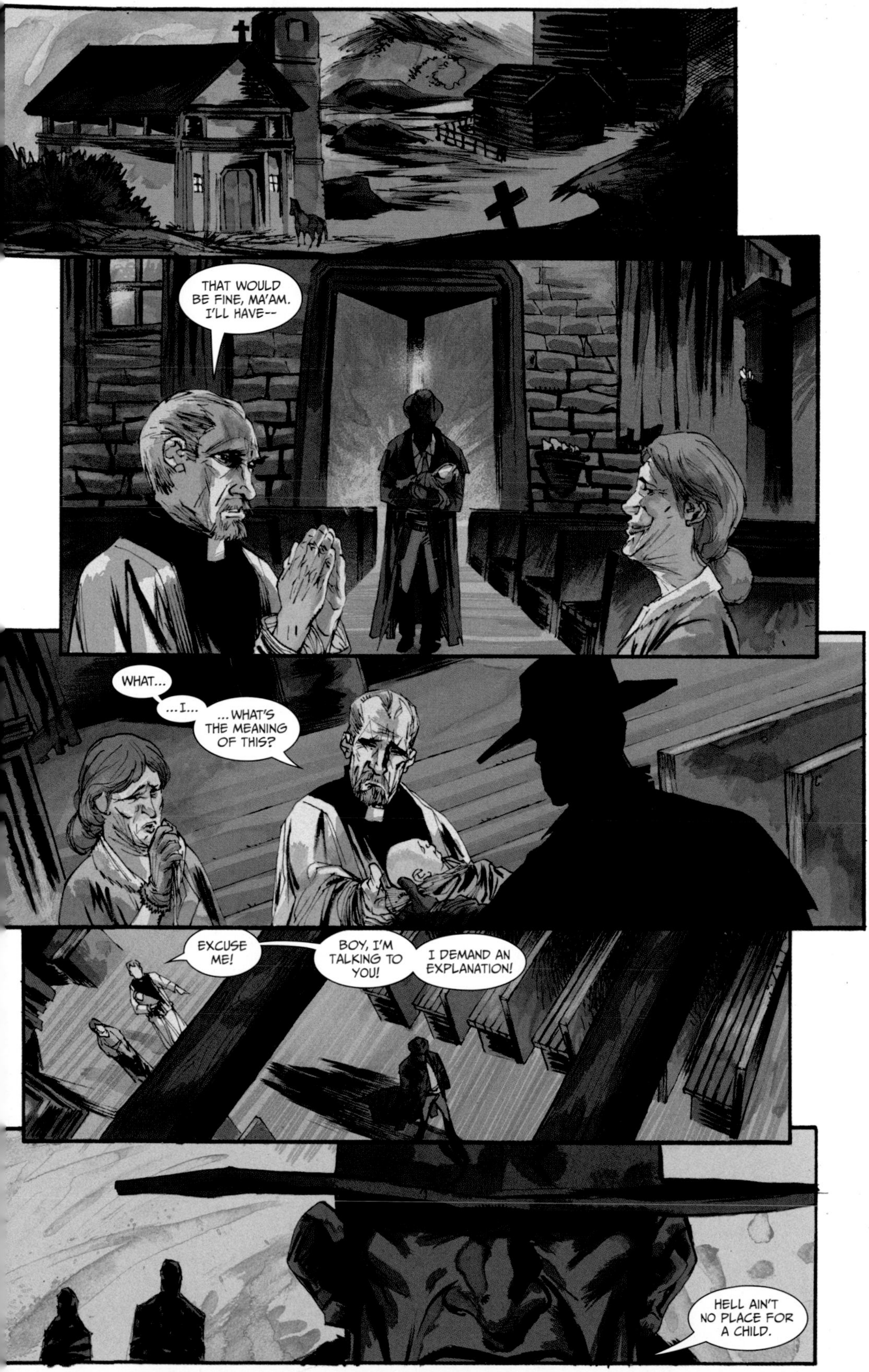
THAT WOULD BE FINE, MA'AM. I'LL HAVE--
WHAT...
...I...
...WHAT'S THE MEANING OF THIS?
EXCUSE ME!
BOY, I'M TALKING TO YOU!
I DEMAND AN EXPLANATION!
HELL AIN'T NO PLACE FOR A CHILD.

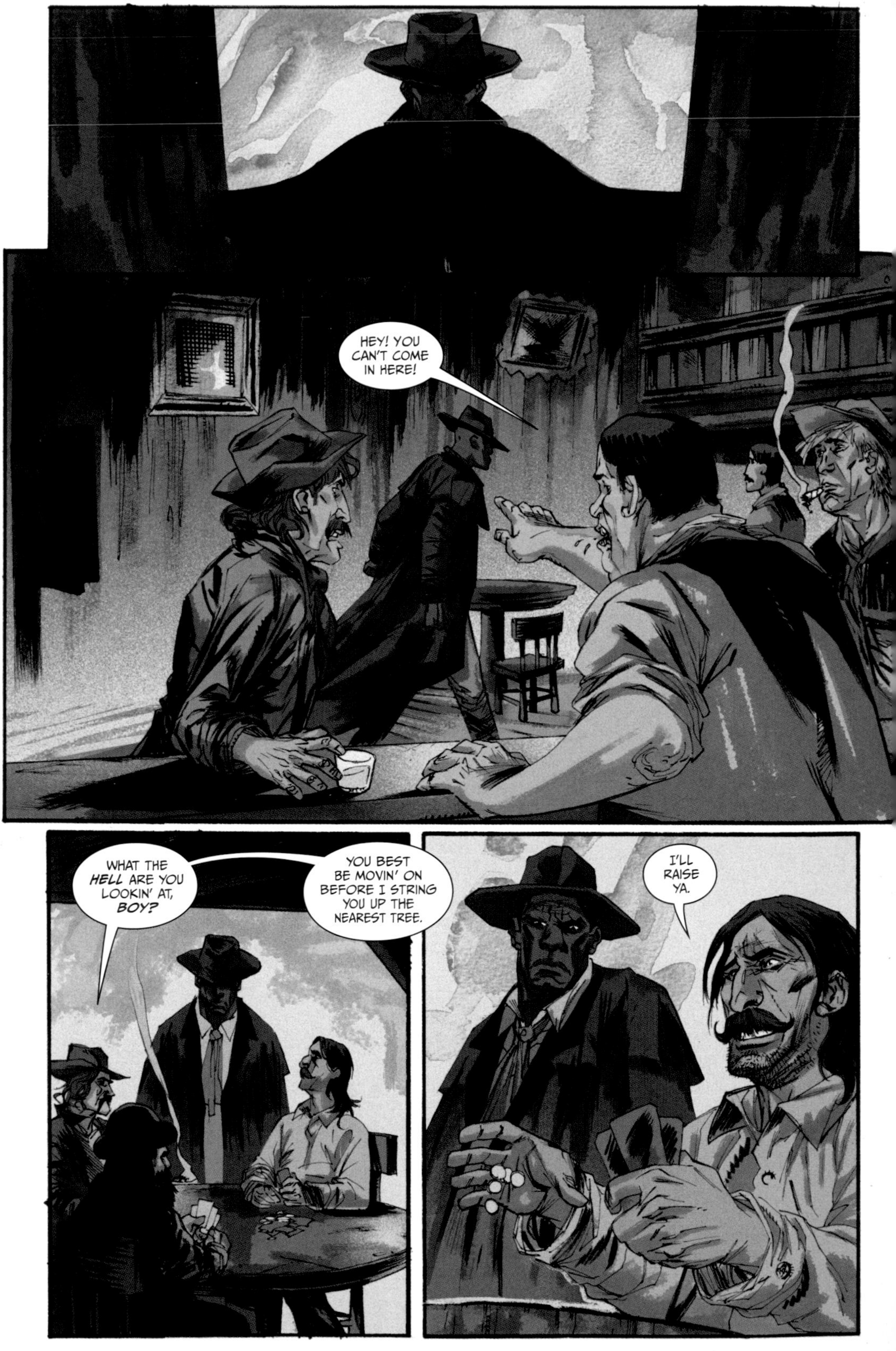
HEY! YOU CAN'T COME IN HERE!
WHAT THE *HELL* ARE YOU LOOKIN' AT, *BOY?*
YOU BEST BE MOVIN' ON BEFORE I STRING YOU UP THE NEAREST TREE.
I'LL RAISE YA.

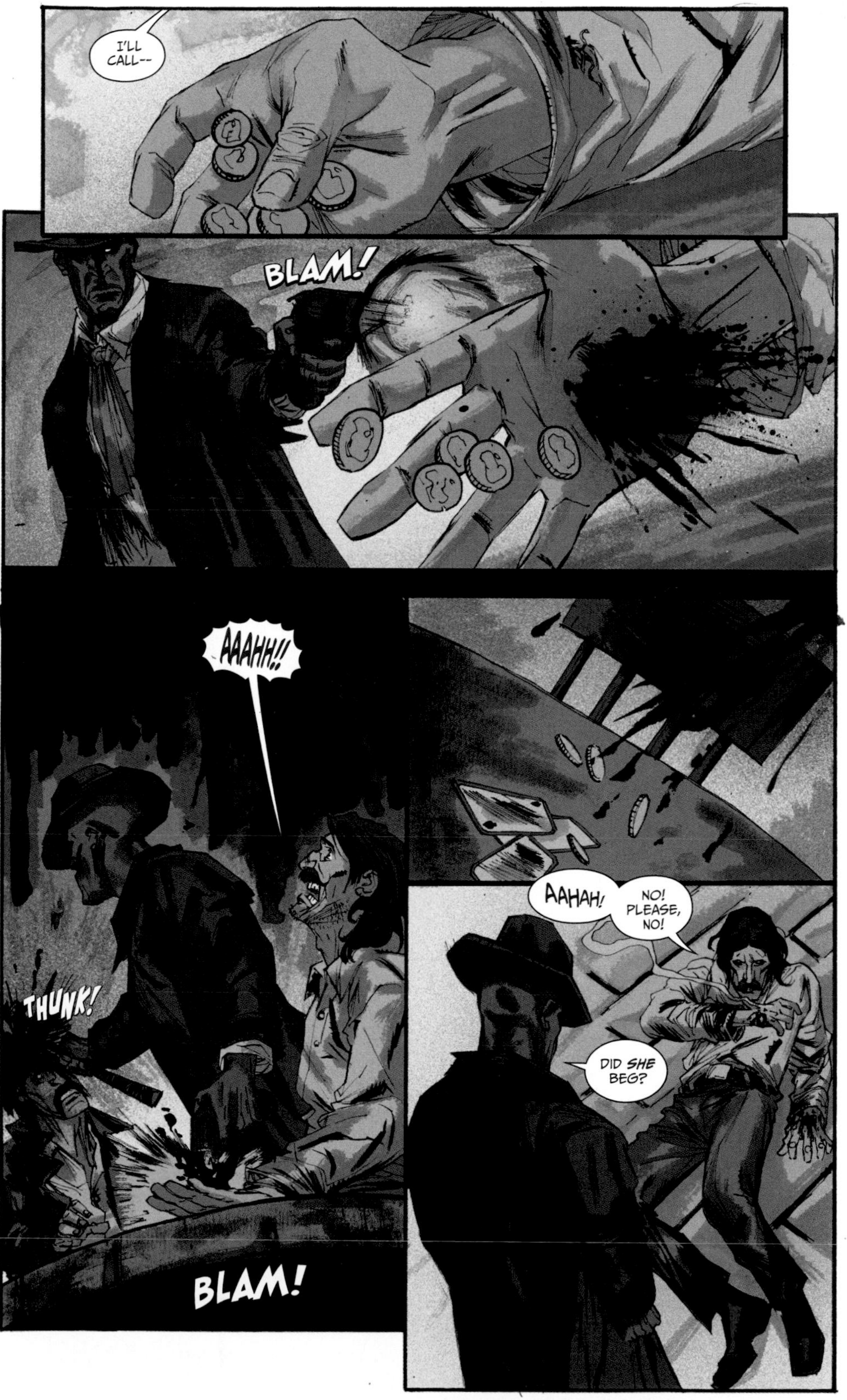
I'LL CALL--
BLAM!
AAAHH!!
THUNK!
BLAM!
AAHAH!
NO! PLEASE, NO!
DID SHE BEG?

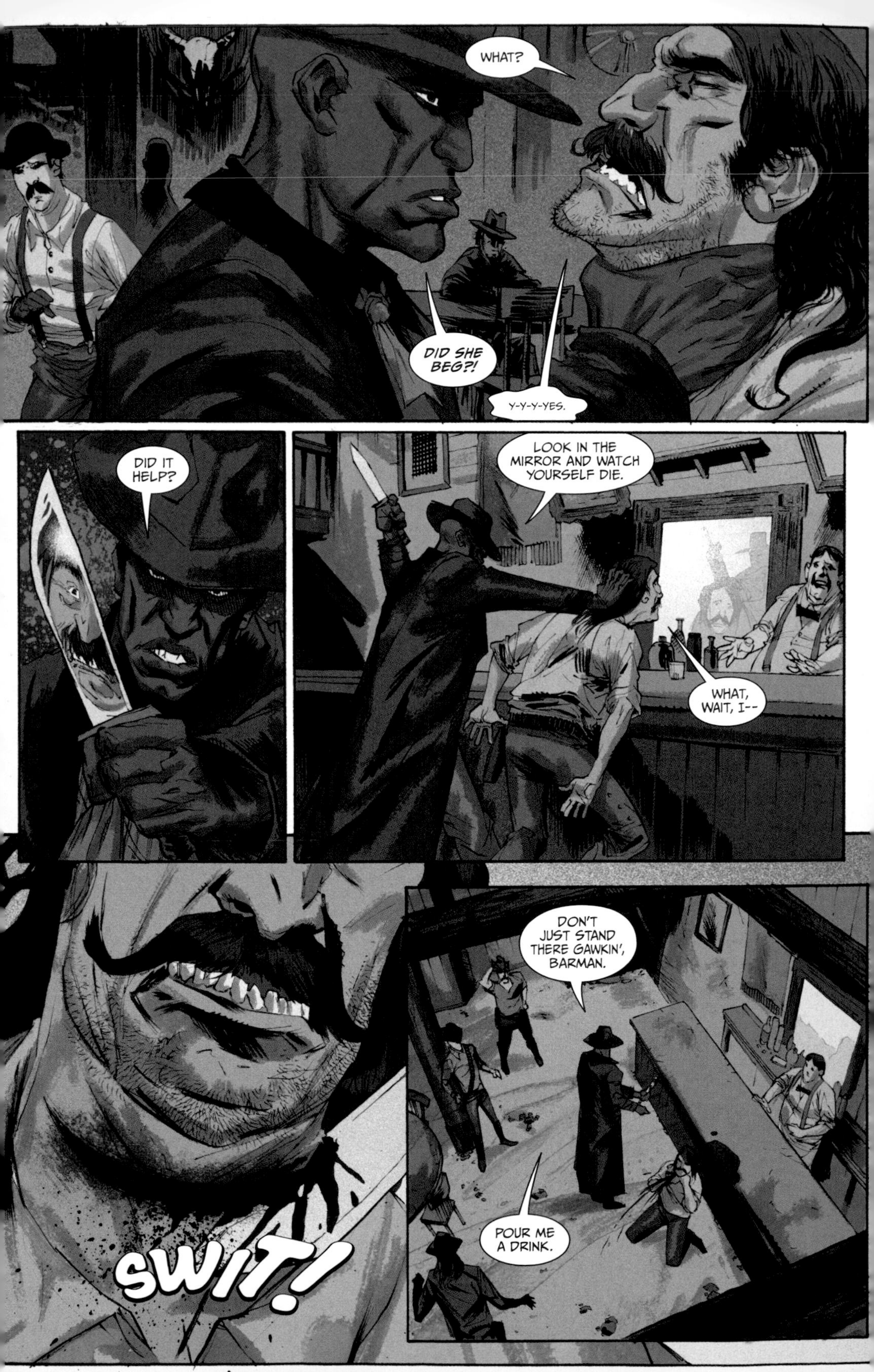
WHAT?
DID SHE BEG?!
Y-Y-Y-YES.
DID IT HELP?
LOOK IN THE MIRROR AND WATCH YOURSELF DIE.
WHAT, WAIT, I--
SWIT!
DON'T JUST STAND THERE GAWKIN', BARMAN.
POUR ME A DRINK.

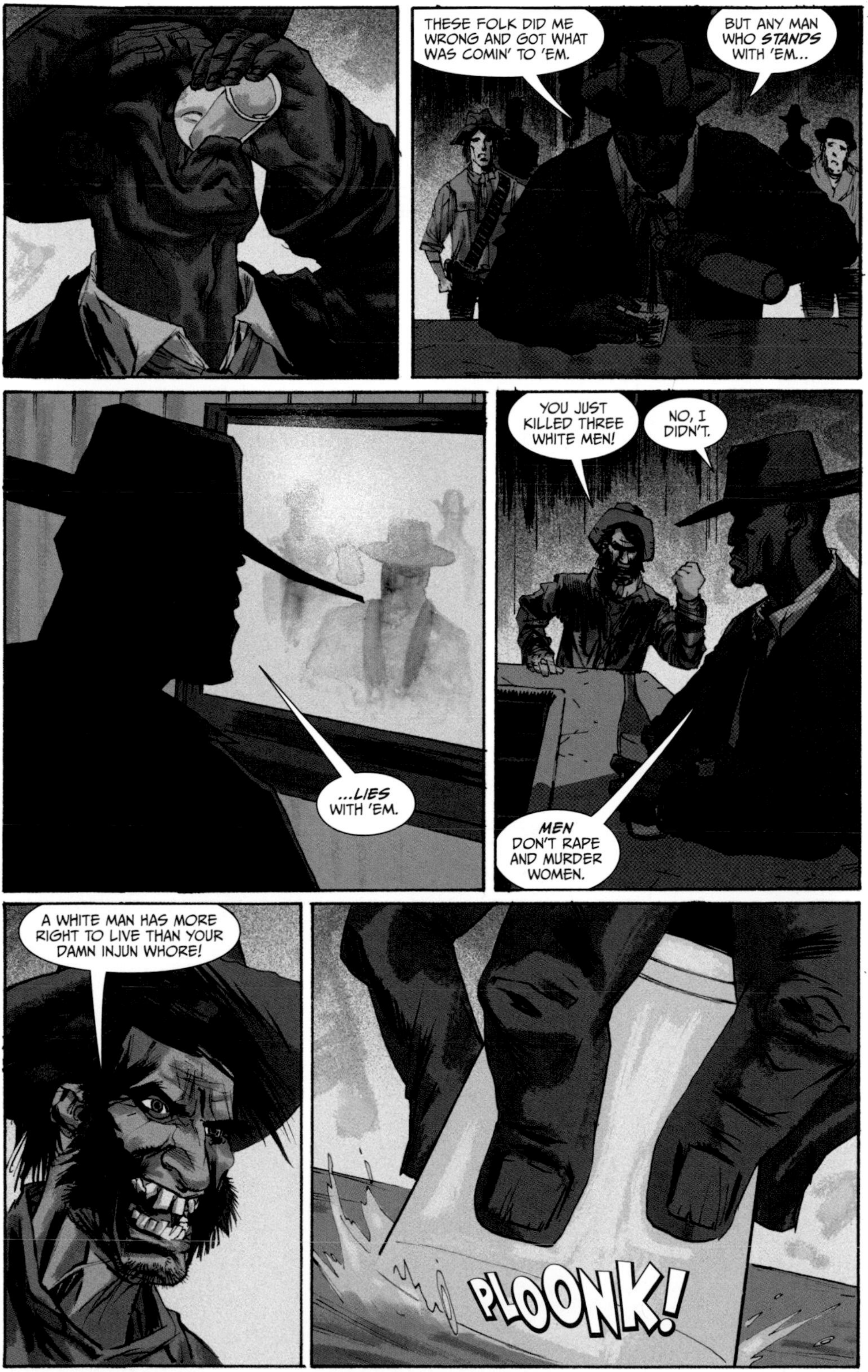
THESE FOLK DID ME WRONG AND GOT WHAT WAS COMIN' TO 'EM.
BUT ANY MAN WHO STANDS WITH 'EM...
...LIES WITH 'EM.
YOU JUST KILLED THREE WHITE MEN!
NO, I DIDN'T.
MEN DON'T RAPE AND MURDER WOMEN.
A WHITE MAN HAS MORE RIGHT TO LIVE THAN YOUR DAMN INJUN WHORE!
PLOONK!

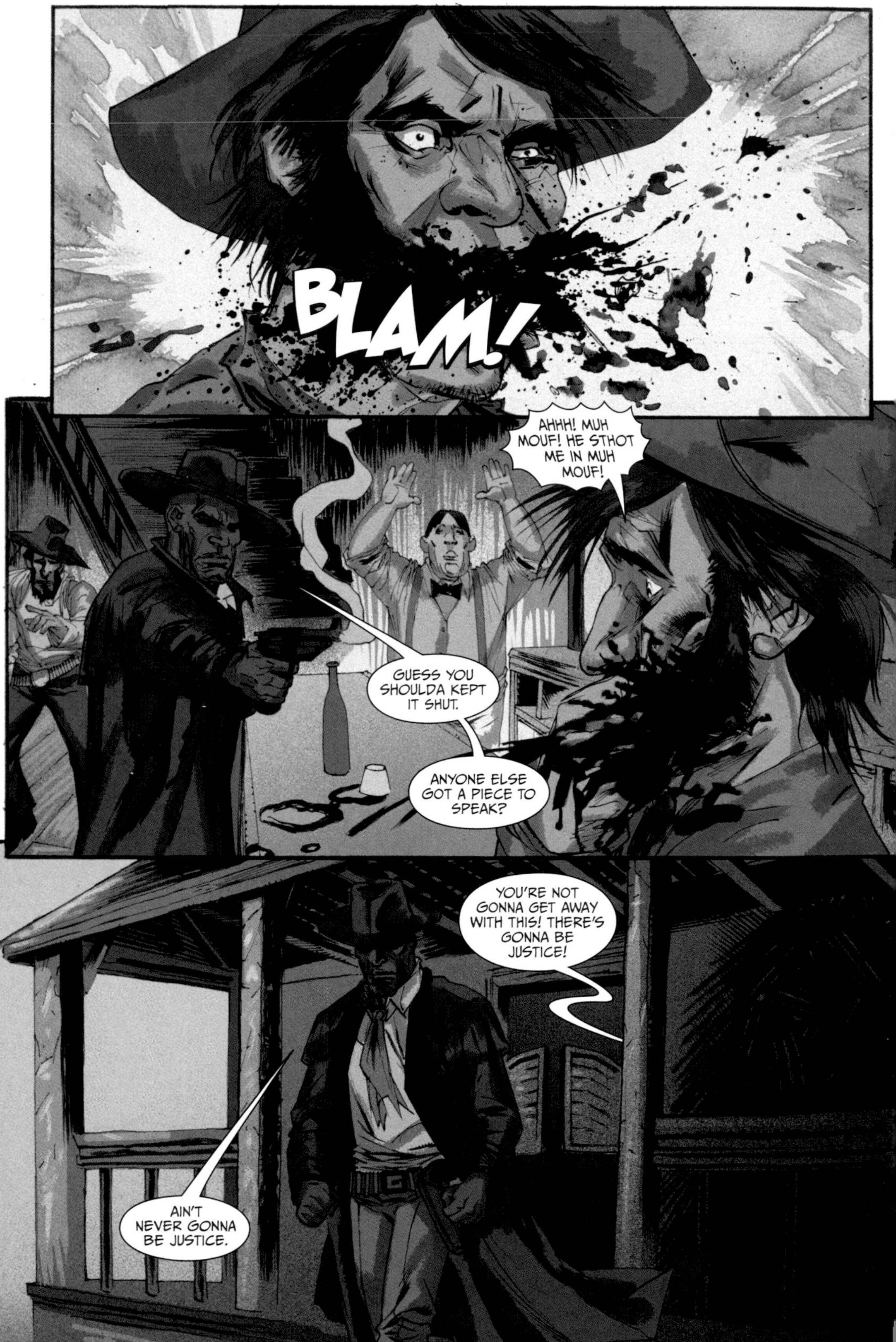
BLAM!
AHHH! MUH MOUF! HE STHOT ME IN MUH MOUF!
GUESS YOU SHOULDA KEPT IT SHUT.
ANYONE ELSE GOT A PIECE TO SPEAK?
YOU'RE NOT GONNA GET AWAY WITH THIS! THERE'S GONNA BE JUSTICE!
AIN'T NEVER GONNA BE JUSTICE.

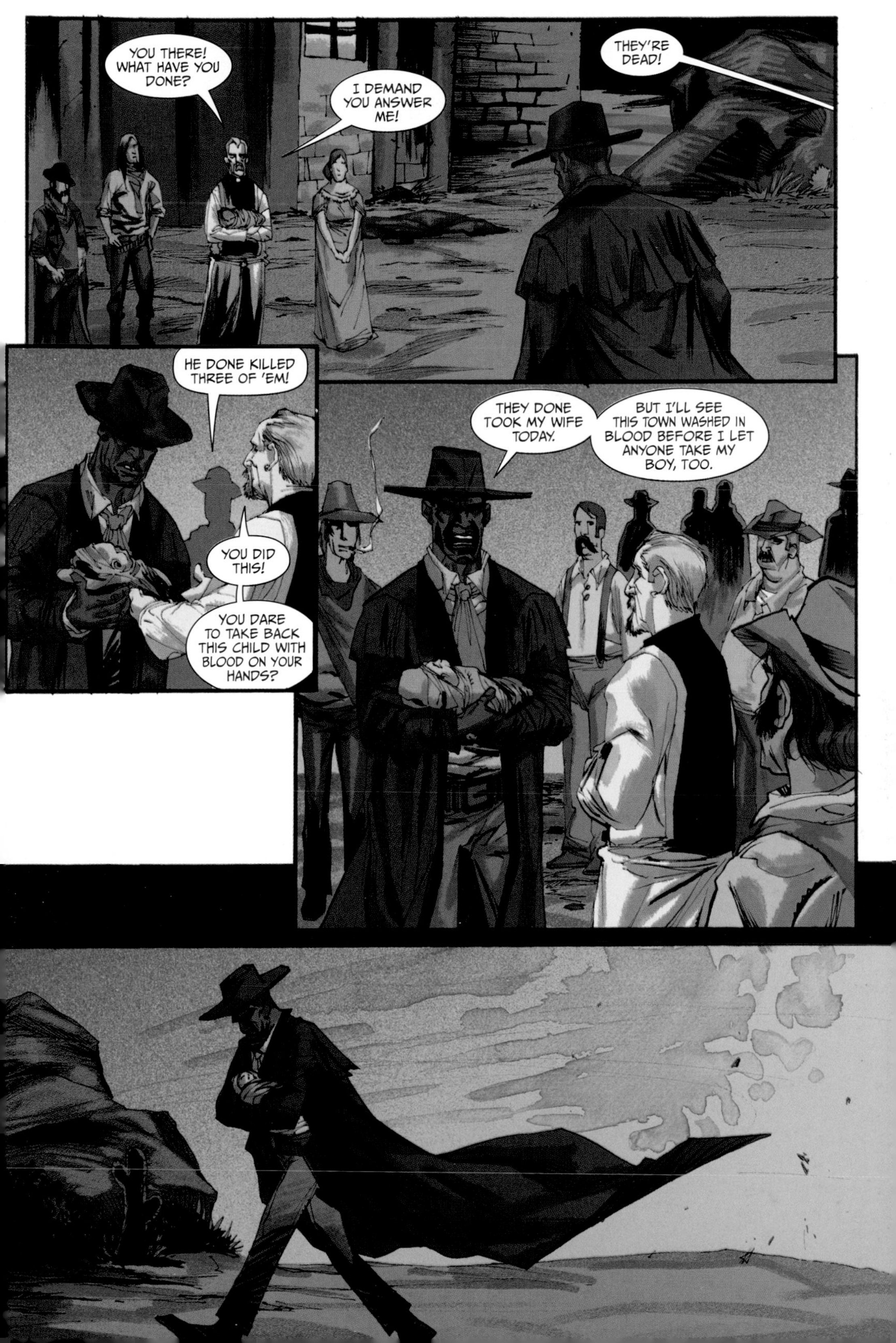
YOU THERE! WHAT HAVE YOU DONE?
I DEMAND YOU ANSWER ME!
THEY'RE DEAD!
HE DONE KILLED THREE OF 'EM!
YOU DID THIS!
YOU DARE TO TAKE BACK THIS CHILD WITH BLOOD ON YOUR HANDS?
THEY DONE TOOK MY WIFE TODAY.
BUT I'LL SEE THIS TOWN WASHED IN BLOOD BEFORE I LET ANYONE TAKE MY BOY, TOO.

THREE YEARS LATER...
WANTED
YOU HERE TO COLLECT THE BOUNTY?

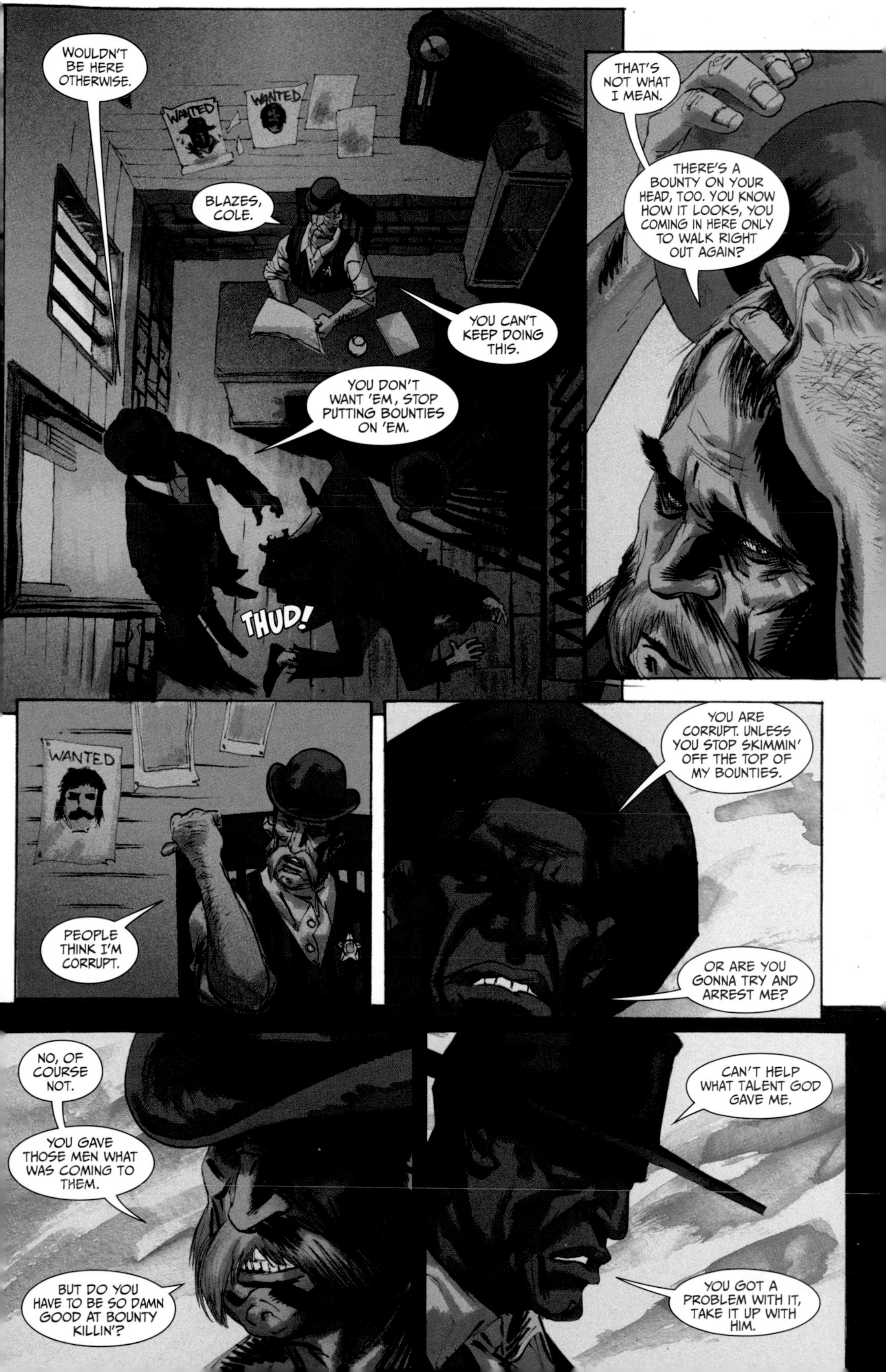

WOULDN'T BE HERE OTHERWISE.
BLAZES, COLE.
YOU CAN'T KEEP DOING THIS.
YOU DON'T WANT 'EM, STOP PUTTING BOUNTIES ON 'EM.
THUD!
THAT'S NOT WHAT I MEAN.
THERE'S A BOUNTY ON YOUR HEAD, TOO. YOU KNOW HOW IT LOOKS, YOU COMING IN HERE ONLY TO WALK RIGHT OUT AGAIN?
WANTED
PEOPLE THINK I'M CORRUPT.
YOU ARE CORRUPT. UNLESS YOU STOP SKIMMIN' OFF THE TOP OF MY BOUNTIES.
OR ARE YOU GONNA TRY AND ARREST ME?
NO, OF COURSE NOT.
YOU GAVE THOSE MEN WHAT WAS COMING TO THEM.
BUT DO YOU HAVE TO BE SO DAMN GOOD AT BOUNTY KILLIN'?
CAN'T HELP WHAT TALENT GOD GAVE ME.
YOU GOT A PROBLEM WITH IT, TAKE IT UP WITH HIM.

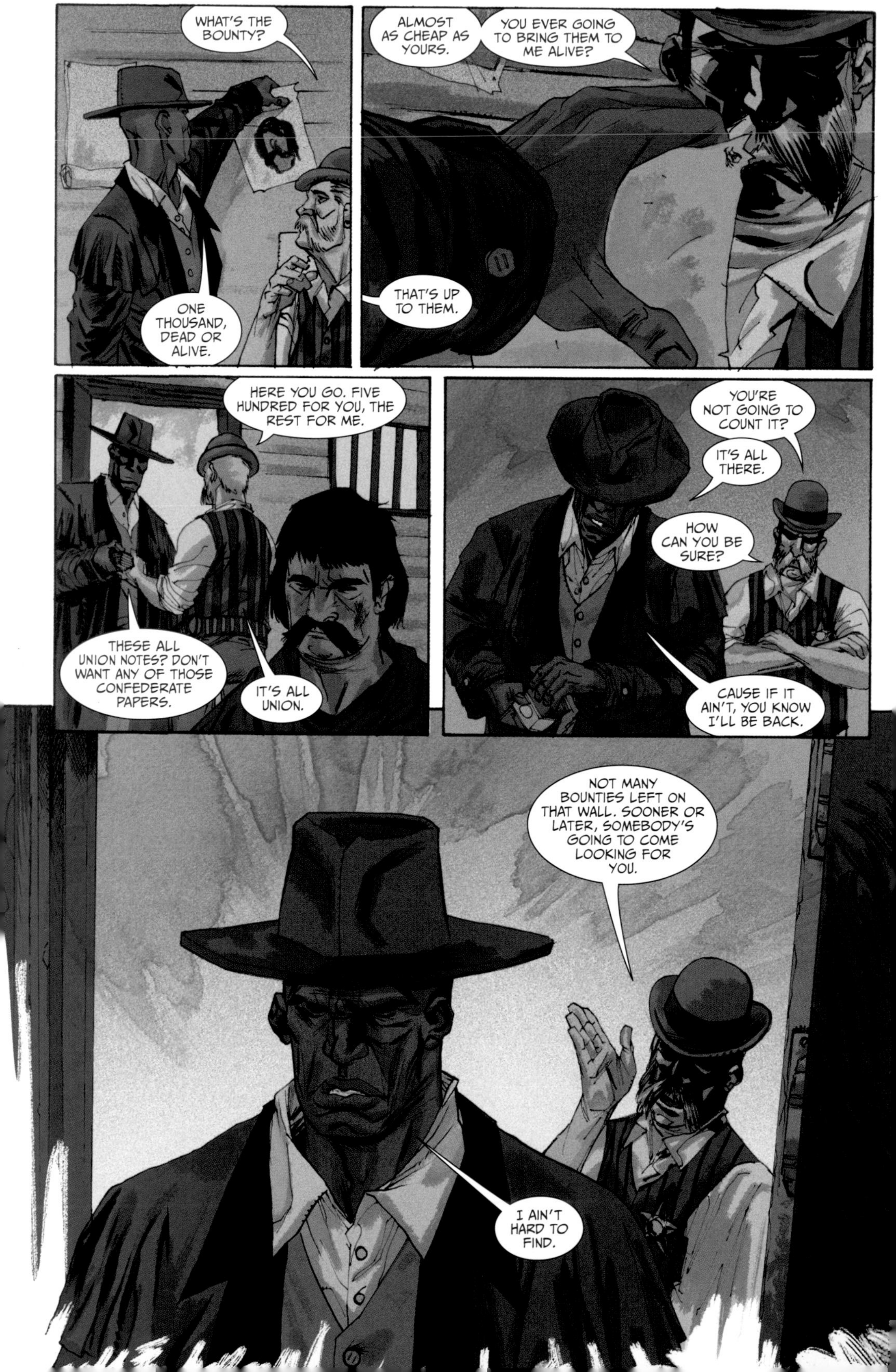
WHAT'S THE BOUNTY?
ONE THOUSAND, DEAD OR ALIVE.
ALMOST AS CHEAP AS YOURS.
YOU EVER GOING TO BRING THEM TO ME ALIVE?
THAT'S UP TO THEM.
HERE YOU GO. FIVE HUNDRED FOR YOU, THE REST FOR ME.
THESE ALL UNION NOTES? DON'T WANT ANY OF THOSE CONFEDERATE PAPERS.
IT'S ALL UNION.
YOU'RE NOT GOING TO COUNT IT?
IT'S ALL THERE.
HOW CAN YOU BE SURE?
CAUSE IF IT AIN'T, YOU KNOW I'LL BE BACK.
NOT MANY BOUNTIES LEFT ON THAT WALL. SOONER OR LATER, SOMEBODY'S GOING TO COME LOOKING FOR YOU.
I AIN'T HARD TO FIND.

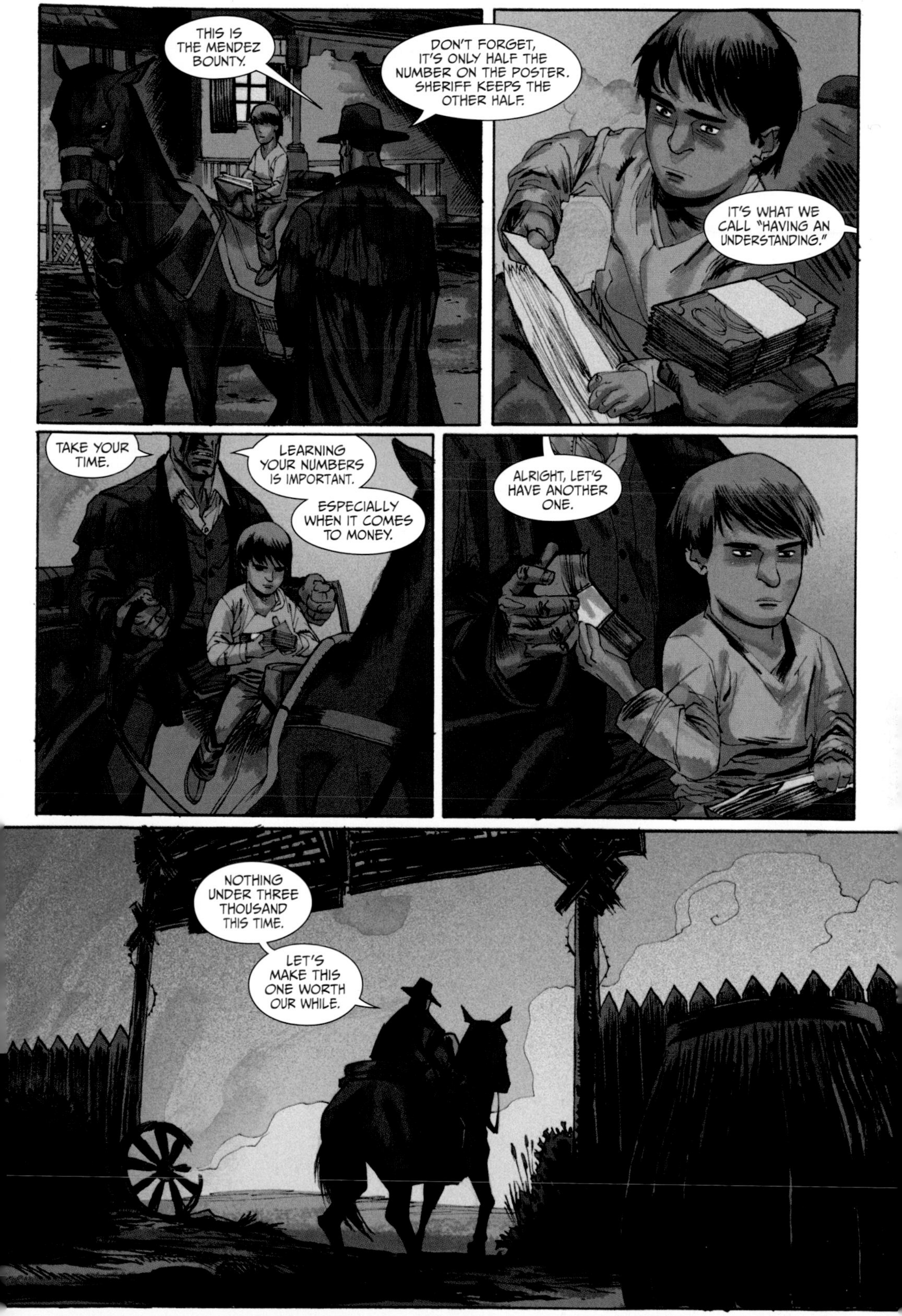
THIS IS THE MENDEZ BOUNTY.
DON'T FORGET, IT'S ONLY HALF THE NUMBER ON THE POSTER. SHERIFF KEEPS THE OTHER HALF.
IT'S WHAT WE CALL "HAVING AN UNDERSTANDING."
TAKE YOUR TIME.
LEARNING YOUR NUMBERS IS IMPORTANT.
ESPECIALLY WHEN IT COMES TO MONEY.
ALRIGHT, LET'S HAVE ANOTHER ONE.
NOTHING UNDER THREE THOUSAND THIS TIME.
LET'S MAKE THIS ONE WORTH OUR WHILE.

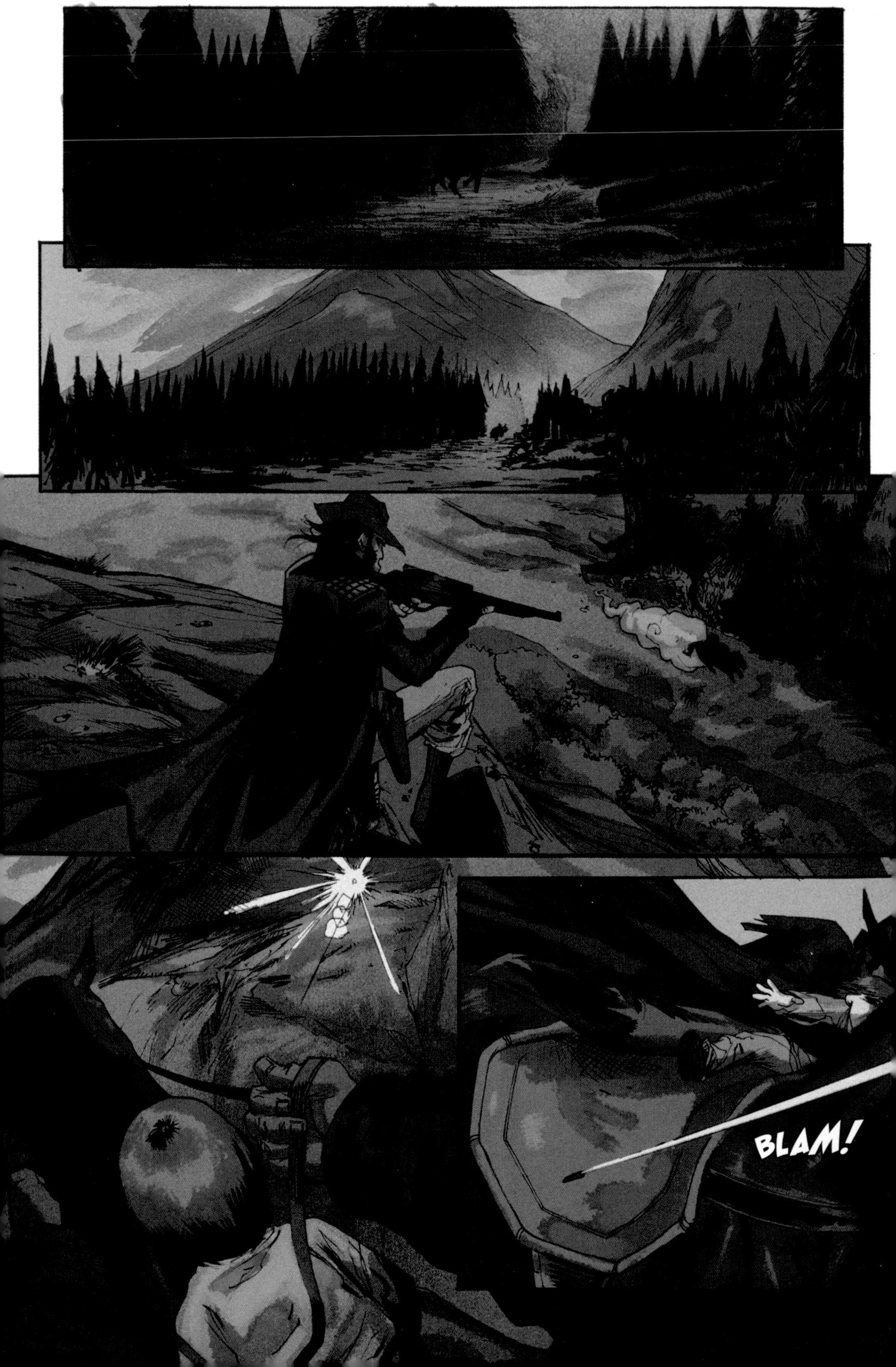
BLAM!

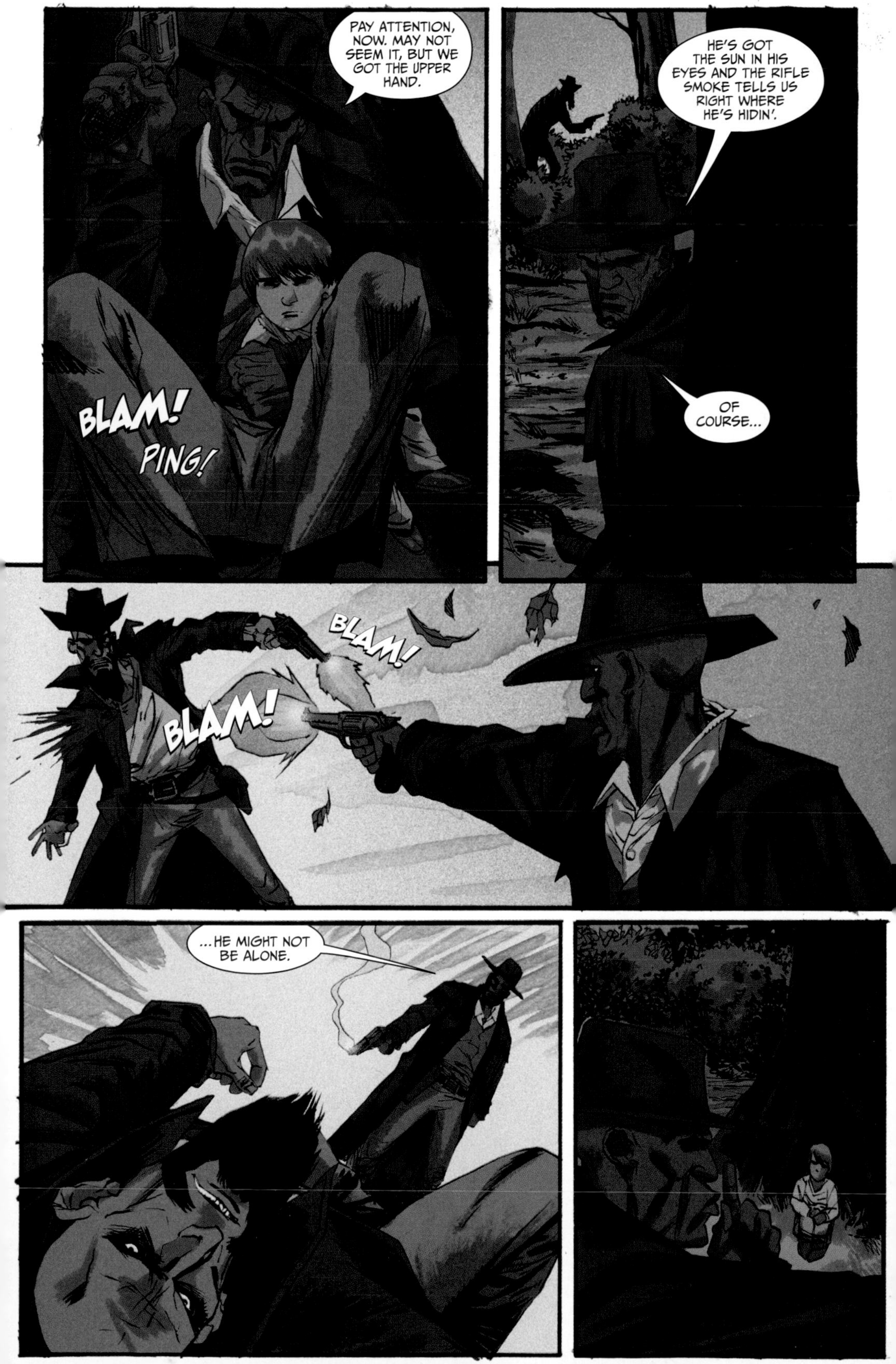
PAY ATTENTION, NOW. MAY NOT SEEM IT, BUT WE GOT THE UPPER HAND.
BLAM!
PING!
HE'S GOT THE SUN IN HIS EYES AND THE RIFLE SMOKE TELLS US RIGHT WHERE HE'S HIDIN'.
OF COURSE...
BLAM!
BLAM!
...HE MIGHT NOT BE ALONE.

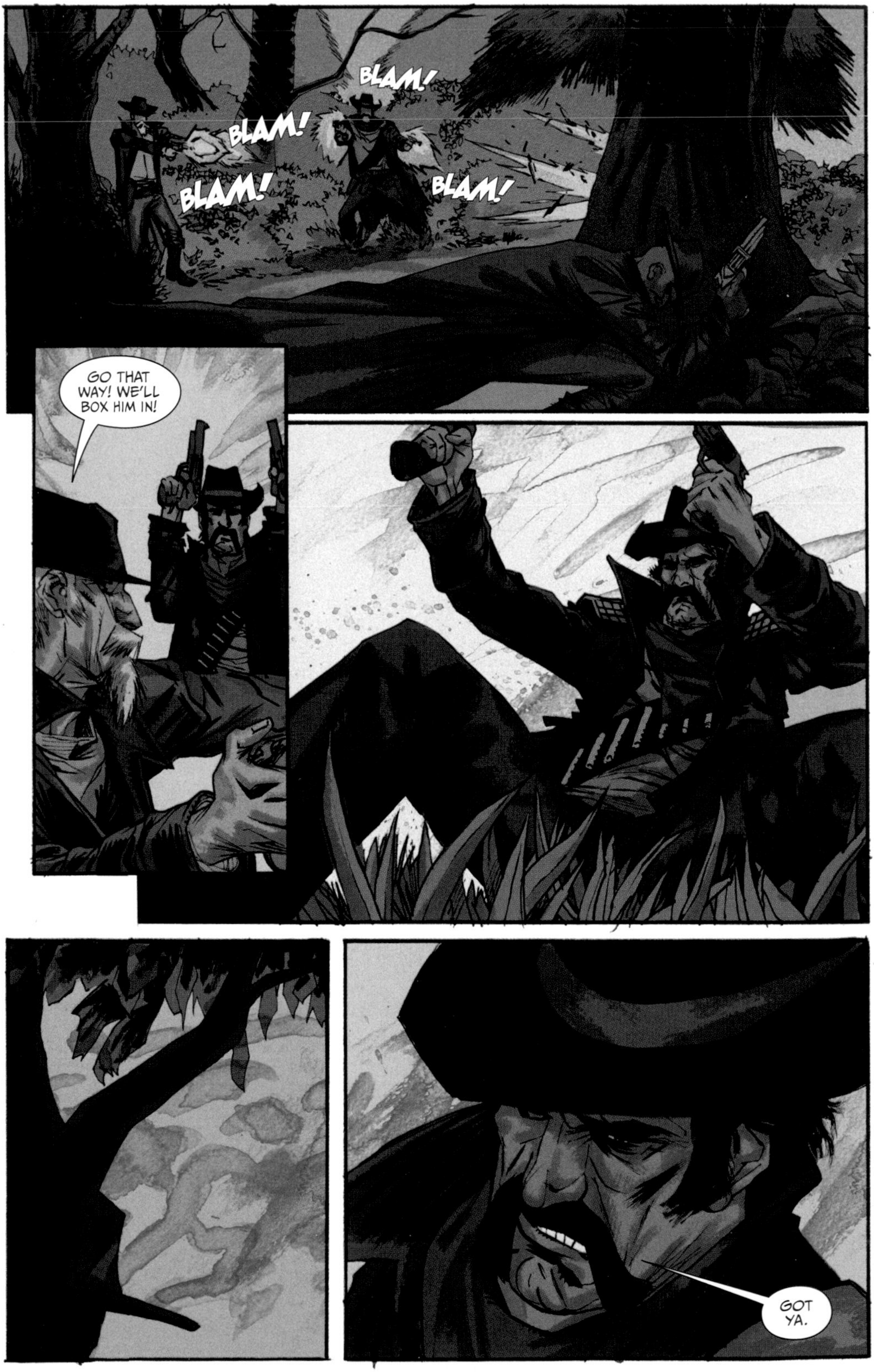
BLAM!
BLAM!
BLAM!
BLAM!
GO THAT WAY! WE'LL BOX HIM IN!
GOT YA.

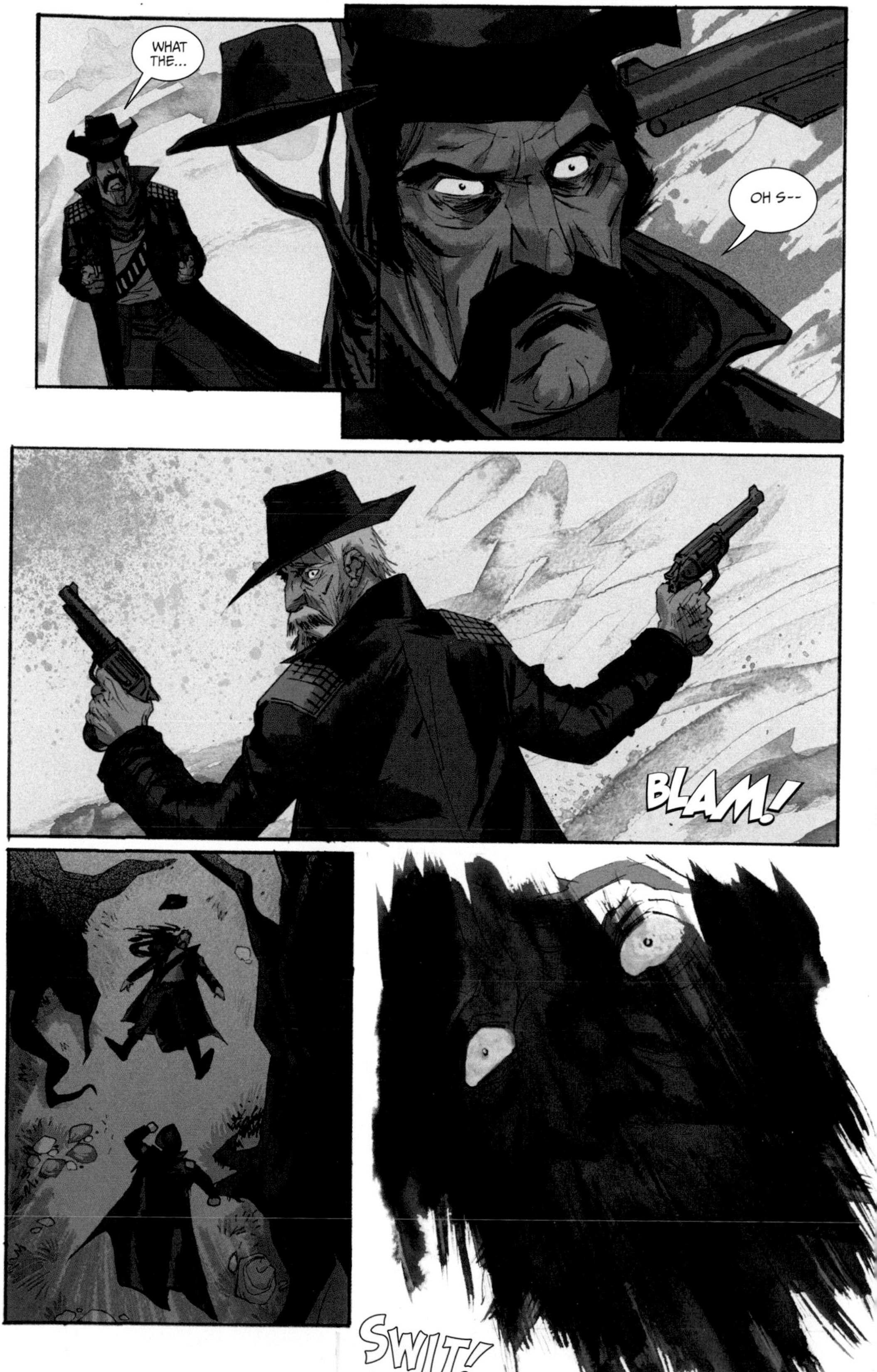
WHAT THE...
OH S--
BLAM!
SWIT!

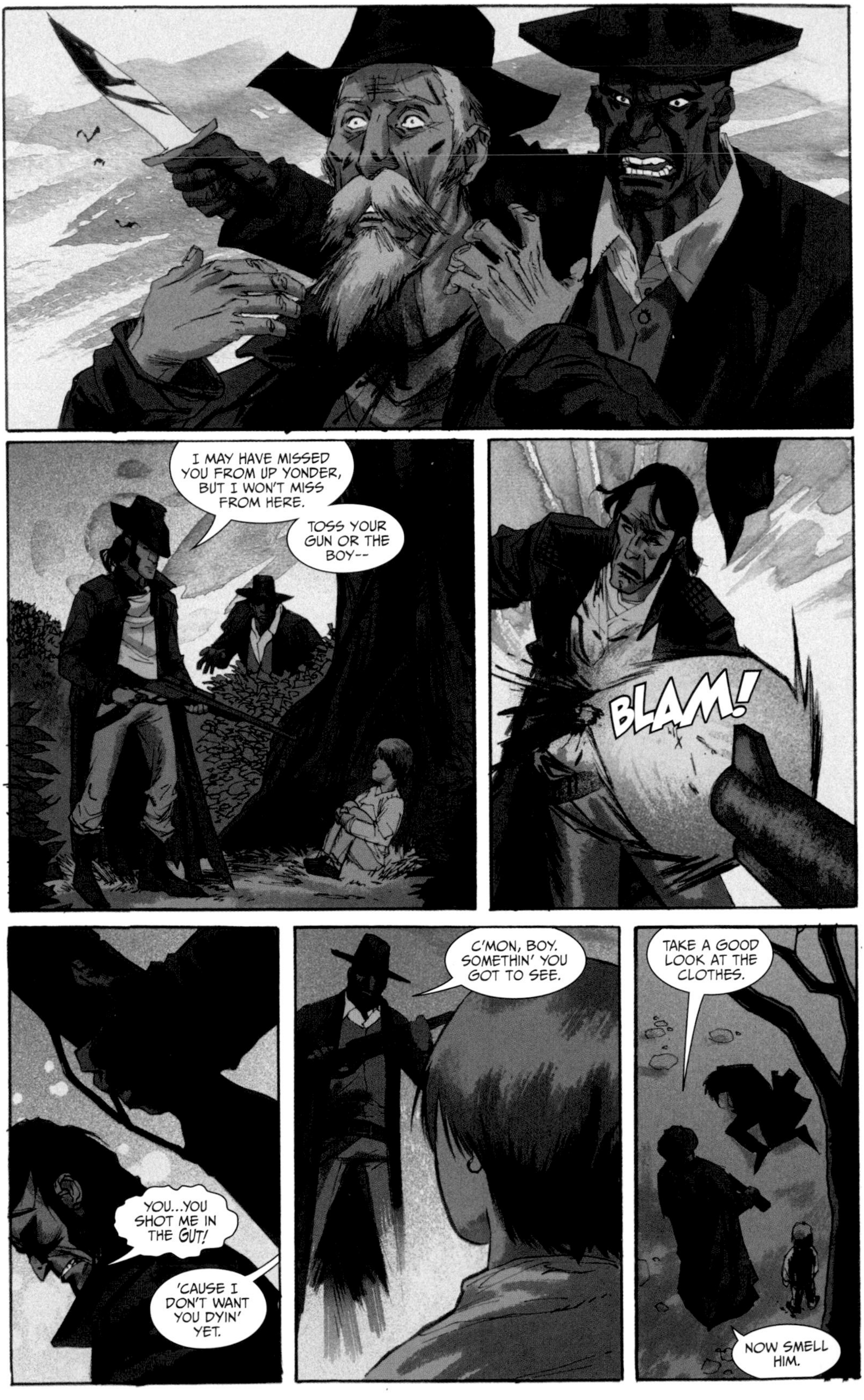
I MAY HAVE MISSED YOU FROM UP YONDER, BUT I WON'T MISS FROM HERE.
TOSS YOUR GUN OR THE BOY--
BLAM!
YOU...YOU SHOT ME IN THE GUT!
'CAUSE I DON'T WANT YOU DYIN' YET.
C'MON, BOY. SOMETHIN' YOU GOT TO SEE.
TAKE A GOOD LOOK AT THE CLOTHES.
NOW SMELL HIM.

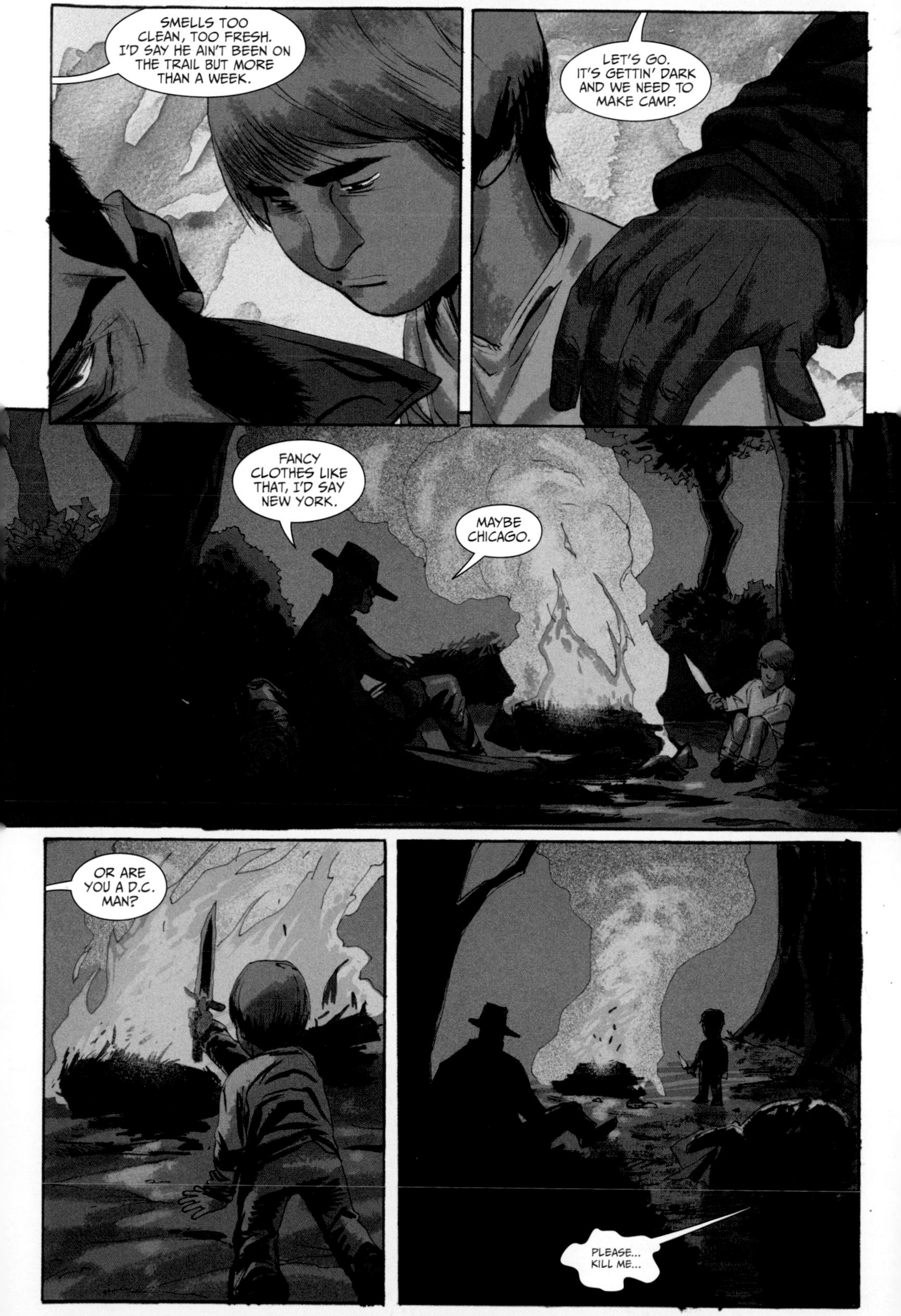
SMELLS TOO CLEAN, TOO FRESH. I'D SAY HE AIN'T BEEN ON THE TRAIL BUT MORE THAN A WEEK.
LET'S GO. IT'S GETTIN' DARK AND WE NEED TO MAKE CAMP.
FANCY CLOTHES LIKE THAT, I'D SAY NEW YORK.
MAYBE CHICAGO.
OR ARE YOU A D.C. MAN?
PLEASE... KILL ME...

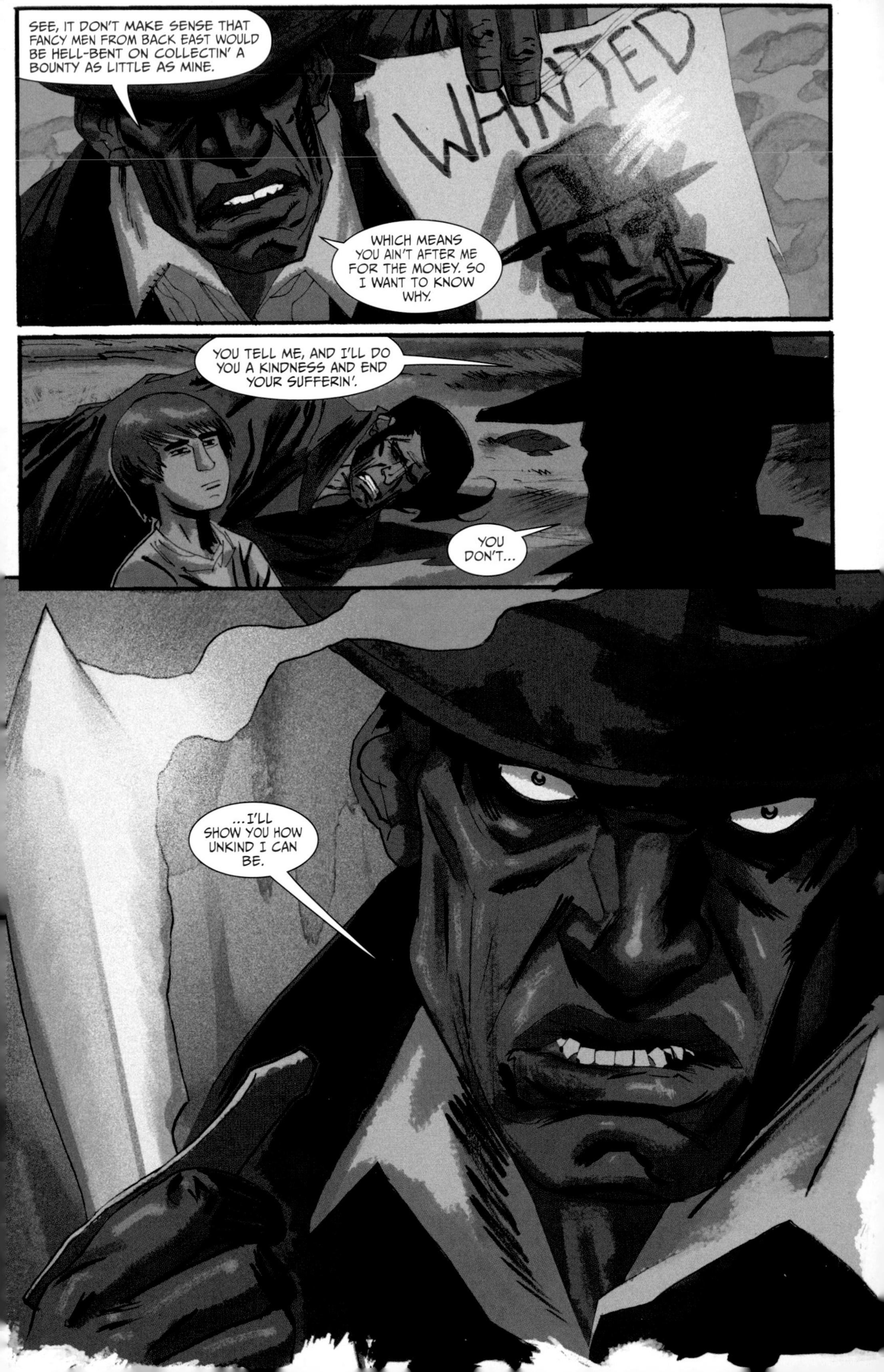
SEE, IT DON'T MAKE SENSE THAT FANCY MEN FROM BACK EAST WOULD BE HELL-BENT ON COLLECTIN' A BOUNTY AS LITTLE AS MINE.
WANTED
WHICH MEANS YOU AIN'T AFTER ME FOR THE MONEY. SO I WANT TO KNOW WHY.
YOU TELL ME, AND I'LL DO YOU A KINDNESS AND END YOUR SUFFERIN'.
YOU DON'T...
...I'LL SHOW YOU HOW UNKIND I CAN BE.

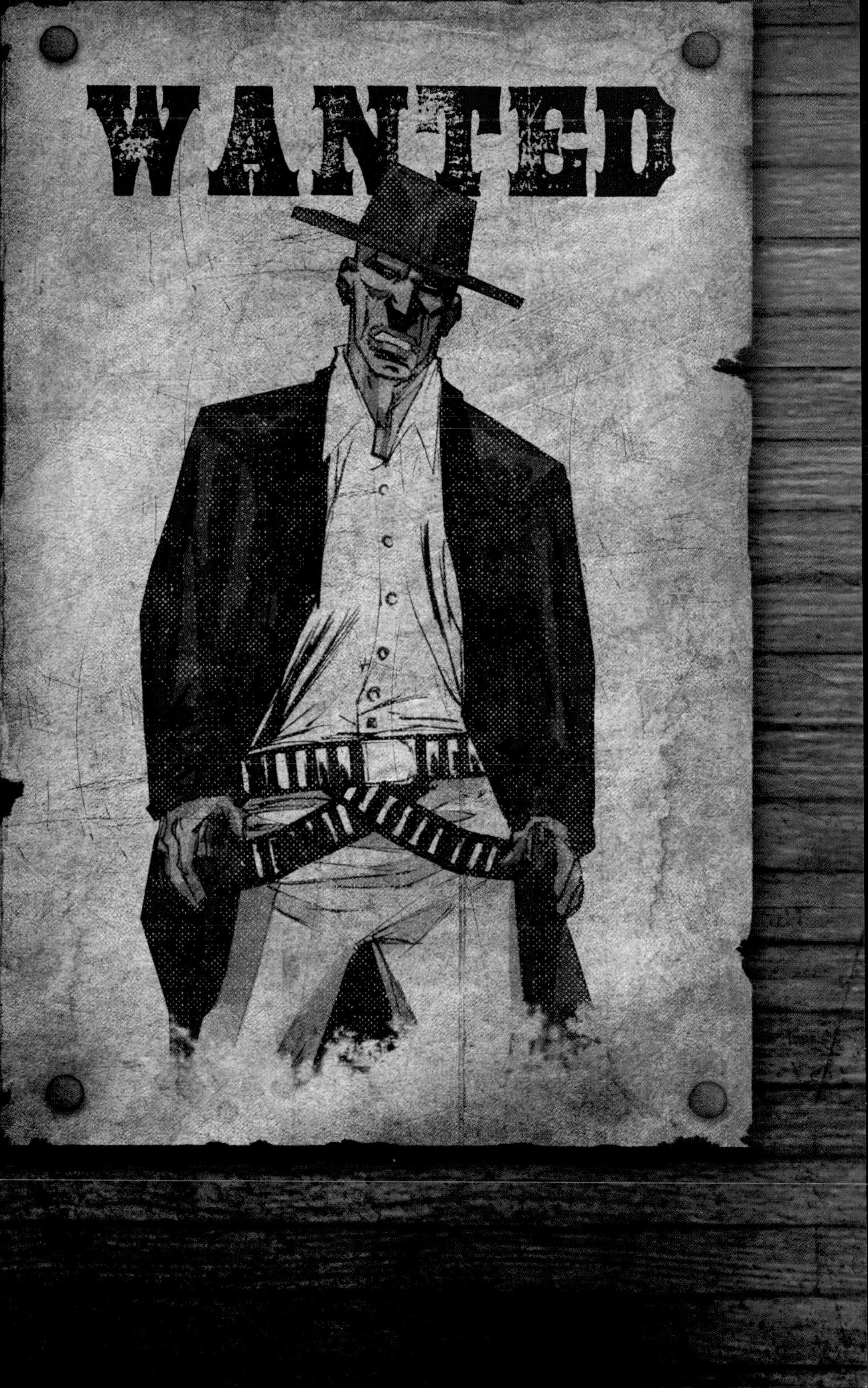
WANTED

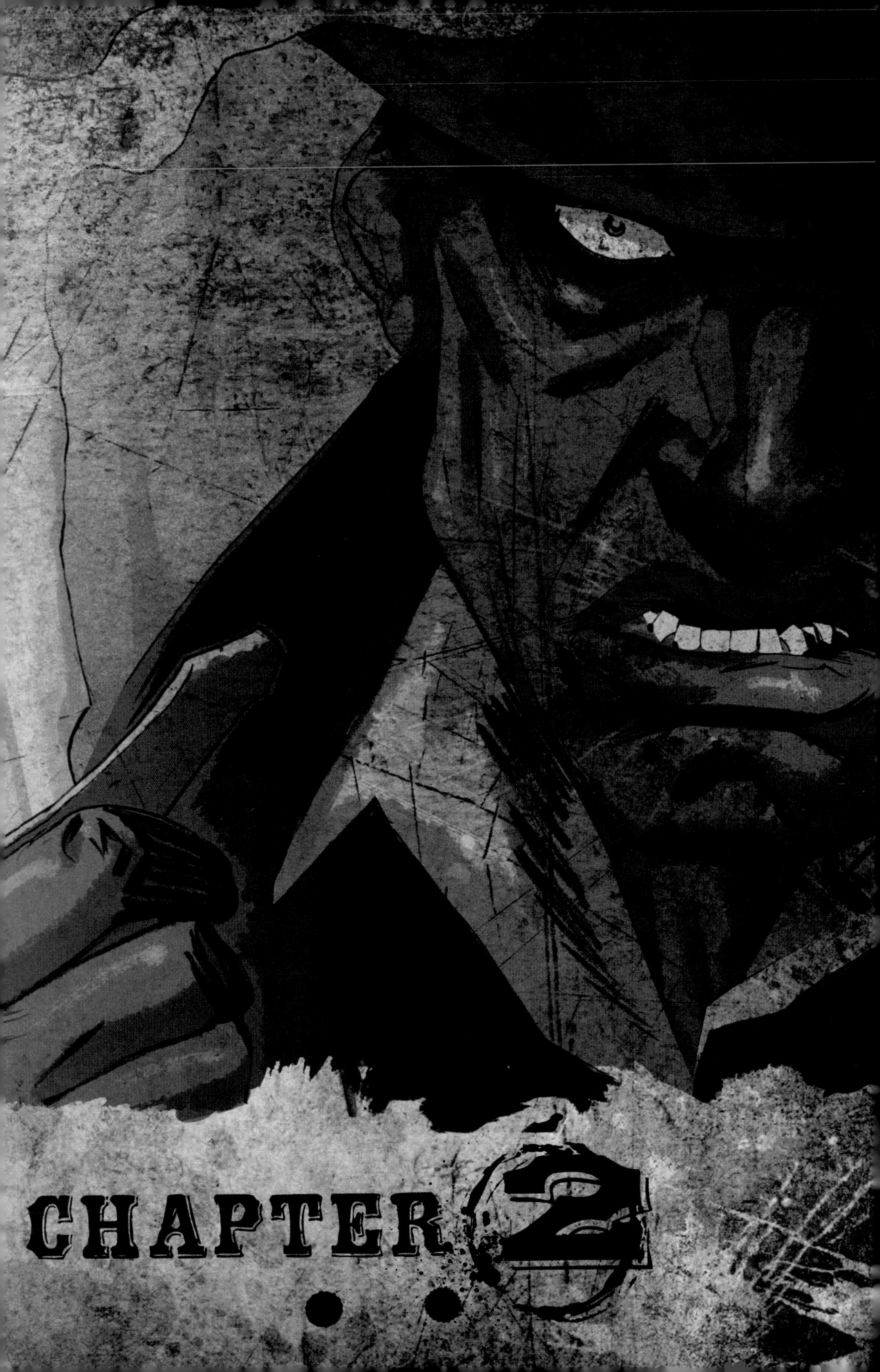
CHAPTER 2

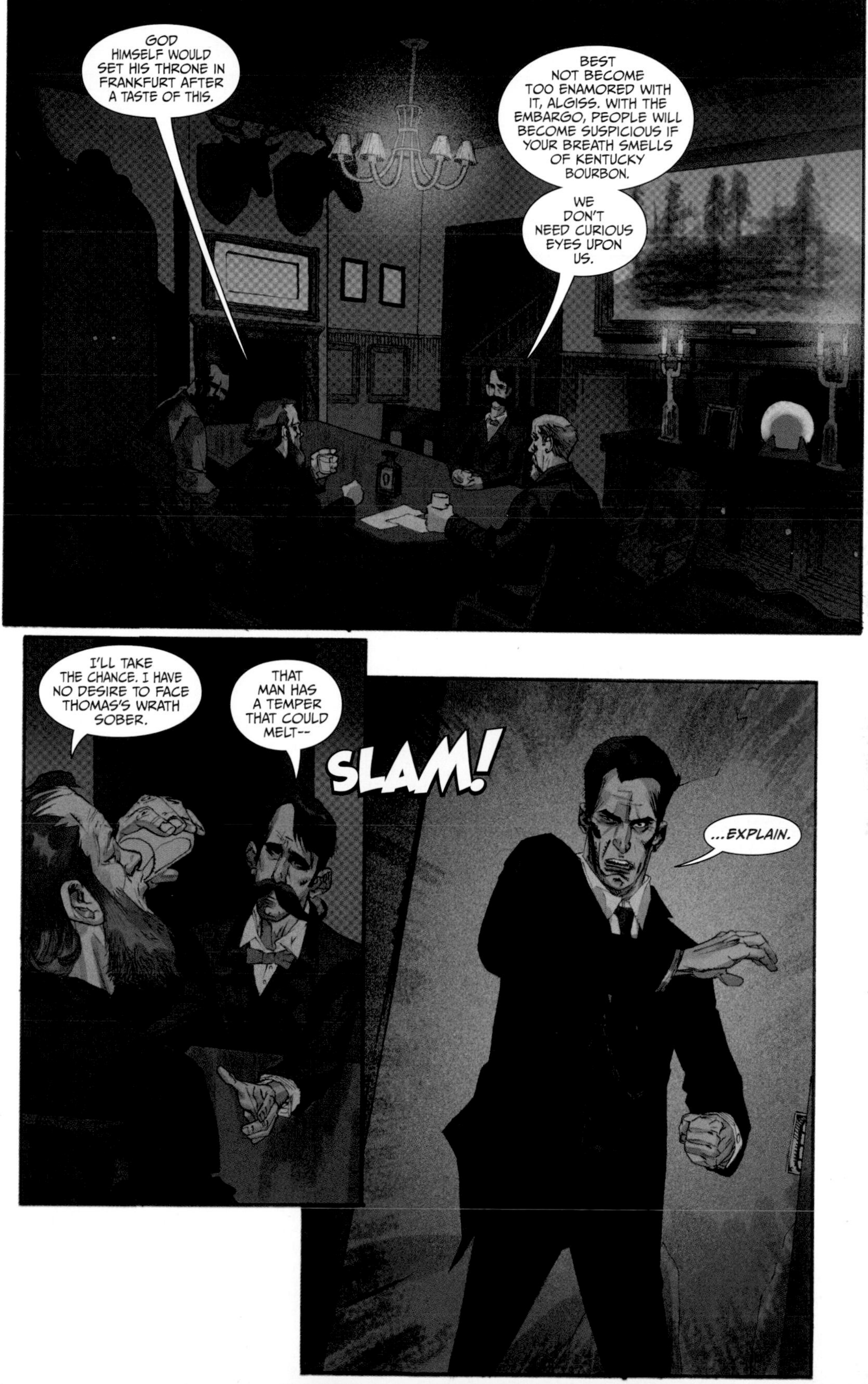
GOD HIMSELF WOULD SET HIS THRONE IN FRANKFURT AFTER A TASTE OF THIS.
BEST NOT BECOME TOO ENAMORED WITH IT, ALGISS. WITH THE EMBARGO, PEOPLE WILL BECOME SUSPICIOUS IF YOUR BREATH SMELLS OF KENTUCKY BOURBON.
WE DON'T NEED CURIOUS EYES UPON US.
I'LL TAKE THE CHANCE. I HAVE NO DESIRE TO FACE THOMAS'S WRATH SOBER.
THAT MAN HAS A TEMPER THAT COULD MELT--
SLAM!
...EXPLAIN.

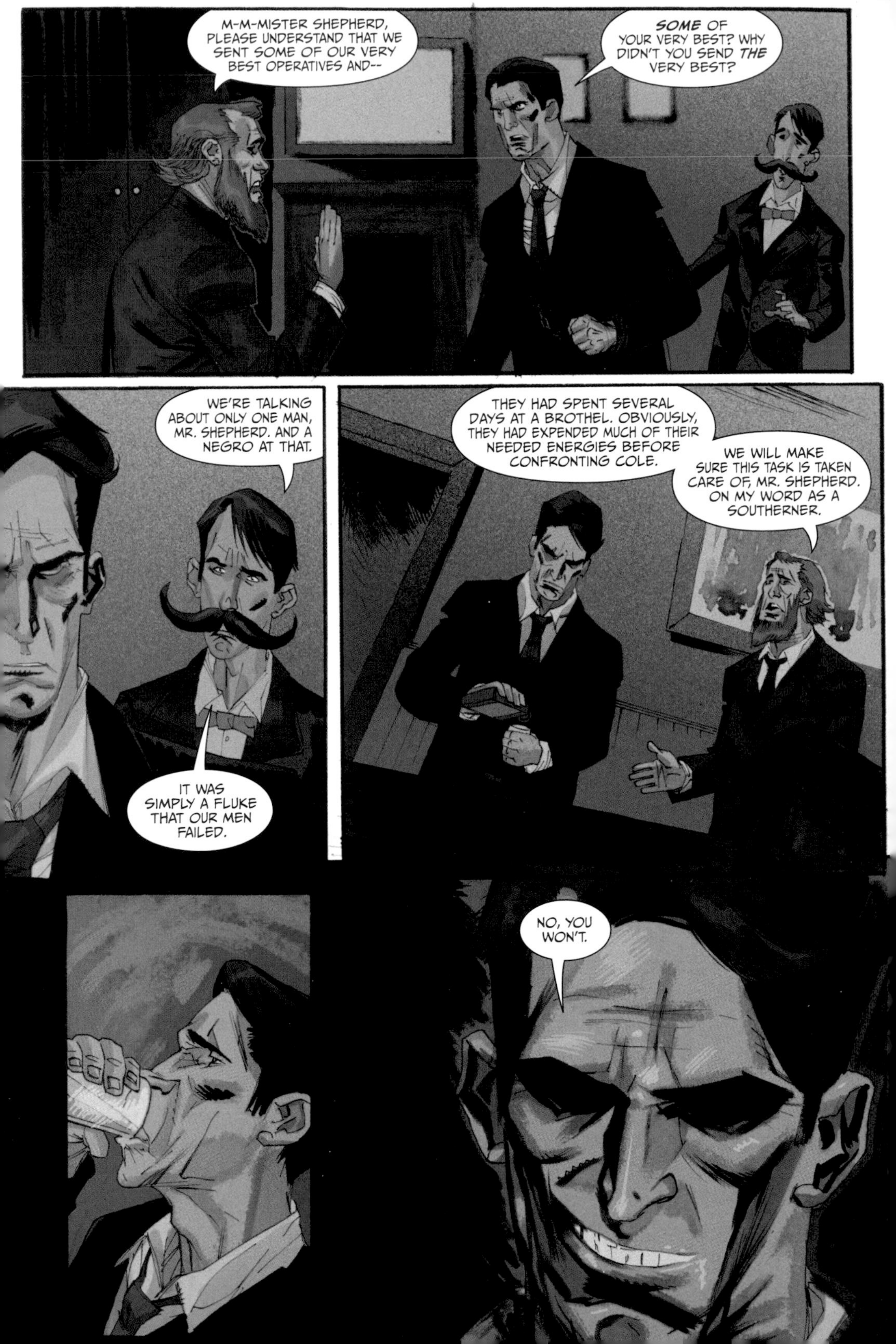
M-M-MISTER SHEPHERD, PLEASE UNDERSTAND THAT WE SENT SOME OF OUR VERY BEST OPERATIVES AND--
SOME OF YOUR VERY BEST? WHY DIDN'T YOU SEND THE VERY BEST?
WE'RE TALKING ABOUT ONLY ONE MAN, MR. SHEPHERD. AND A NEGRO AT THAT.
IT WAS SIMPLY A FLUKE THAT OUR MEN FAILED.
THEY HAD SPENT SEVERAL DAYS AT A BROTHEL. OBVIOUSLY, THEY HAD EXPENDED MUCH OF THEIR NEEDED ENERGIES BEFORE CONFRONTING COLE.
WE WILL MAKE SURE THIS TASK IS TAKEN CARE OF, MR. SHEPHERD. ON MY WORD AS A SOUTHERNER.
NO, YOU WON'T.

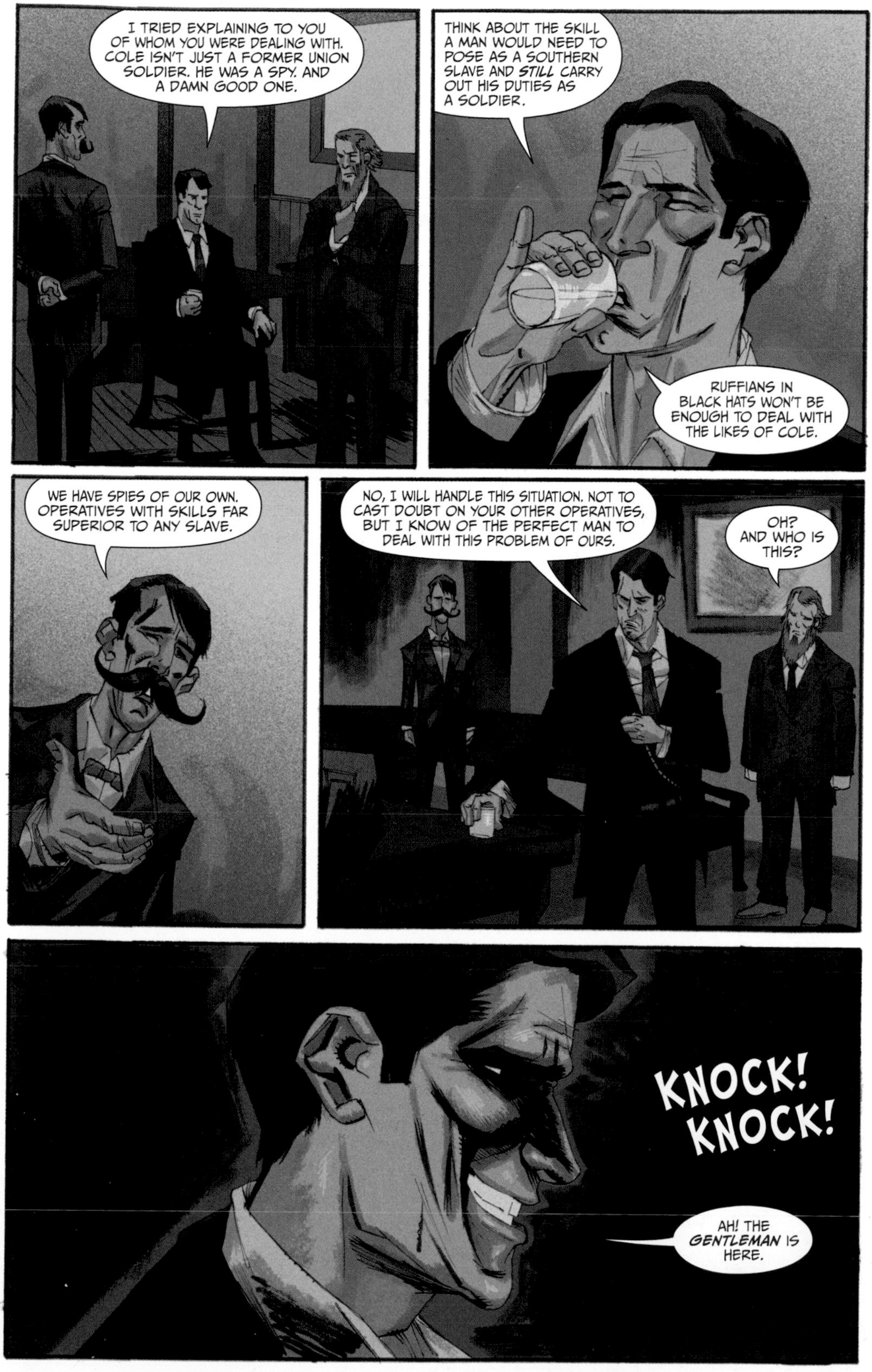
I TRIED EXPLAINING TO YOU OF WHOM YOU WERE DEALING WITH. COLE ISN'T JUST A FORMER UNION SOLDIER. HE WAS A SPY. AND A DAMN GOOD ONE.
THINK ABOUT THE SKILL A MAN WOULD NEED TO POSE AS A SOUTHERN SLAVE AND STILL CARRY OUT HIS DUTIES AS A SOLDIER.
RUFFIANS IN BLACK HATS WON'T BE ENOUGH TO DEAL WITH THE LIKES OF COLE.
WE HAVE SPIES OF OUR OWN. OPERATIVES WITH SKILLS FAR SUPERIOR TO ANY SLAVE.
NO, I WILL HANDLE THIS SITUATION. NOT TO CAST DOUBT ON YOUR OTHER OPERATIVES, BUT I KNOW OF THE PERFECT MAN TO DEAL WITH THIS PROBLEM OF OURS.
OH? AND WHO IS THIS?
KNOCK! KNOCK!
AH! THE GENTLEMAN IS HERE.

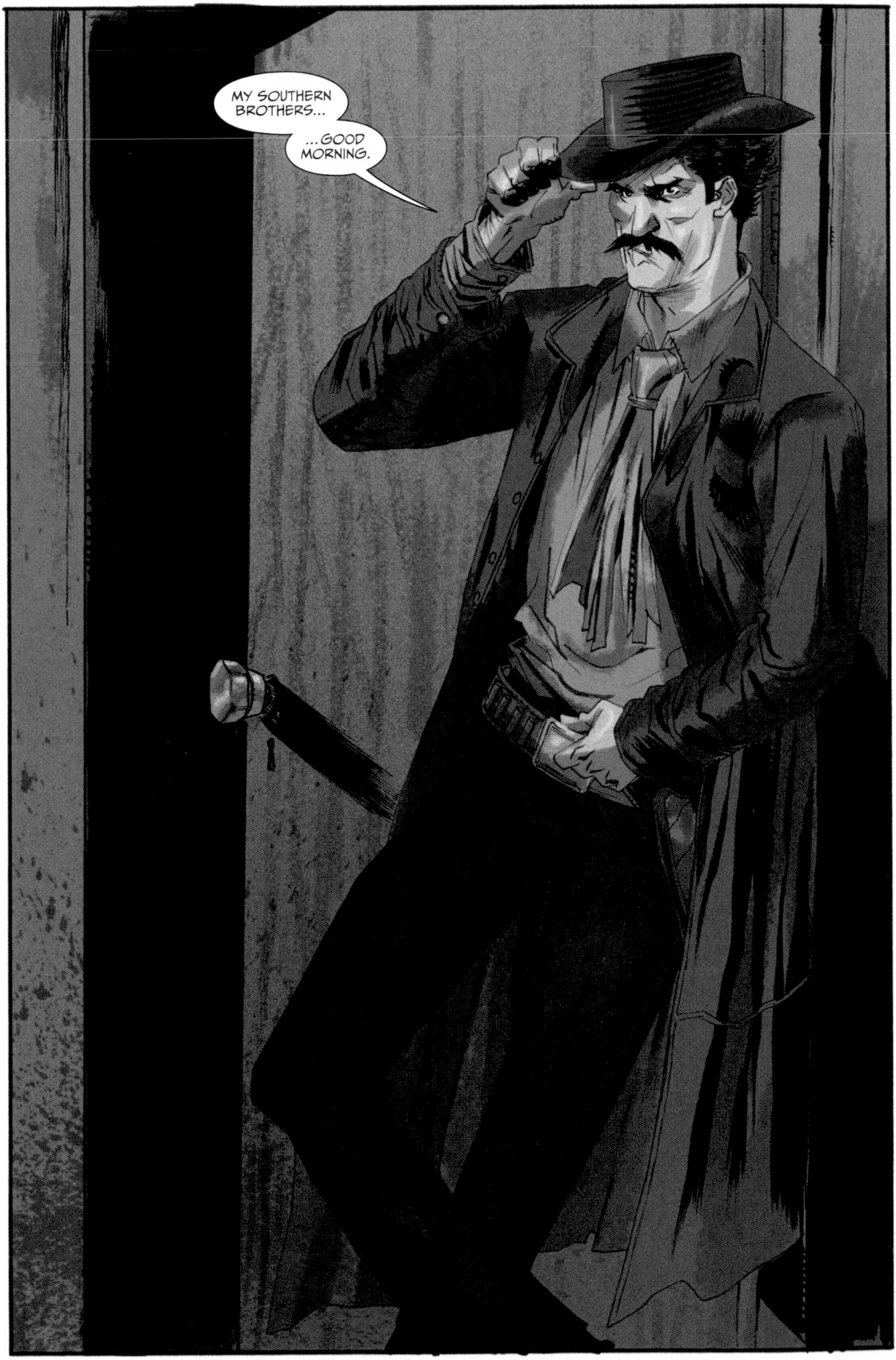
MY SOUTHERN BROTHERS...
...GOOD MORNING.

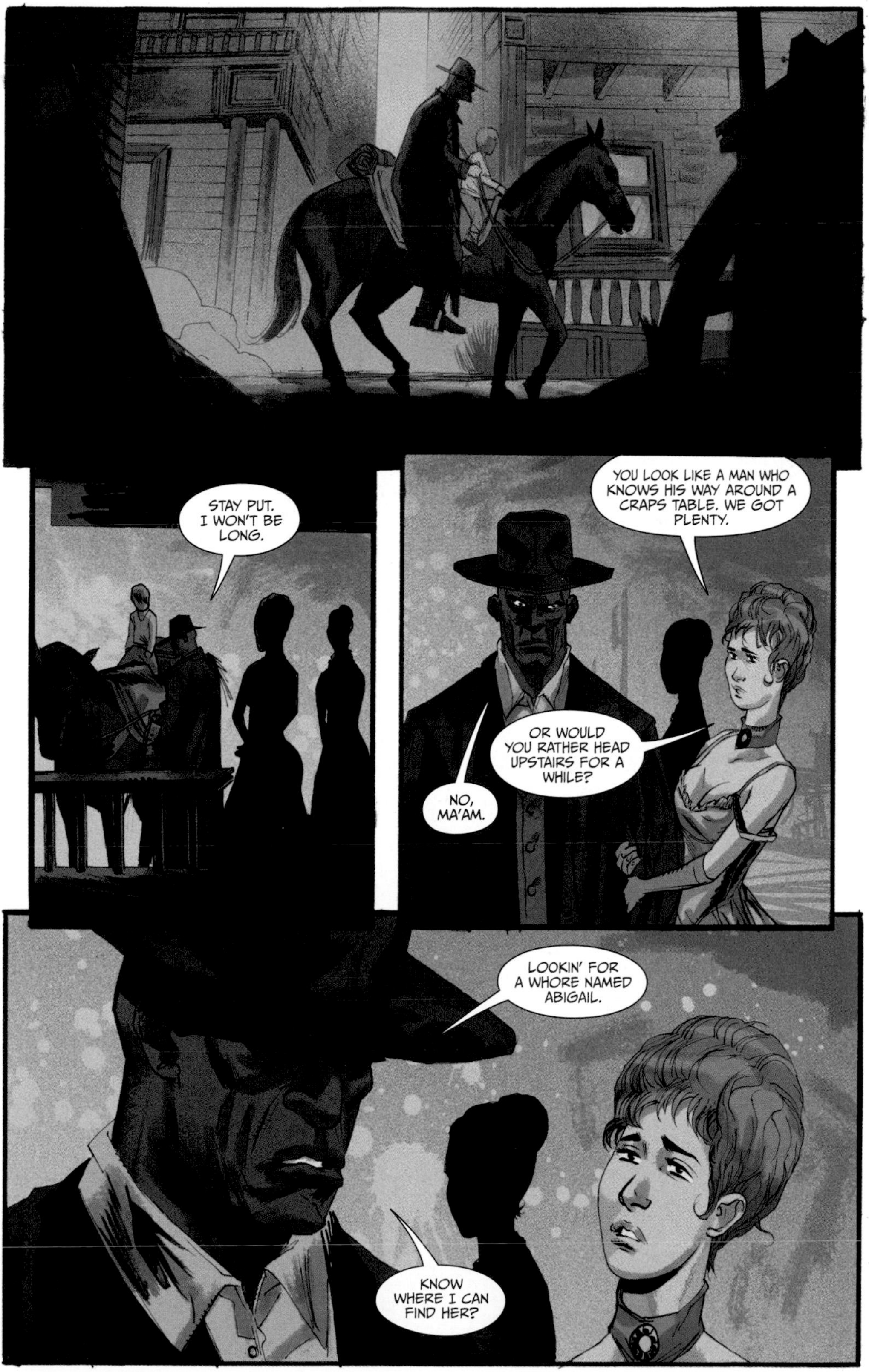
STAY PUT. I WON'T BE LONG.
YOU LOOK LIKE A MAN WHO KNOWS HIS WAY AROUND A CRAPS TABLE. WE GOT PLENTY.
OR WOULD YOU RATHER HEAD UPSTAIRS FOR A WHILE?
NO, MA'AM.
LOOKIN' FOR A WHORE NAMED ABIGAIL.
KNOW WHERE I CAN FIND HER?

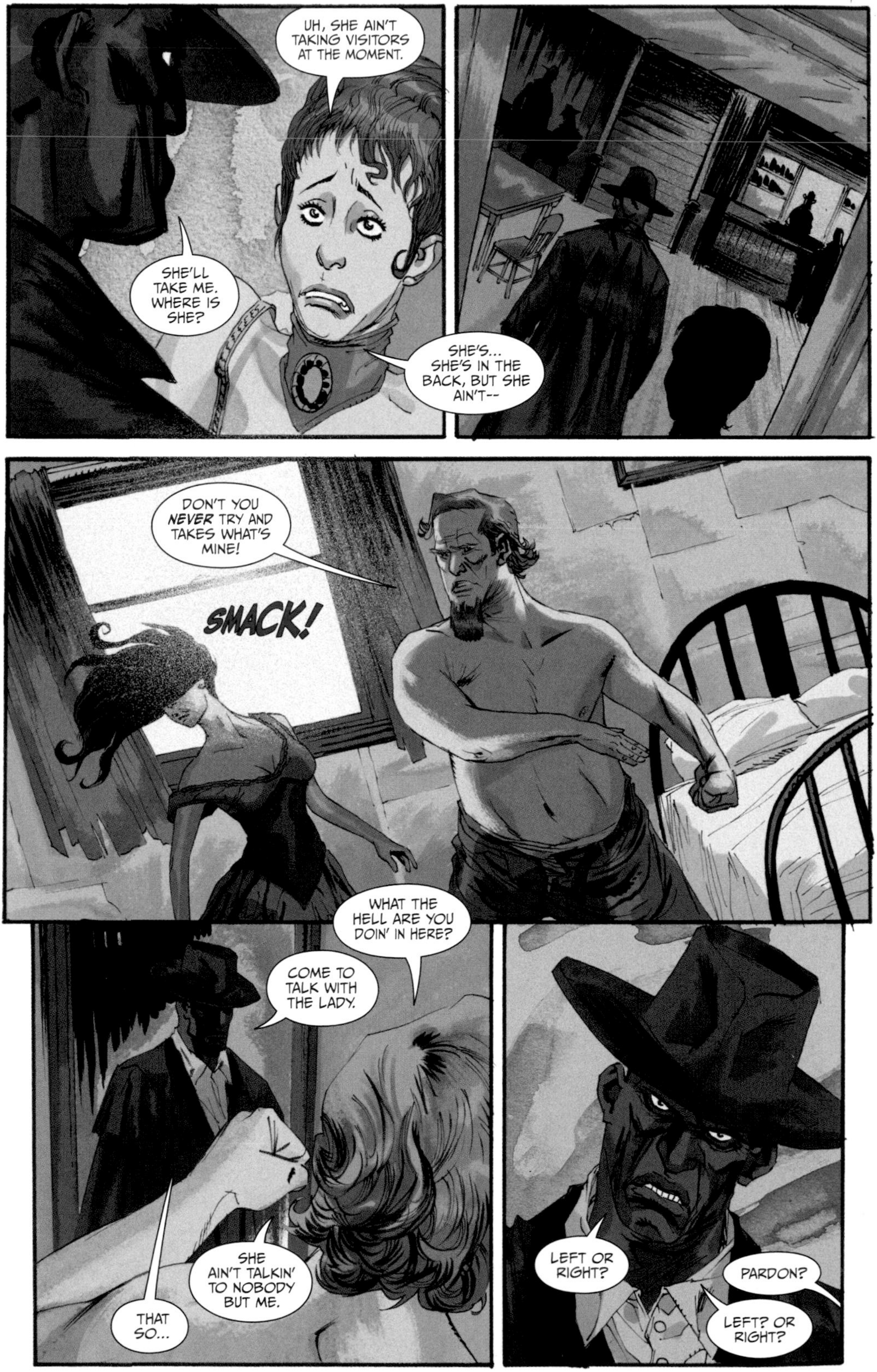
UH, SHE AIN'T TAKING VISITORS AT THE MOMENT.
SHE'LL TAKE ME. WHERE IS SHE?
SHE'S... SHE'S IN THE BACK, BUT SHE AIN'T--
DON'T YOU *NEVER* TRY AND TAKES WHAT'S MINE!
SMACK!
WHAT THE HELL ARE YOU DOIN' IN HERE?
COME TO TALK WITH THE LADY.
SHE AIN'T TALKIN' TO NOBODY BUT ME.
THAT SO...
LEFT OR RIGHT?
PARDON?
LEFT? OR RIGHT?

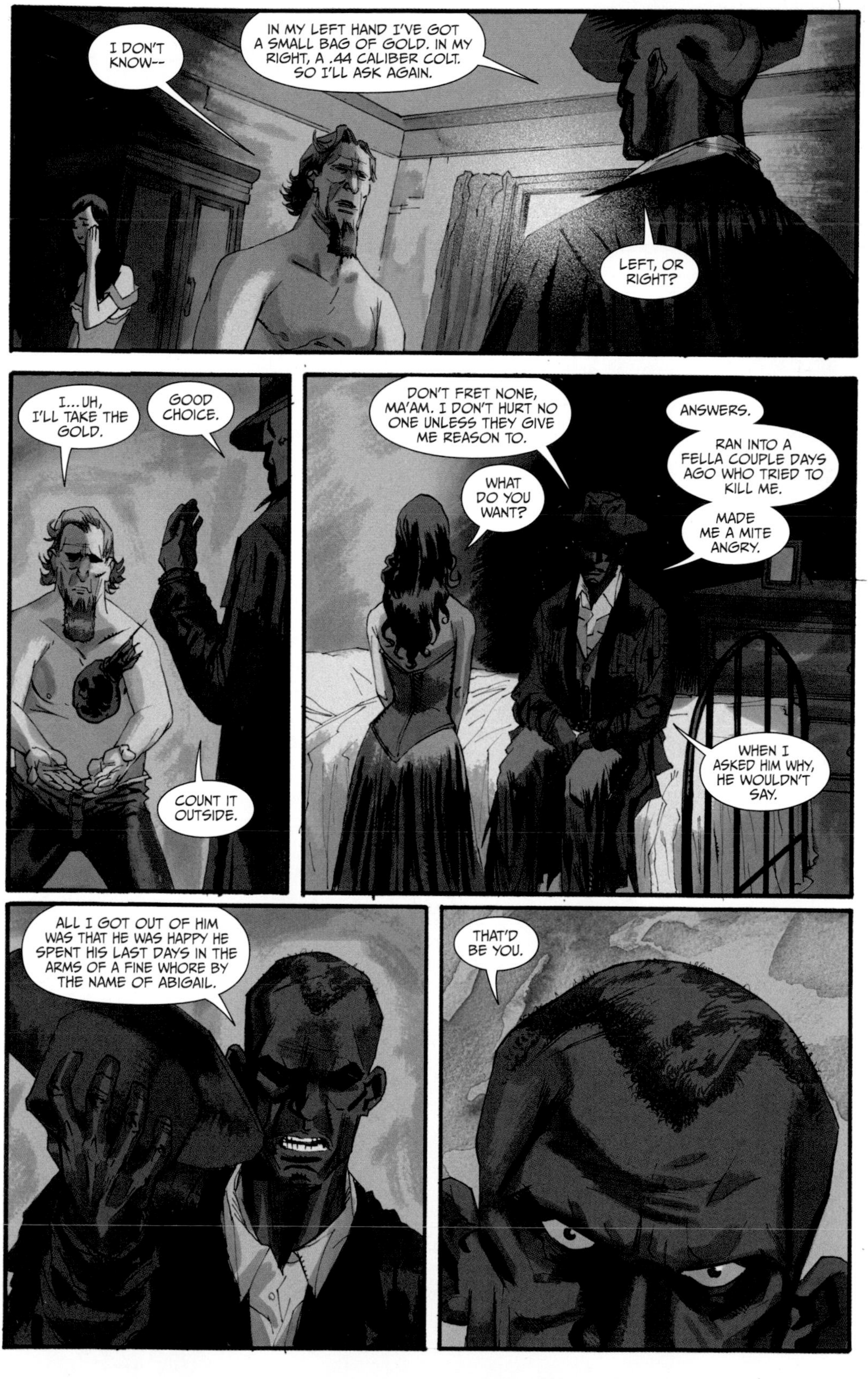
I DON'T KNOW--
IN MY LEFT HAND I'VE GOT A SMALL BAG OF GOLD. IN MY RIGHT, A .44 CALIBER COLT. SO I'LL ASK AGAIN.
LEFT, OR RIGHT?
I...UH, I'LL TAKE THE GOLD.
GOOD CHOICE.
COUNT IT OUTSIDE.
DON'T FRET NONE, MA'AM. I DON'T HURT NO ONE UNLESS THEY GIVE ME REASON TO.
WHAT DO YOU WANT?
ANSWERS.
RAN INTO A FELLA COUPLE DAYS AGO WHO TRIED TO KILL ME.
MADE ME A MITE ANGRY.
WHEN I ASKED HIM WHY, HE WOULDN'T SAY.
ALL I GOT OUT OF HIM WAS THAT HE WAS HAPPY HE SPENT HIS LAST DAYS IN THE ARMS OF A FINE WHORE BY THE NAME OF ABIGAIL.
THAT'D BE YOU.

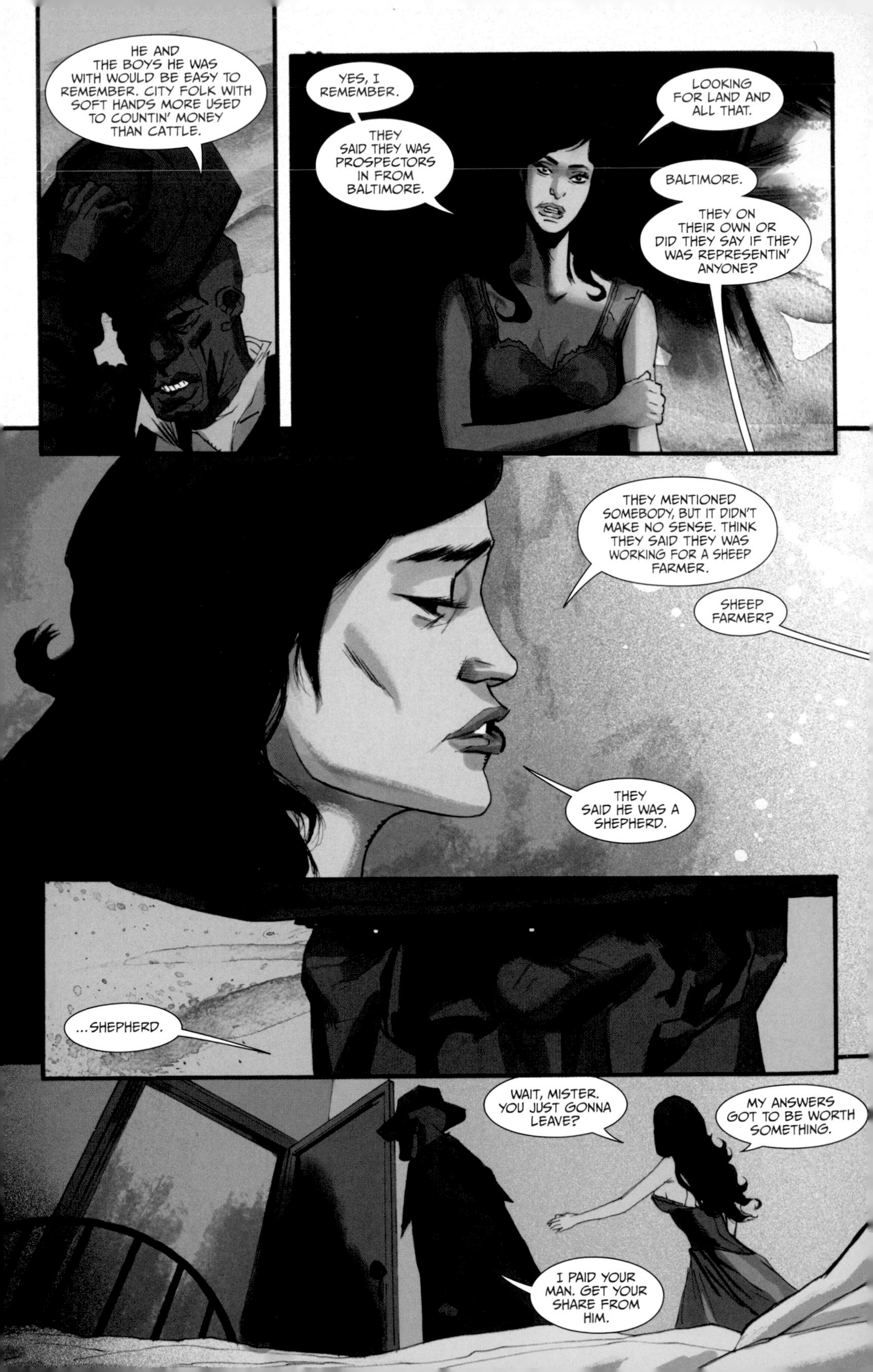
HE AND THE BOYS HE WAS WITH WOULD BE EASY TO REMEMBER. CITY FOLK WITH SOFT HANDS MORE USED TO COUNTIN' MONEY THAN CATTLE.
YES, I REMEMBER.
THEY SAID THEY WAS PROSPECTORS IN FROM BALTIMORE.
LOOKING FOR LAND AND ALL THAT.
BALTIMORE.
THEY ON THEIR OWN OR DID THEY SAY IF THEY WAS REPRESENTIN' ANYONE?
THEY MENTIONED SOMEBODY, BUT IT DIDN'T MAKE NO SENSE. THINK THEY SAID THEY WAS WORKING FOR A SHEEP FARMER.
SHEEP FARMER?
THEY SAID HE WAS A SHEPHERD.
...SHEPHERD.
WAIT, MISTER. YOU JUST GONNA LEAVE?
MY ANSWERS GOT TO BE WORTH SOMETHING.
I PAID YOUR MAN. GET YOUR SHARE FROM HIM.

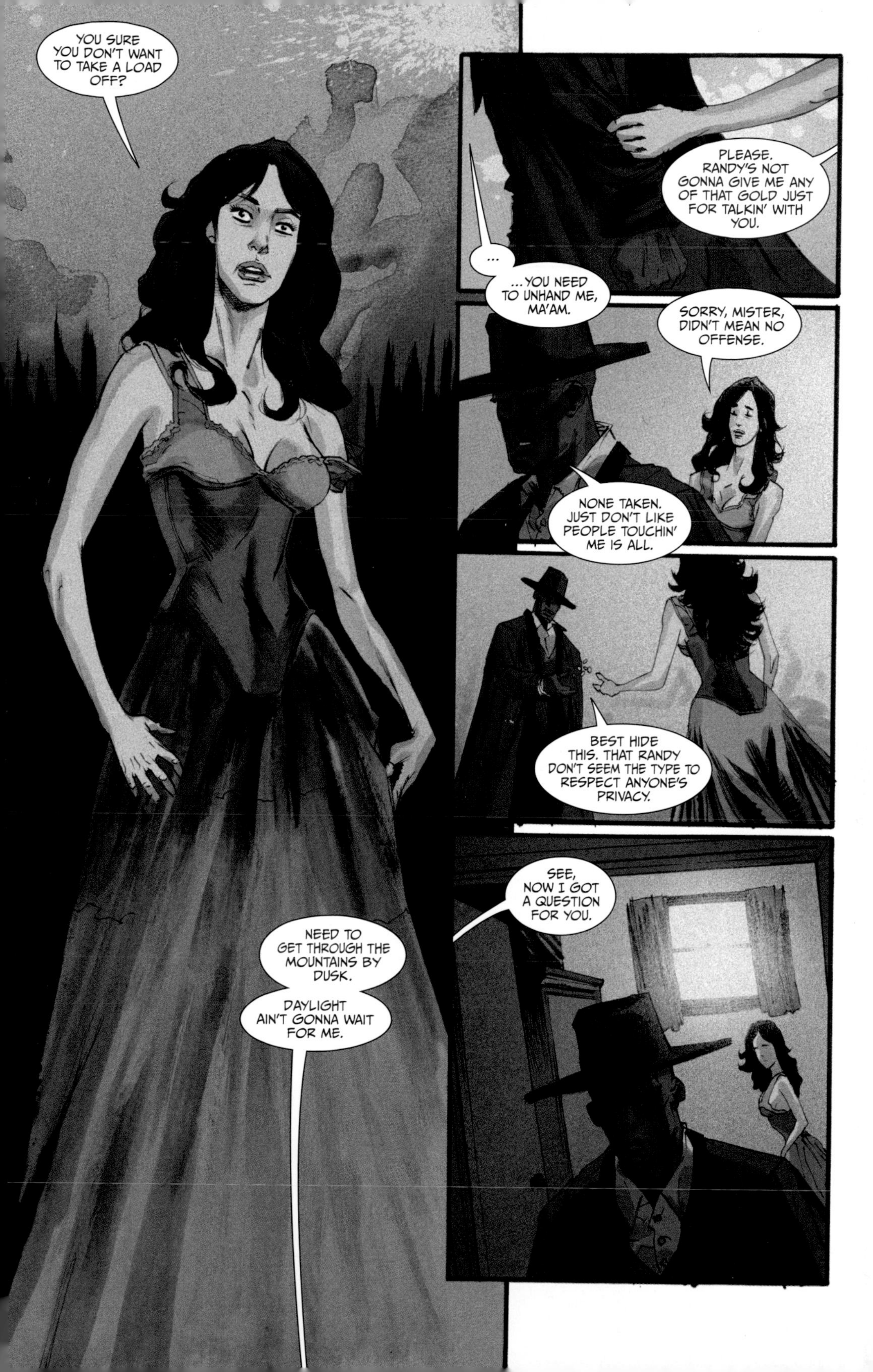
YOU SURE YOU DON'T WANT TO TAKE A LOAD OFF?
NEED TO GET THROUGH THE MOUNTAINS BY DUSK.
DAYLIGHT AIN'T GONNA WAIT FOR ME.
PLEASE. RANDY'S NOT GONNA GIVE ME ANY OF THAT GOLD JUST FOR TALKIN' WITH YOU.
...
...YOU NEED TO UNHAND ME, MA'AM.
SORRY, MISTER, DIDN'T MEAN NO OFFENSE.
NONE TAKEN. JUST DON'T LIKE PEOPLE TOUCHIN' ME IS ALL.
BEST HIDE THIS. THAT RANDY DON'T SEEM THE TYPE TO RESPECT ANYONE'S PRIVACY.
SEE, NOW I GOT A QUESTION FOR YOU.

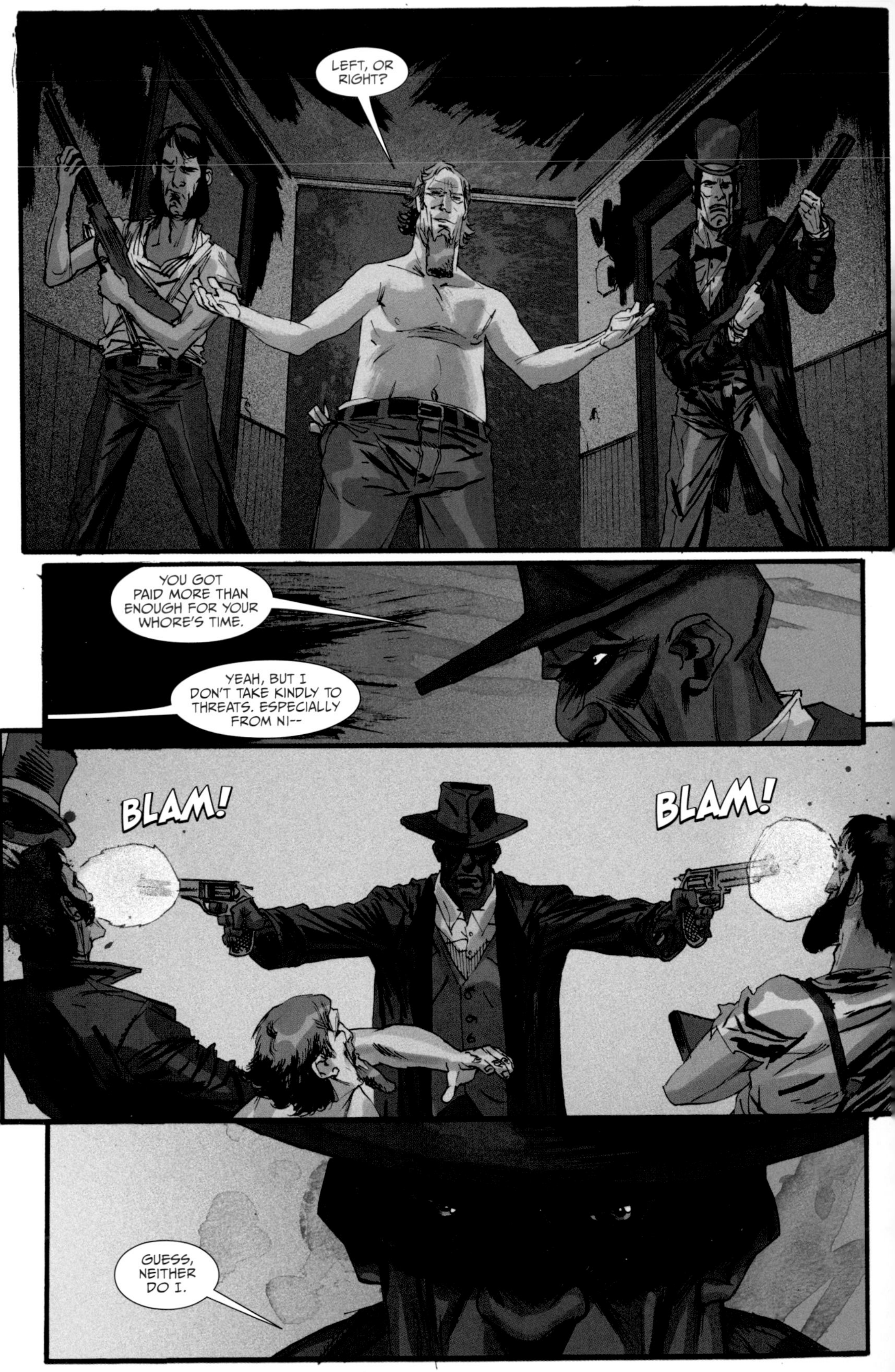
LEFT, OR RIGHT?
YOU GOT PAID MORE THAN ENOUGH FOR YOUR WHORE'S TIME.
YEAH, BUT I DON'T TAKE KINDLY TO THREATS. ESPECIALLY FROM NI--
BLAM!
BLAM!
GUESS, NEITHER DO I.

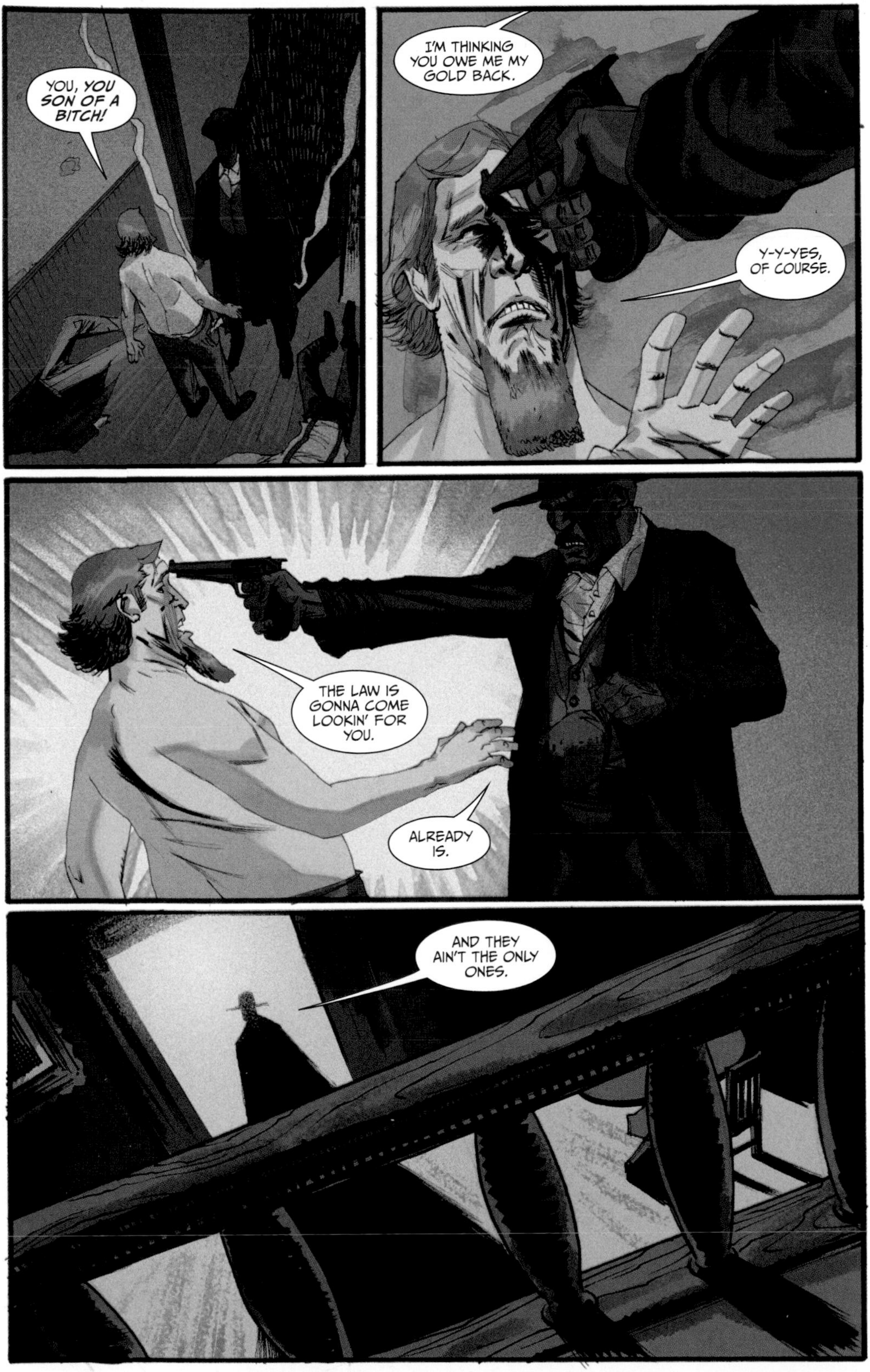
YOU, YOU SON OF A BITCH!
I'M THINKING YOU OWE ME MY GOLD BACK.
Y-Y-YES, OF COURSE.
THE LAW IS GONNA COME LOOKIN' FOR YOU.
ALREADY IS.
AND THEY AIN'T THE ONLY ONES.

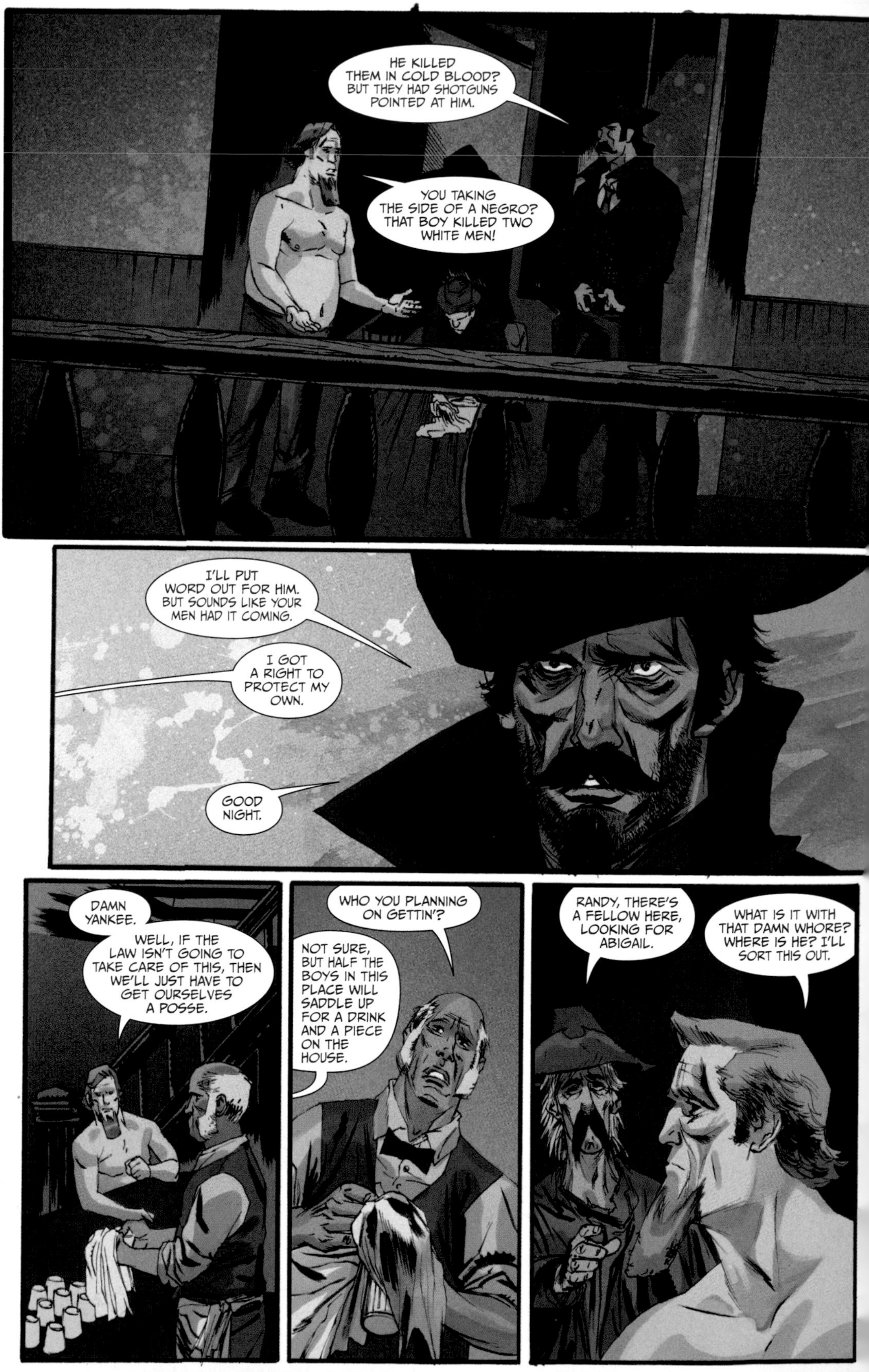
HE KILLED THEM IN COLD BLOOD? BUT THEY HAD SHOTGUNS POINTED AT HIM.
YOU TAKING THE SIDE OF A NEGRO? THAT BOY KILLED TWO WHITE MEN!
I'LL PUT WORD OUT FOR HIM. BUT SOUNDS LIKE YOUR MEN HAD IT COMING.
I GOT A RIGHT TO PROTECT MY OWN.
GOOD NIGHT.
DAMN YANKEE.
WELL, IF THE LAW ISN'T GOING TO TAKE CARE OF THIS, THEN WE'LL JUST HAVE TO GET OURSELVES A POSSE.
WHO YOU PLANNING ON GETTIN'?
NOT SURE, BUT HALF THE BOYS IN THIS PLACE WILL SADDLE UP FOR A DRINK AND A PIECE ON THE HOUSE.
RANDY, THERE'S A FELLOW HERE, LOOKING FOR ABIGAIL.
WHAT IS IT WITH THAT DAMN WHORE? WHERE IS HE? I'LL SORT THIS OUT.

NOW YOU BE A GOOD BOY AND GO WIN SOME WHISKEY MONEY ON THOSE TABLES OUT THERE.

OH, YOU BETCHA!

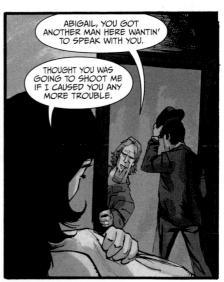

ABIGAIL, YOU GOT ANOTHER MAN HERE WANTIN' TO SPEAK WITH YOU.

THOUGHT YOU WAS GOING TO SHOOT ME IF I CAUSED YOU ANY MORE TROUBLE.

THIS MAN PAID ME RIGHT AND PROPER. NOW, YOU GET CLEANED UP REAL QUICK FOR HIM.

THIS MAN'S A *GENTLEMAN*.

ABIGAIL?

YES, THAT'S ME. COME ON IN AND MAKE YOURSELF COMFORTABLE.

OH, THAT WON'T BE NECESSARY.

I JUST WANT TO ASK YOU A FEW QUESTIONS.

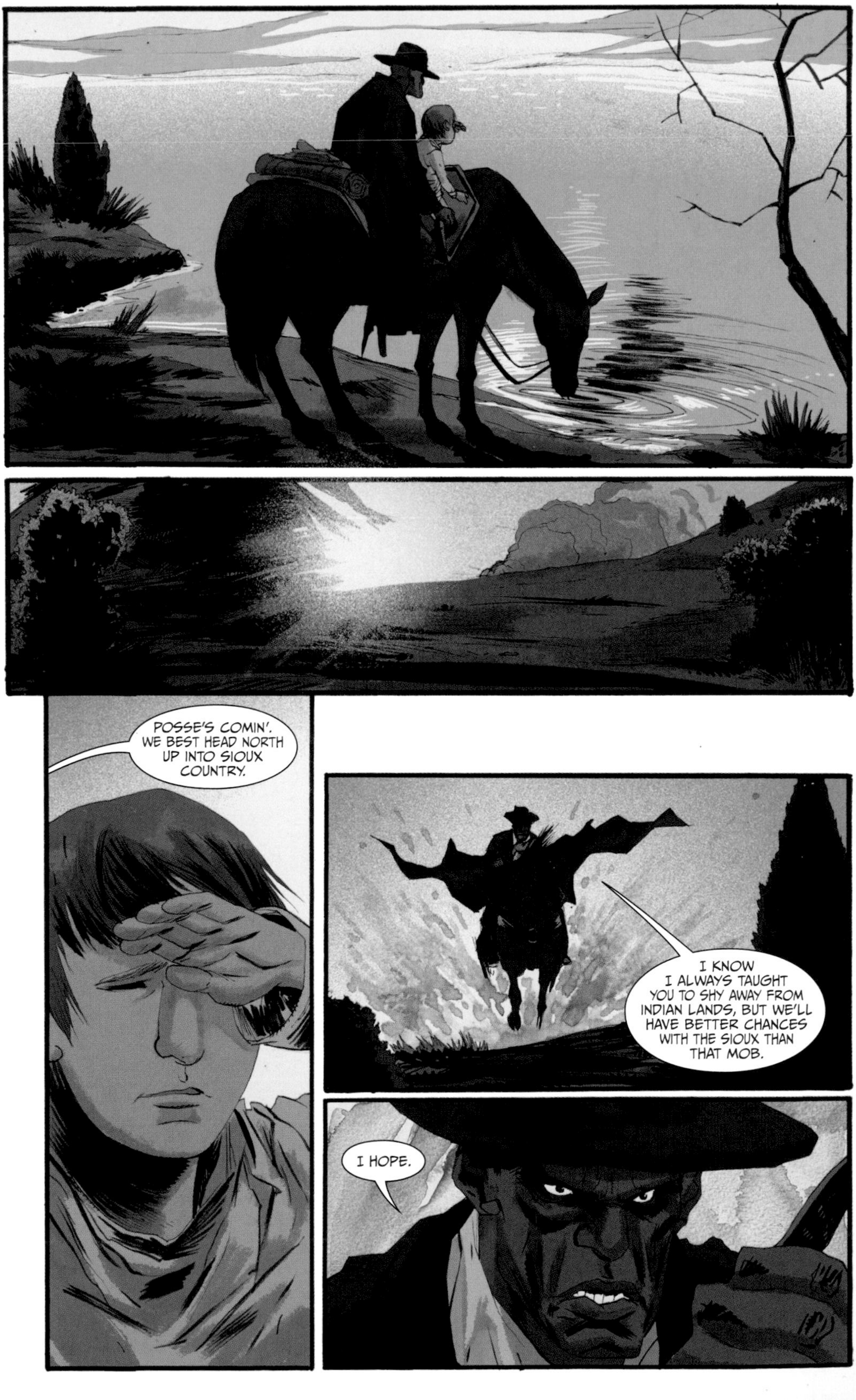
POSSE'S COMIN'. WE BEST HEAD NORTH UP INTO SIOUX COUNTRY.
I KNOW I ALWAYS TAUGHT YOU TO SHY AWAY FROM INDIAN LANDS, BUT WE'LL HAVE BETTER CHANCES WITH THE SIOUX THAN THAT MOB.
I HOPE.

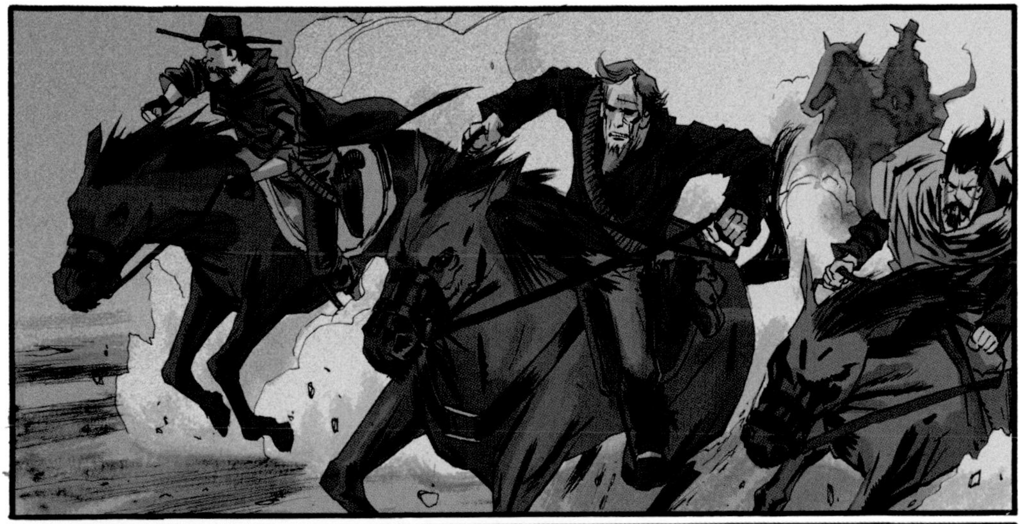
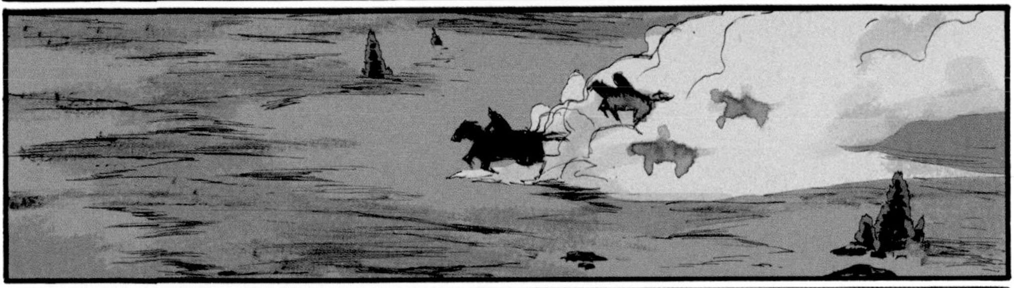
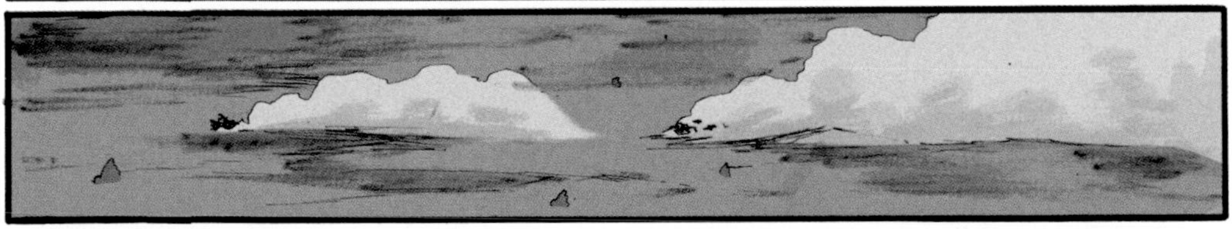
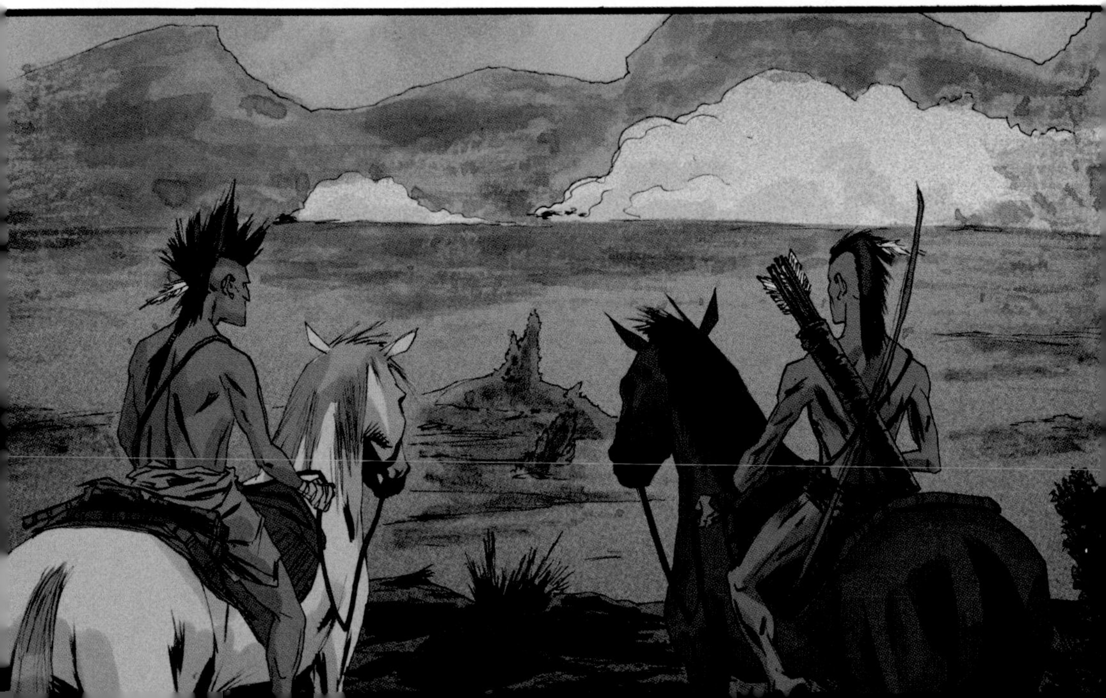

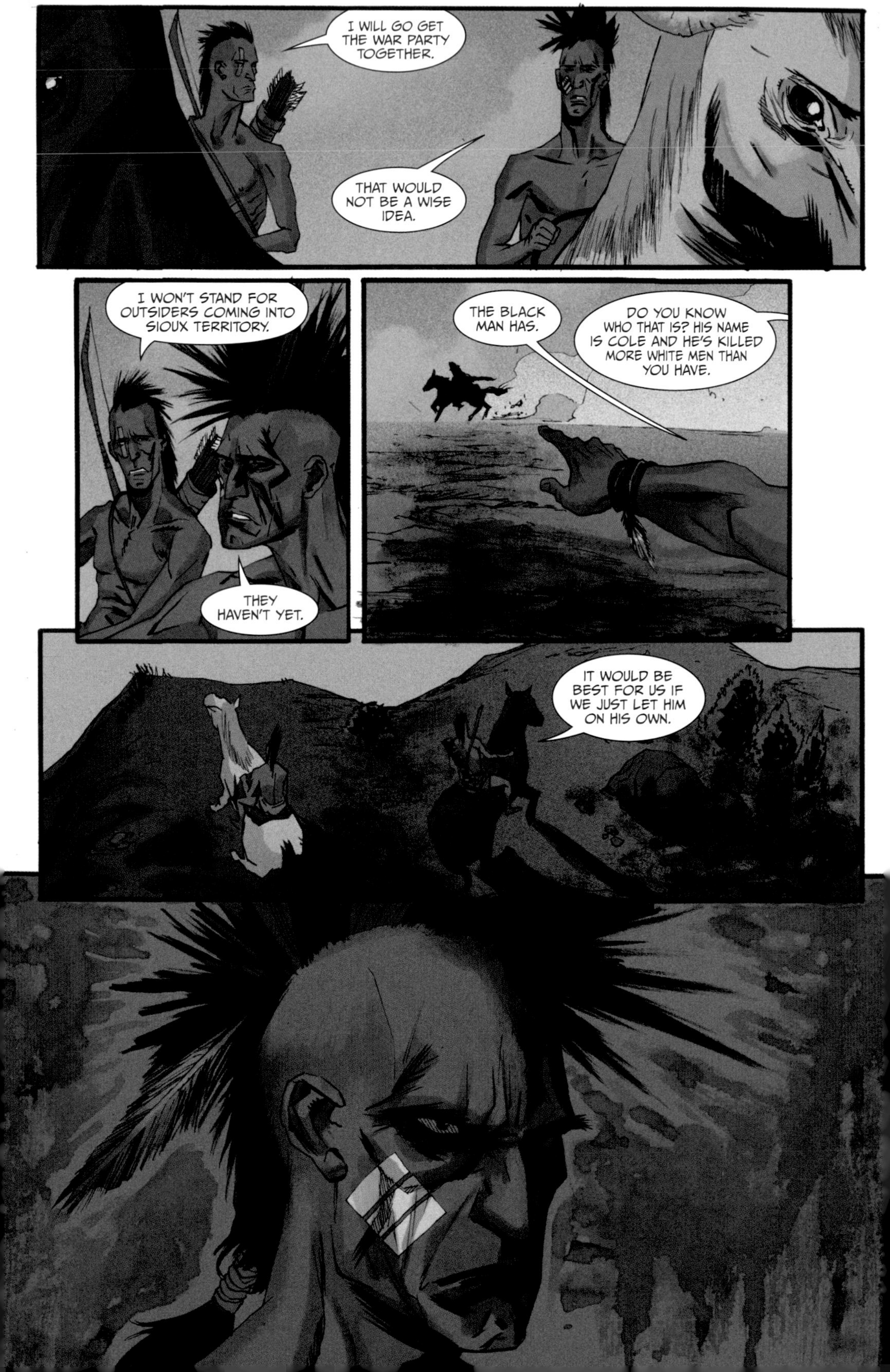
I WILL GO GET THE WAR PARTY TOGETHER.
THAT WOULD NOT BE A WISE IDEA.
I WON'T STAND FOR OUTSIDERS COMING INTO SIOUX TERRITORY.
THEY HAVEN'T YET.
THE BLACK MAN HAS.
DO YOU KNOW WHO THAT IS? HIS NAME IS COLE AND HE'S KILLED MORE WHITE MEN THAN YOU HAVE.
IT WOULD BE BEST FOR US IF WE JUST LET HIM ON HIS OWN.

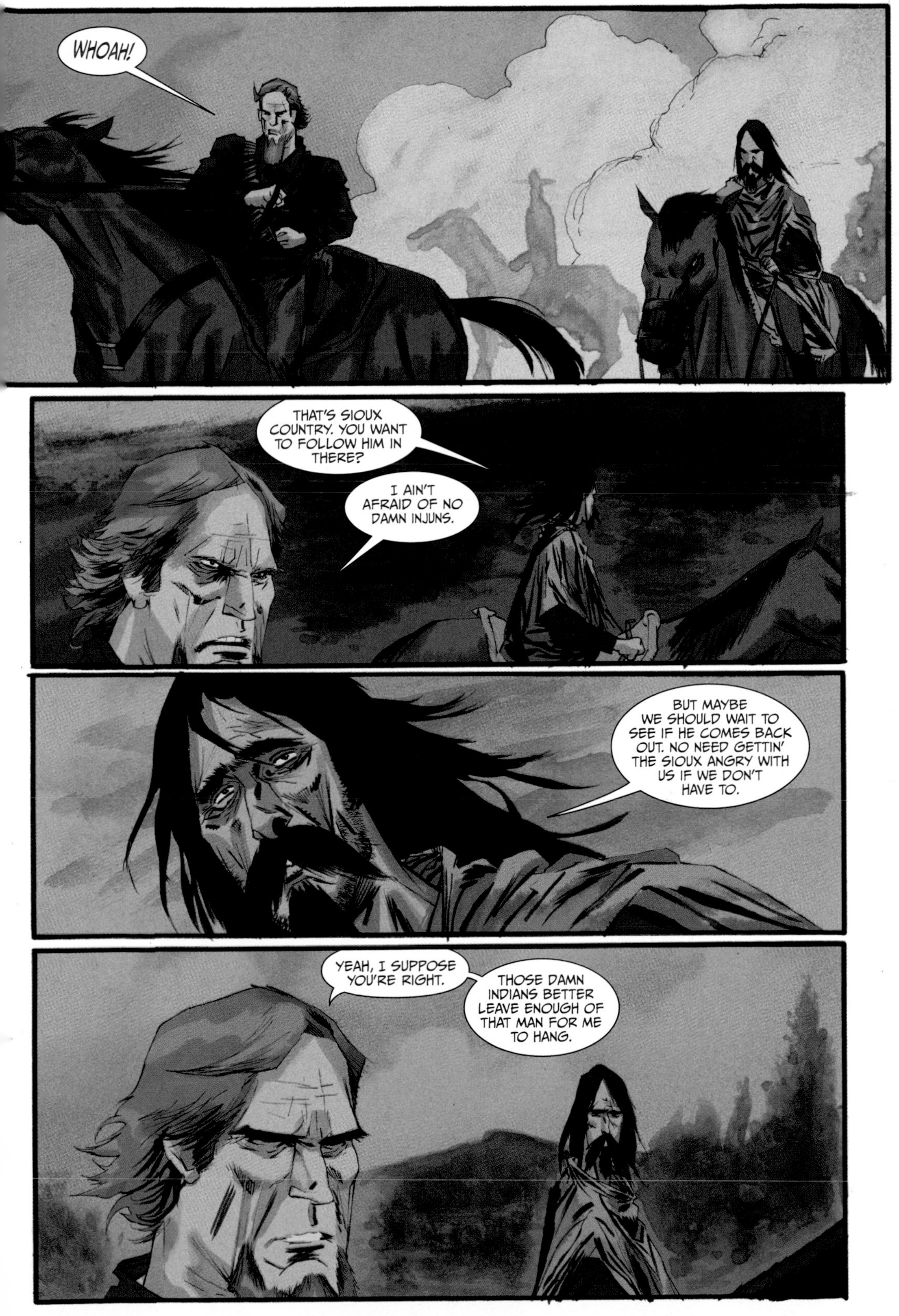
WHOAH!
THAT'S SIOUX COUNTRY. YOU WANT TO FOLLOW HIM IN THERE?
I AIN'T AFRAID OF NO DAMN INJUNS.
BUT MAYBE WE SHOULD WAIT TO SEE IF HE COMES BACK OUT. NO NEED GETTIN' THE SIOUX ANGRY WITH US IF WE DON'T HAVE TO.
YEAH, I SUPPOSE YOU'RE RIGHT.
THOSE DAMN INDIANS BETTER LEAVE ENOUGH OF THAT MAN FOR ME TO HANG.

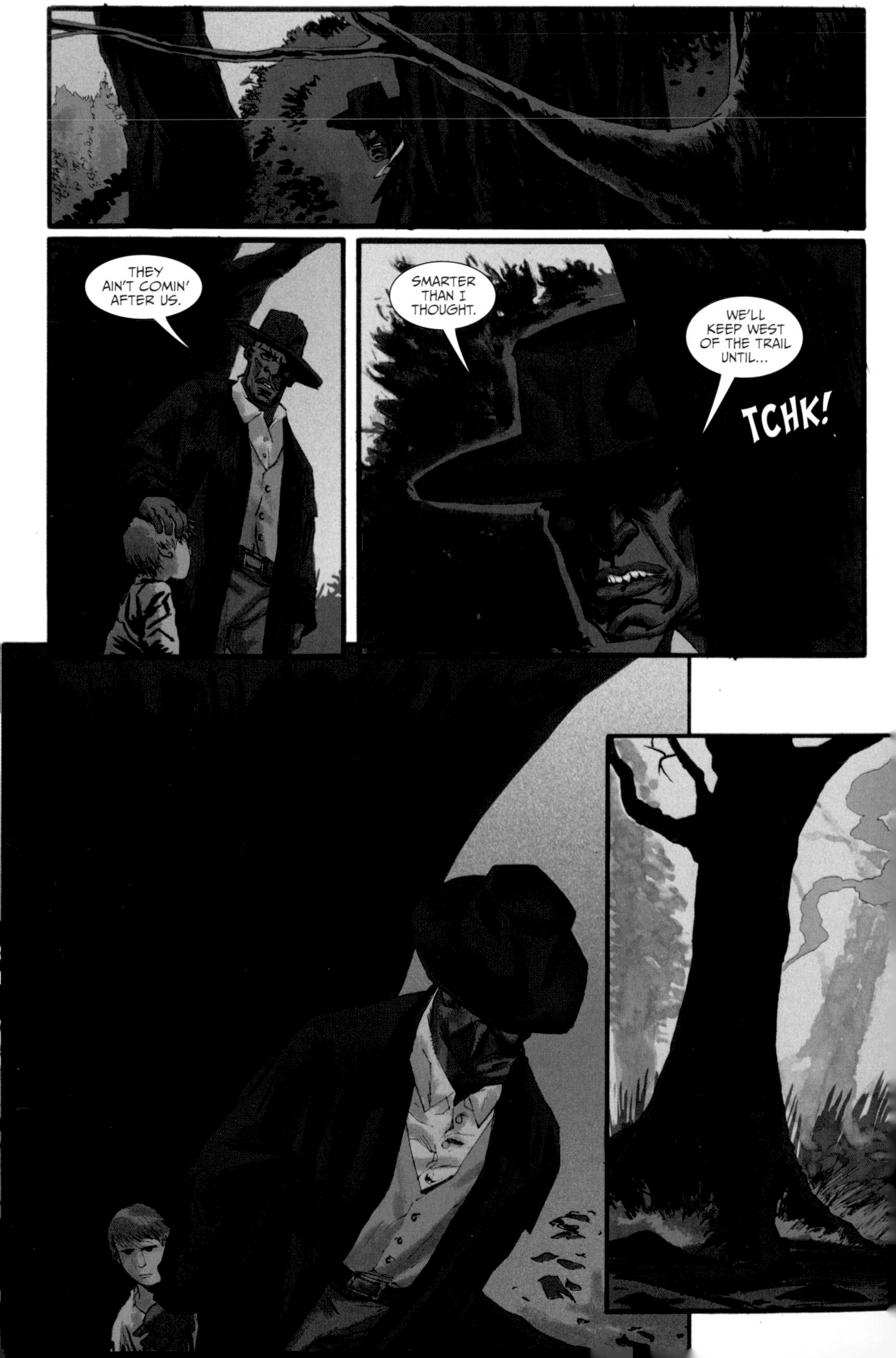
THEY AIN'T COMIN' AFTER US.
SMARTER THAN I THOUGHT.
WE'LL KEEP WEST OF THE TRAIL UNTIL...
TCHK!

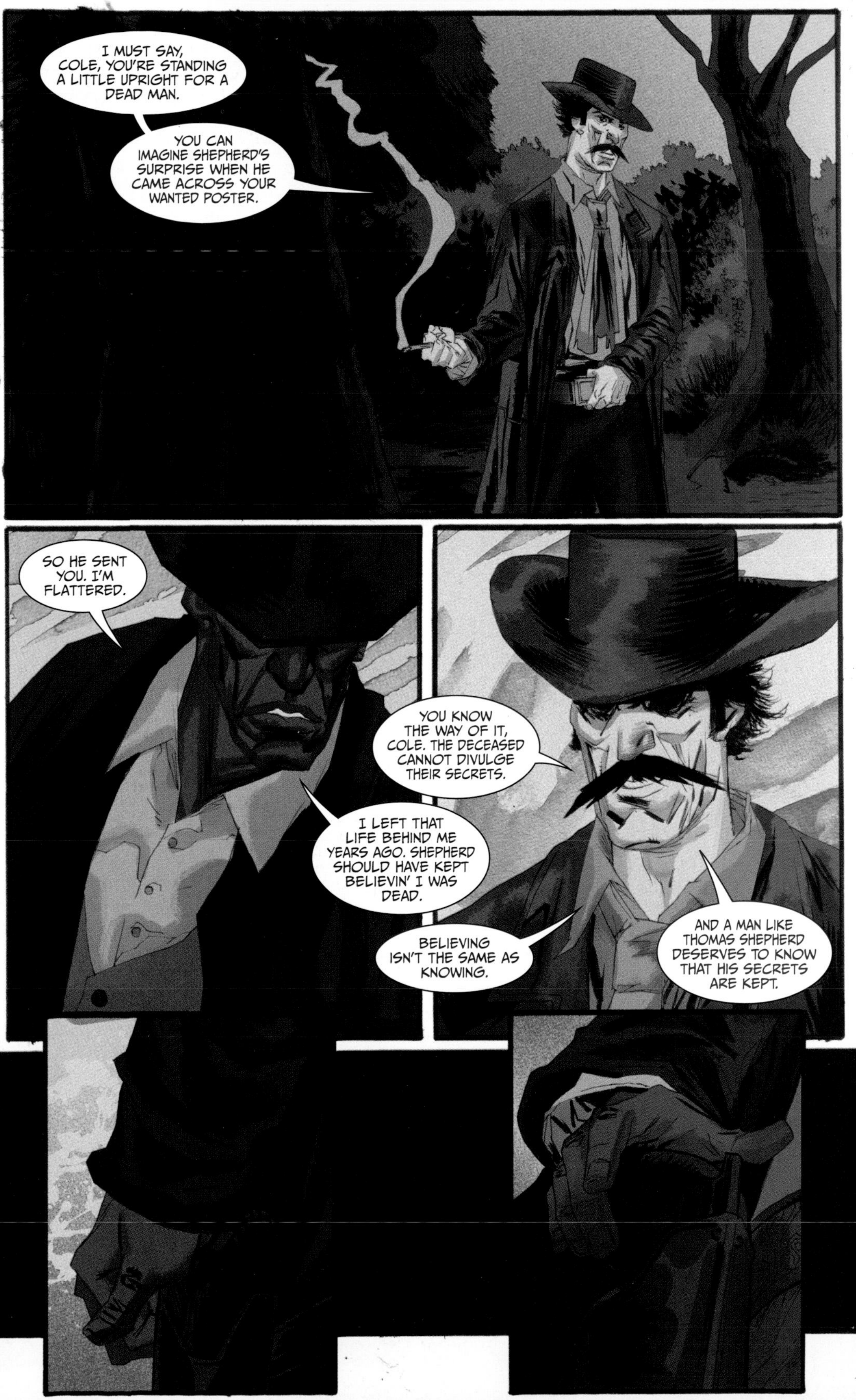
I MUST SAY, COLE, YOU'RE STANDING A LITTLE UPRIGHT FOR A DEAD MAN.
YOU CAN IMAGINE SHEPHERD'S SURPRISE WHEN HE CAME ACROSS YOUR WANTED POSTER.
SO HE SENT YOU. I'M FLATTERED.
YOU KNOW THE WAY OF IT, COLE. THE DECEASED CANNOT DIVULGE THEIR SECRETS.
I LEFT THAT LIFE BEHIND ME YEARS AGO. SHEPHERD SHOULD HAVE KEPT BELIEVIN' I WAS DEAD.
BELIEVING ISN'T THE SAME AS KNOWING.
AND A MAN LIKE THOMAS SHEPHERD DESERVES TO KNOW THAT HIS SECRETS ARE KEPT.

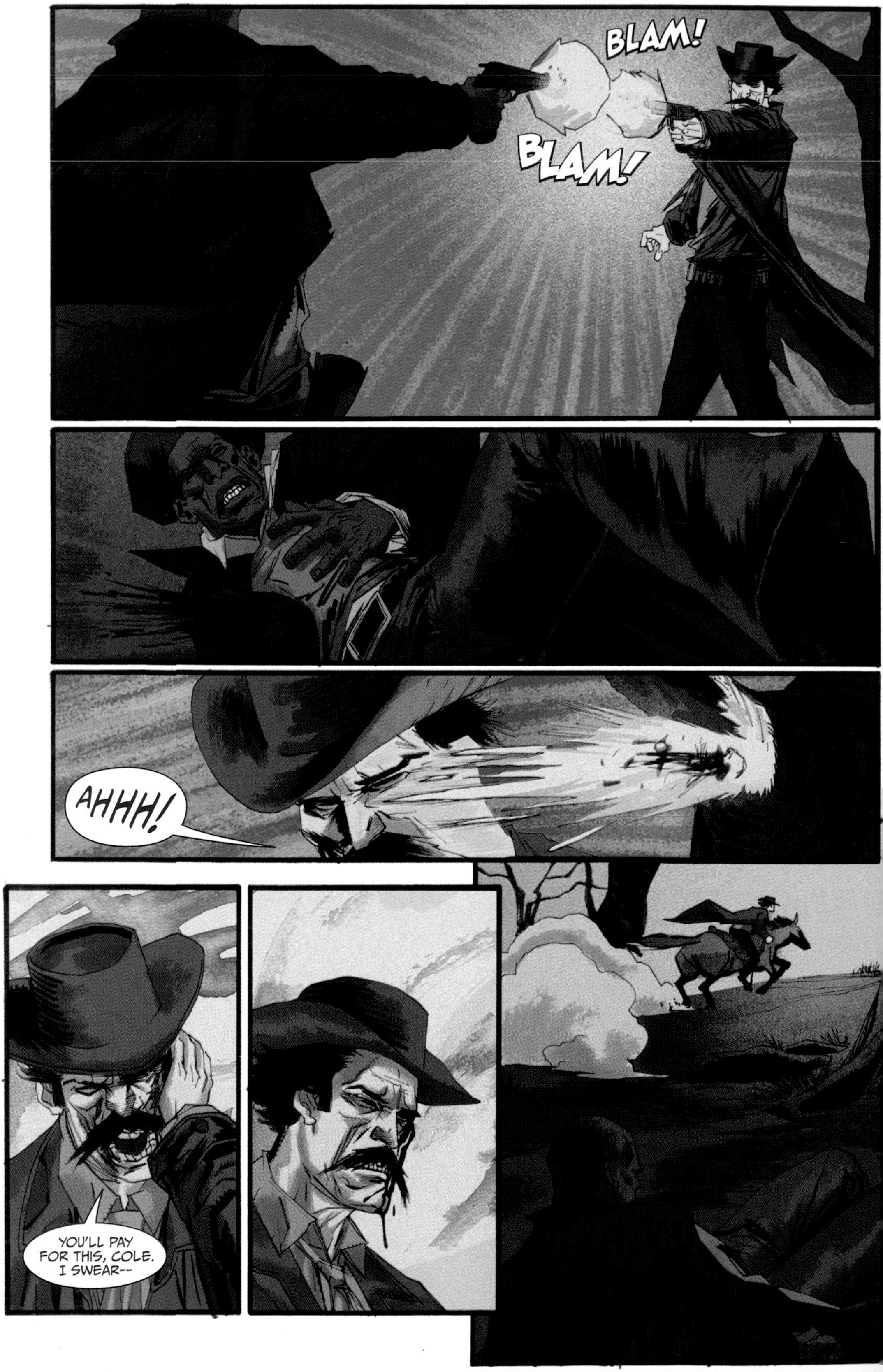
BLAM!
BLAM!
AHHH!
YOU'LL PAY FOR THIS, COLE. I SWEAR--

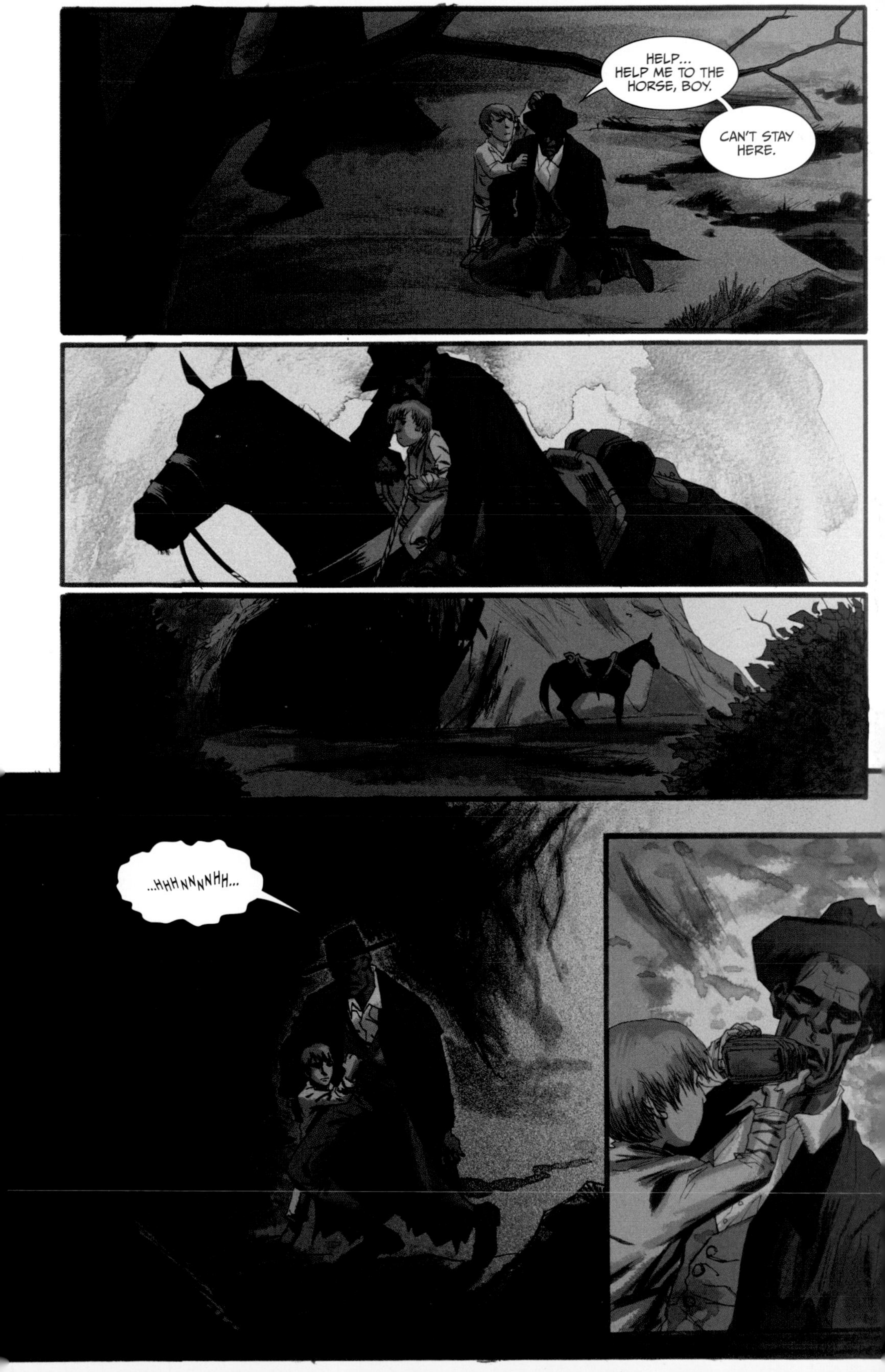
HELP... HELP ME TO THE HORSE, BOY.
CAN'T STAY HERE.
...HHHNNNNHH...

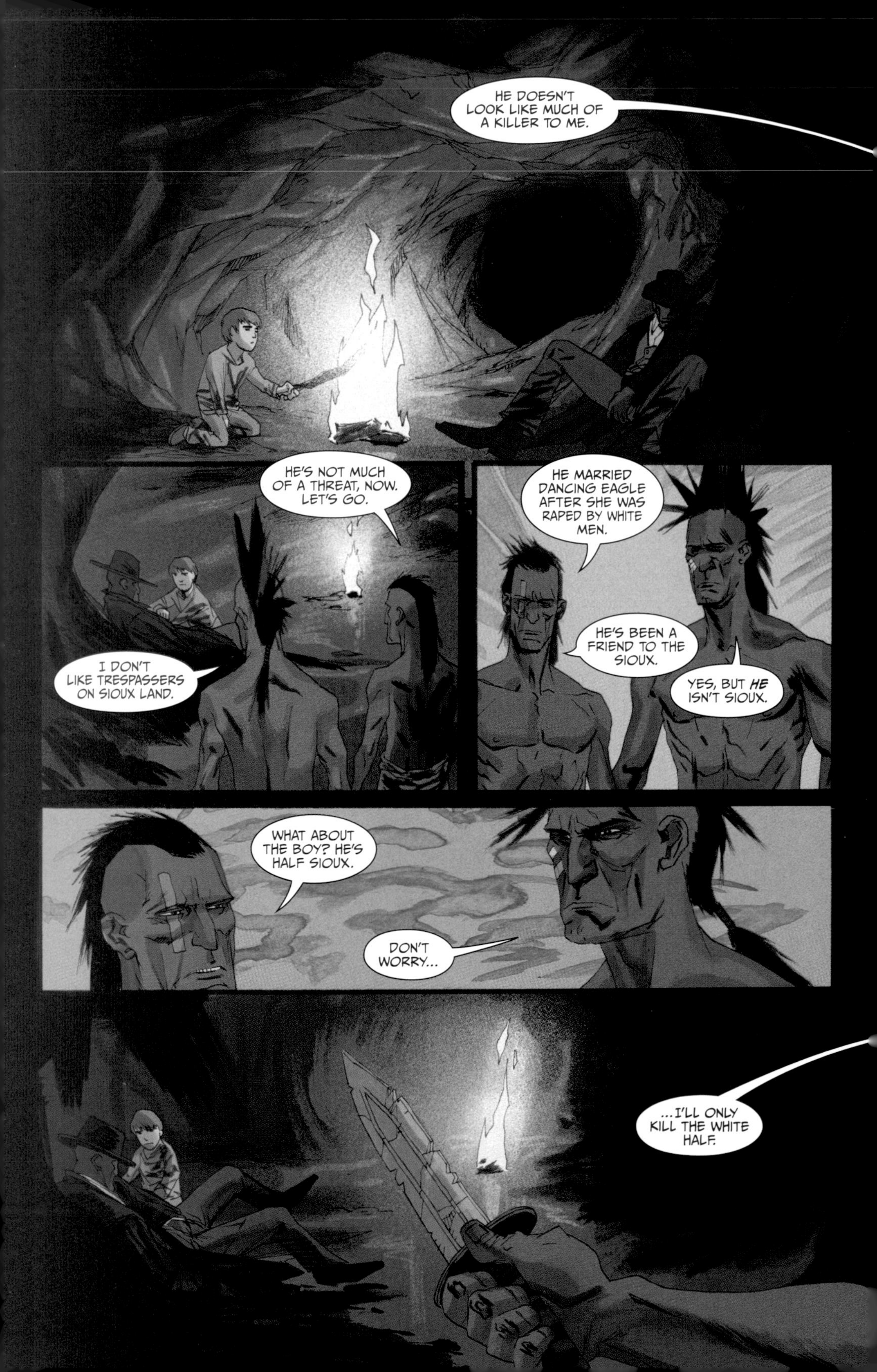
HE DOESN'T LOOK LIKE MUCH OF A KILLER TO ME.
HE'S NOT MUCH OF A THREAT, NOW. LET'S GO.
I DON'T LIKE TRESPASSERS ON SIOUX LAND.
HE MARRIED DANCING EAGLE AFTER SHE WAS RAPED BY WHITE MEN.
HE'S BEEN A FRIEND TO THE SIOUX.
YES, BUT HE ISN'T SIOUX.
WHAT ABOUT THE BOY? HE'S HALF SIOUX.
DON'T WORRY...
...I'LL ONLY KILL THE WHITE HALF.

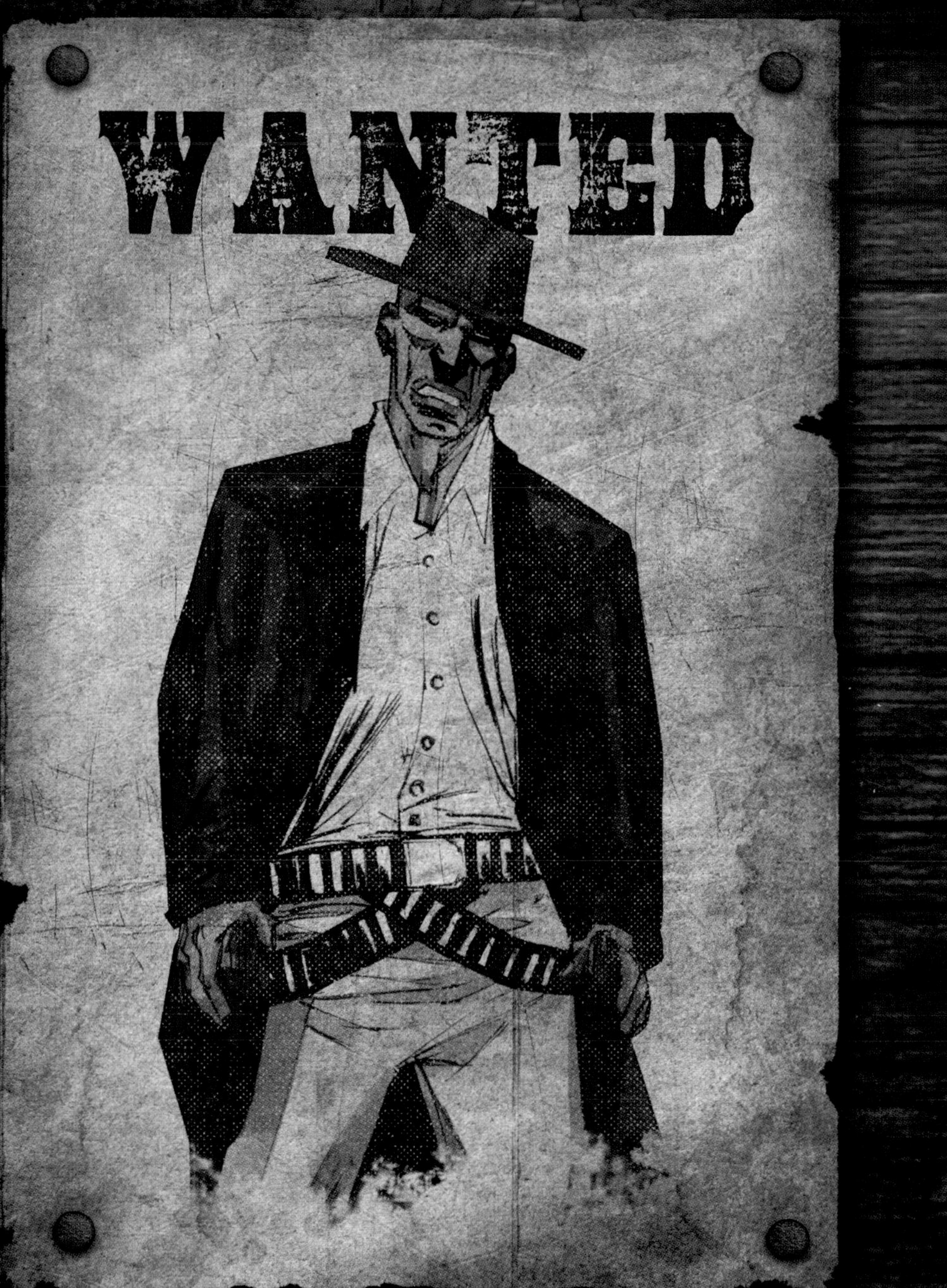
WANTED

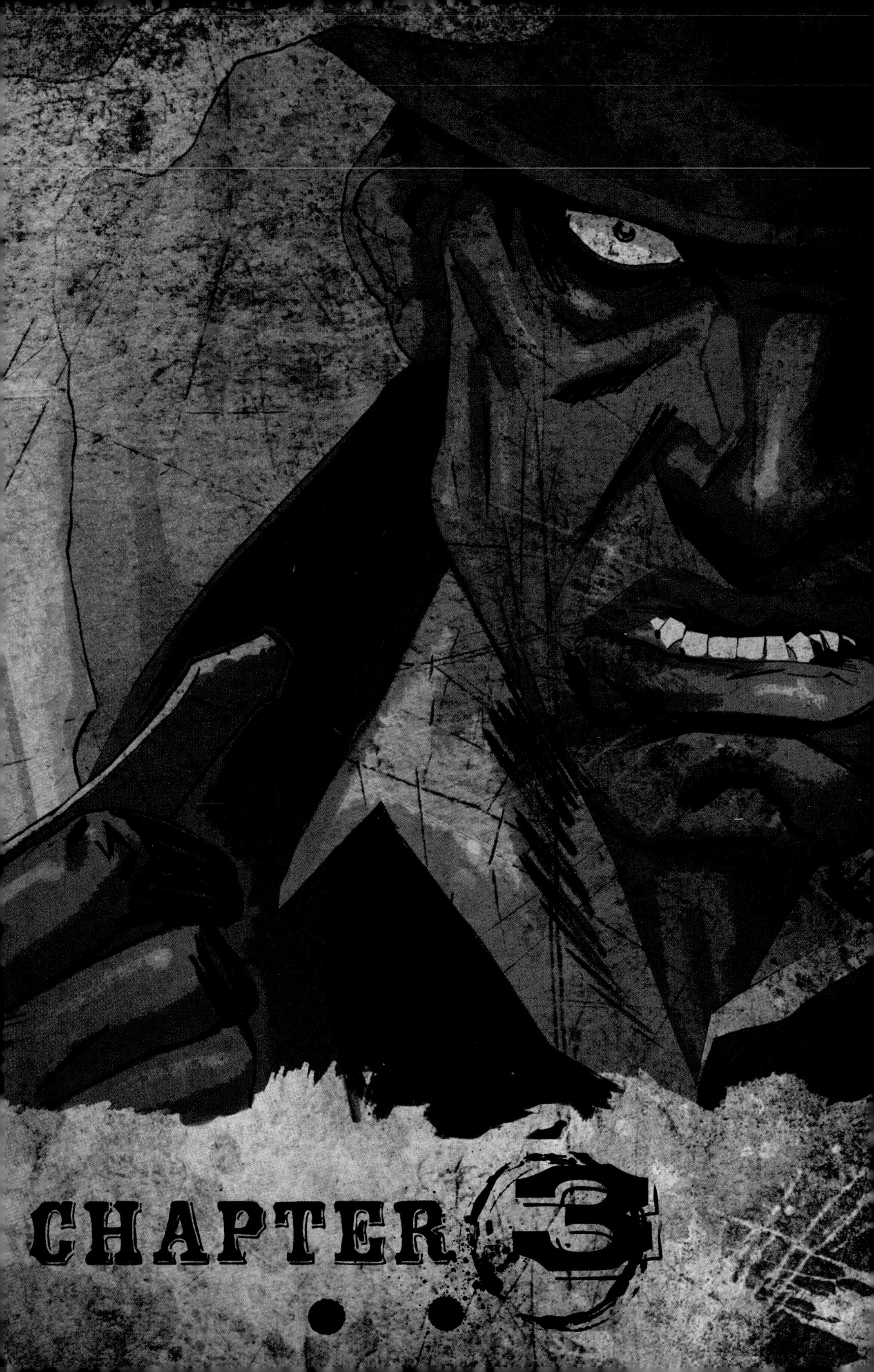
CHAPTER 3

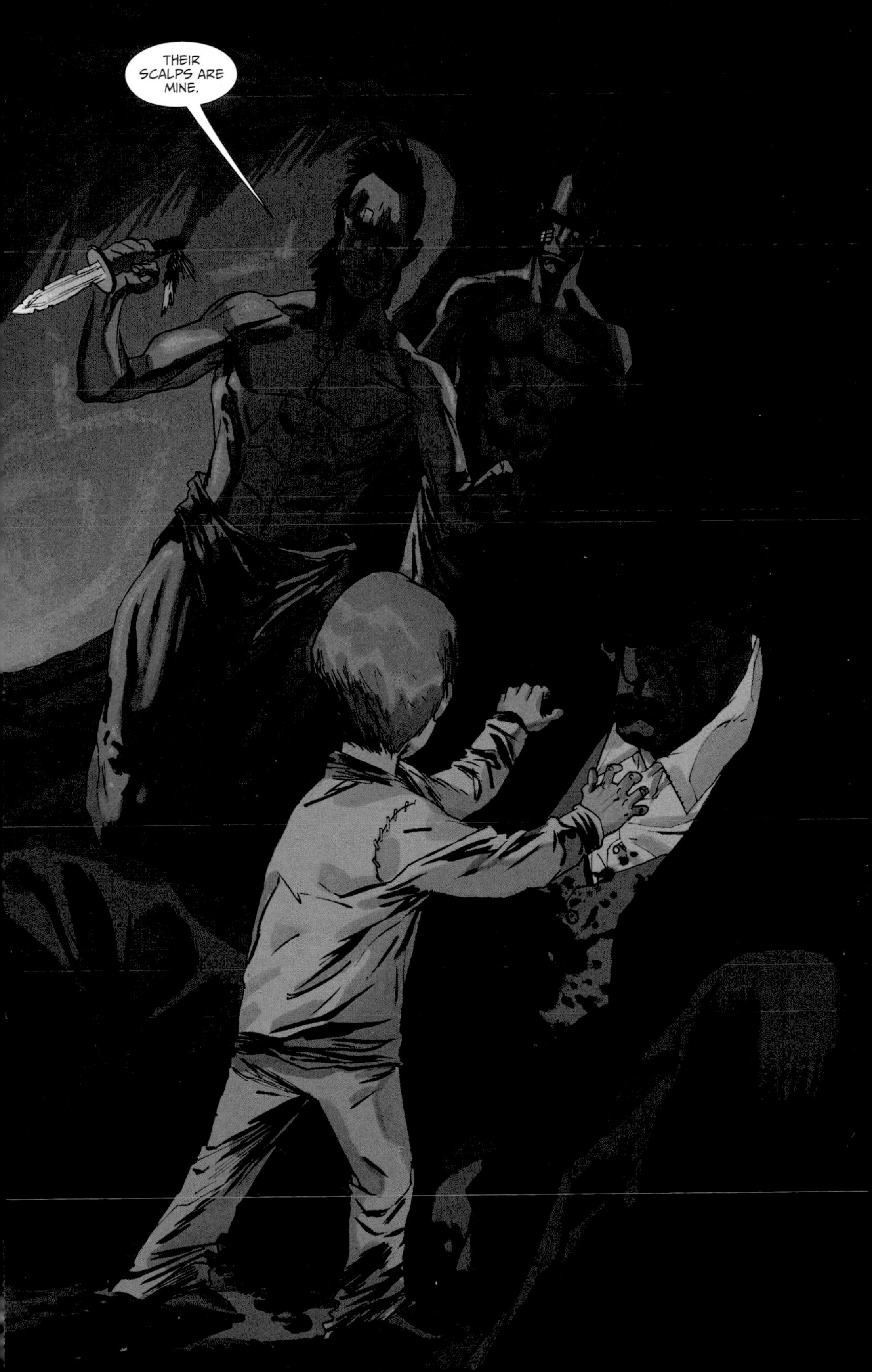
THEIR SCALPS ARE MINE.

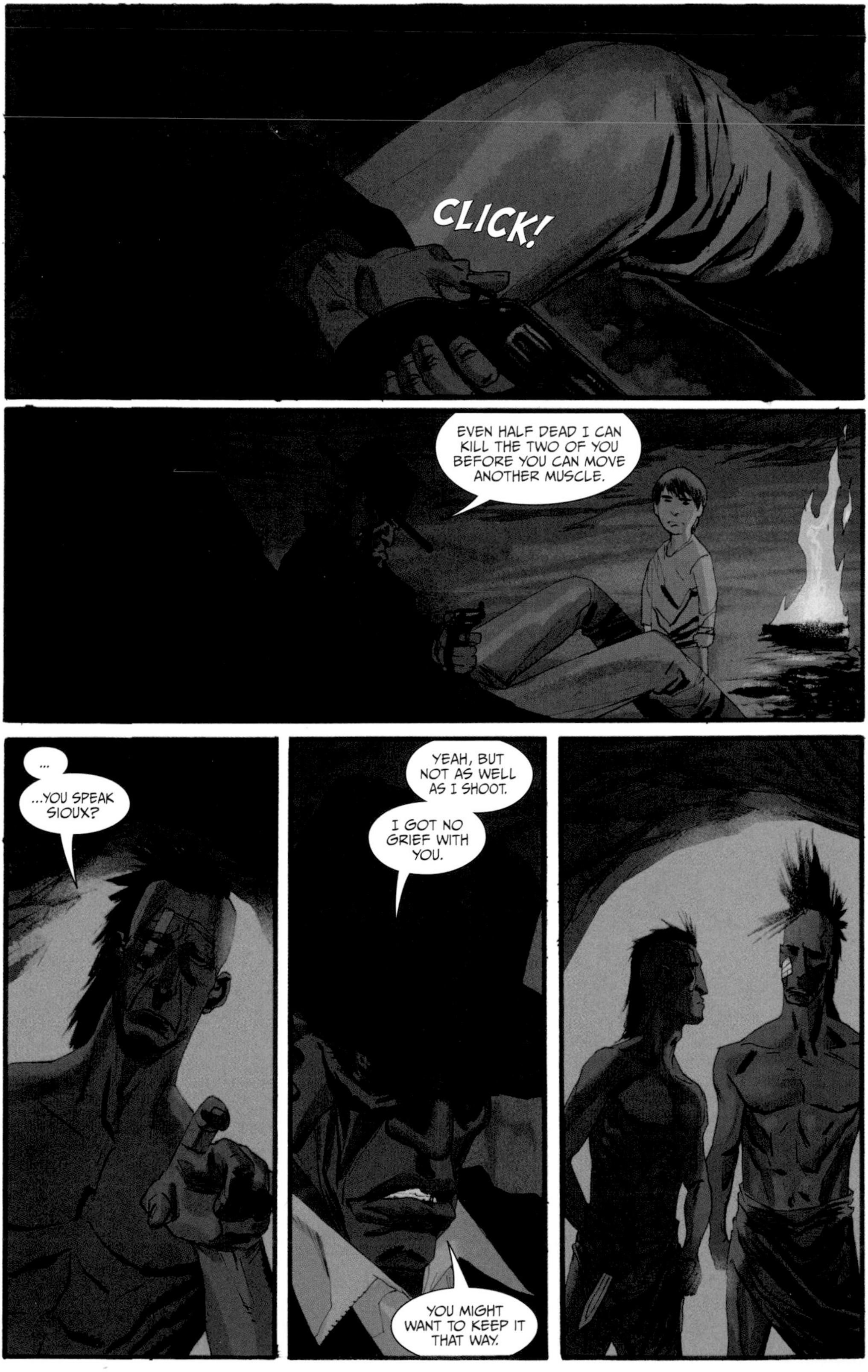
CLICK!
EVEN HALF DEAD I CAN KILL THE TWO OF YOU BEFORE YOU CAN MOVE ANOTHER MUSCLE.
...
...YOU SPEAK SIOUX?
YEAH, BUT NOT AS WELL AS I SHOOT.
I GOT NO GRIEF WITH YOU.
YOU MIGHT WANT TO KEEP IT THAT WAY.

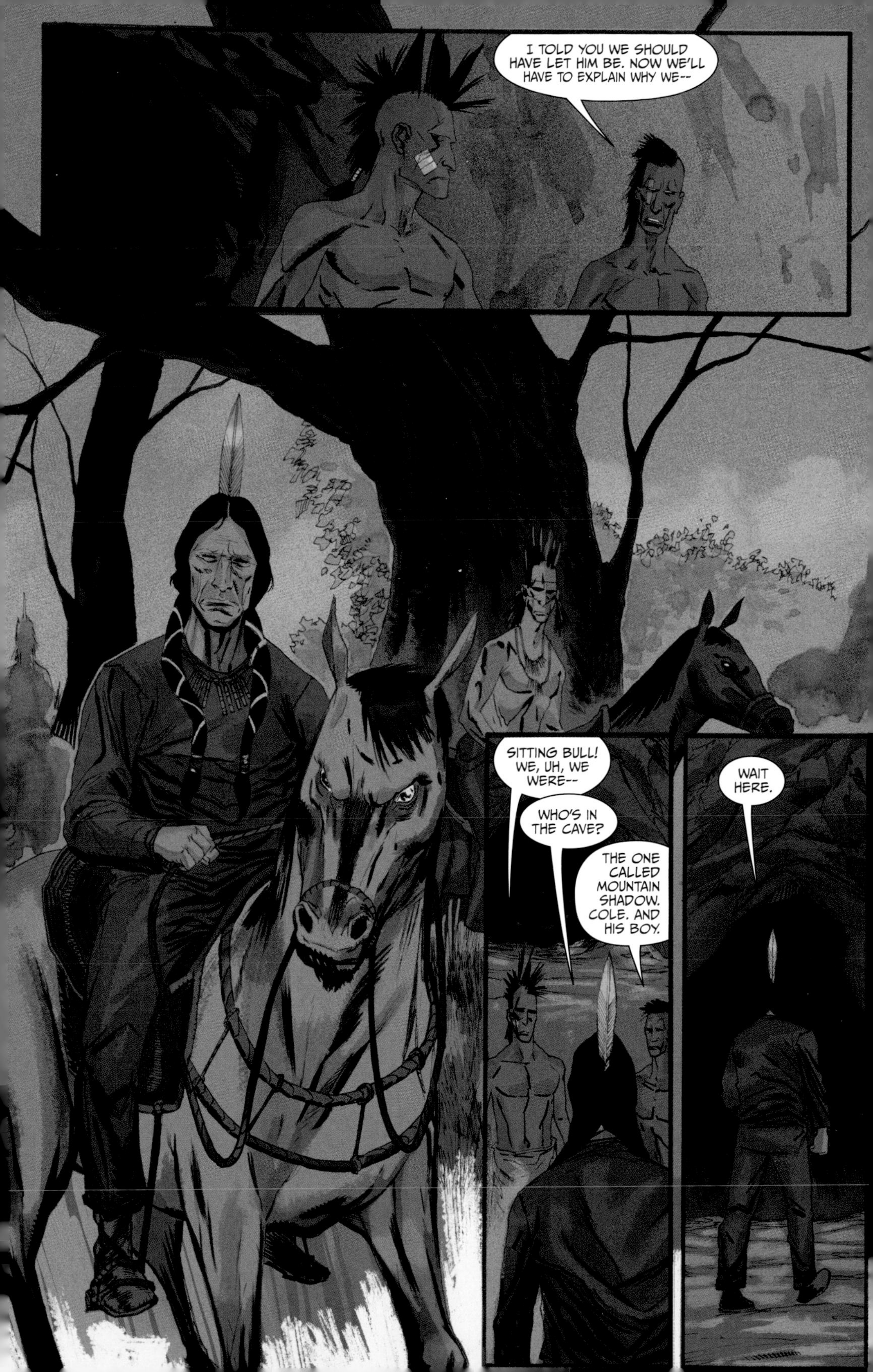
I TOLD YOU WE SHOULD HAVE LET HIM BE. NOW WE'LL HAVE TO EXPLAIN WHY WE--
SITTING BULL! WE, UH, WE WERE--
WHO'S IN THE CAVE?
THE ONE CALLED MOUNTAIN SHADOW. COLE. AND HIS BOY.
WAIT HERE.

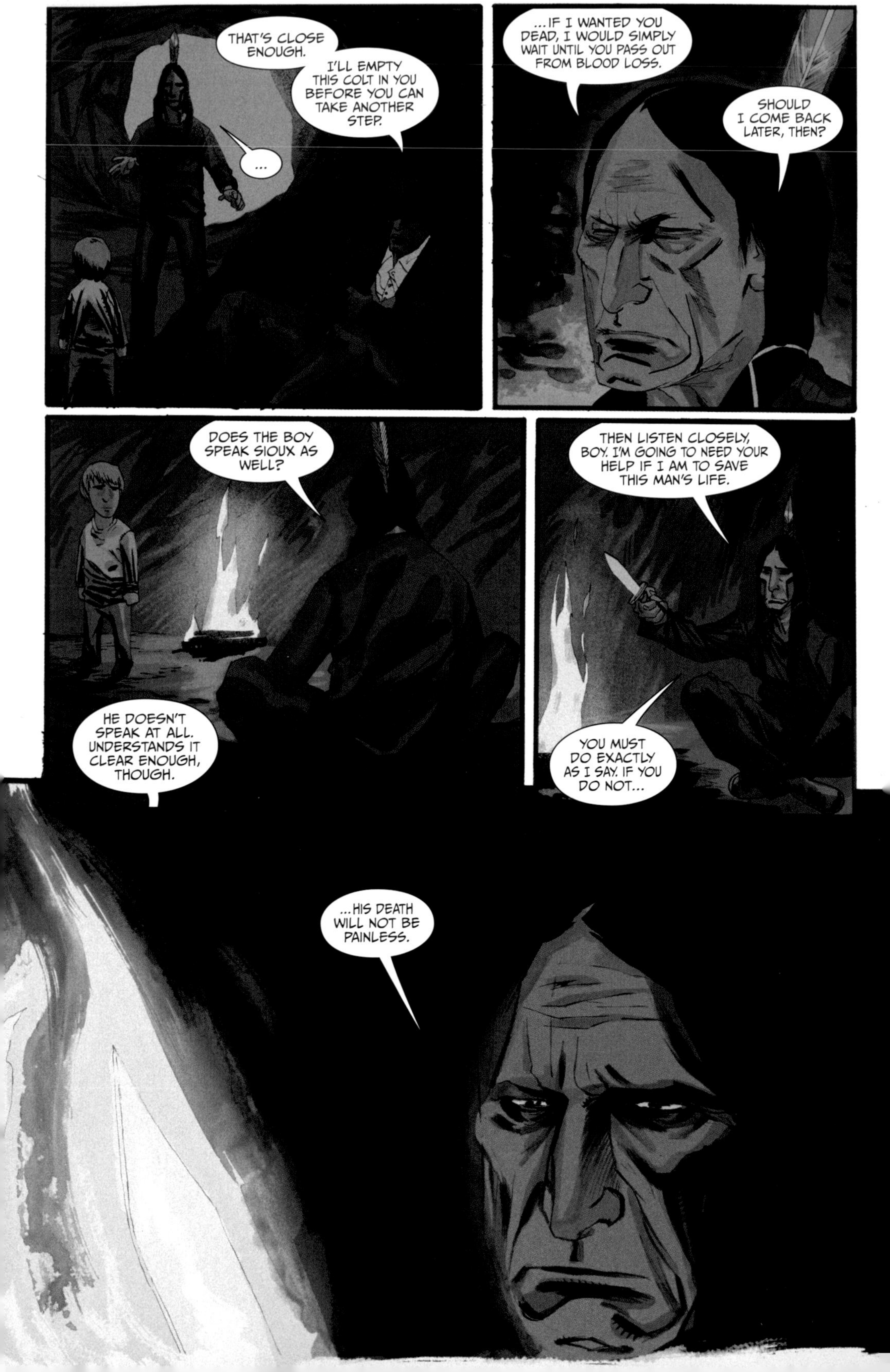
THAT'S CLOSE ENOUGH.
I'LL EMPTY THIS COLT IN YOU BEFORE YOU CAN TAKE ANOTHER STEP.
...
...IF I WANTED YOU DEAD, I WOULD SIMPLY WAIT UNTIL YOU PASS OUT FROM BLOOD LOSS.
SHOULD I COME BACK LATER, THEN?
DOES THE BOY SPEAK SIOUX AS WELL?
HE DOESN'T SPEAK AT ALL. UNDERSTANDS IT CLEAR ENOUGH, THOUGH.
THEN LISTEN CLOSELY, BOY. I'M GOING TO NEED YOUR HELP IF I AM TO SAVE THIS MAN'S LIFE.
YOU MUST DO EXACTLY AS I SAY. IF YOU DO NOT...
...HIS DEATH WILL NOT BE PAINLESS.

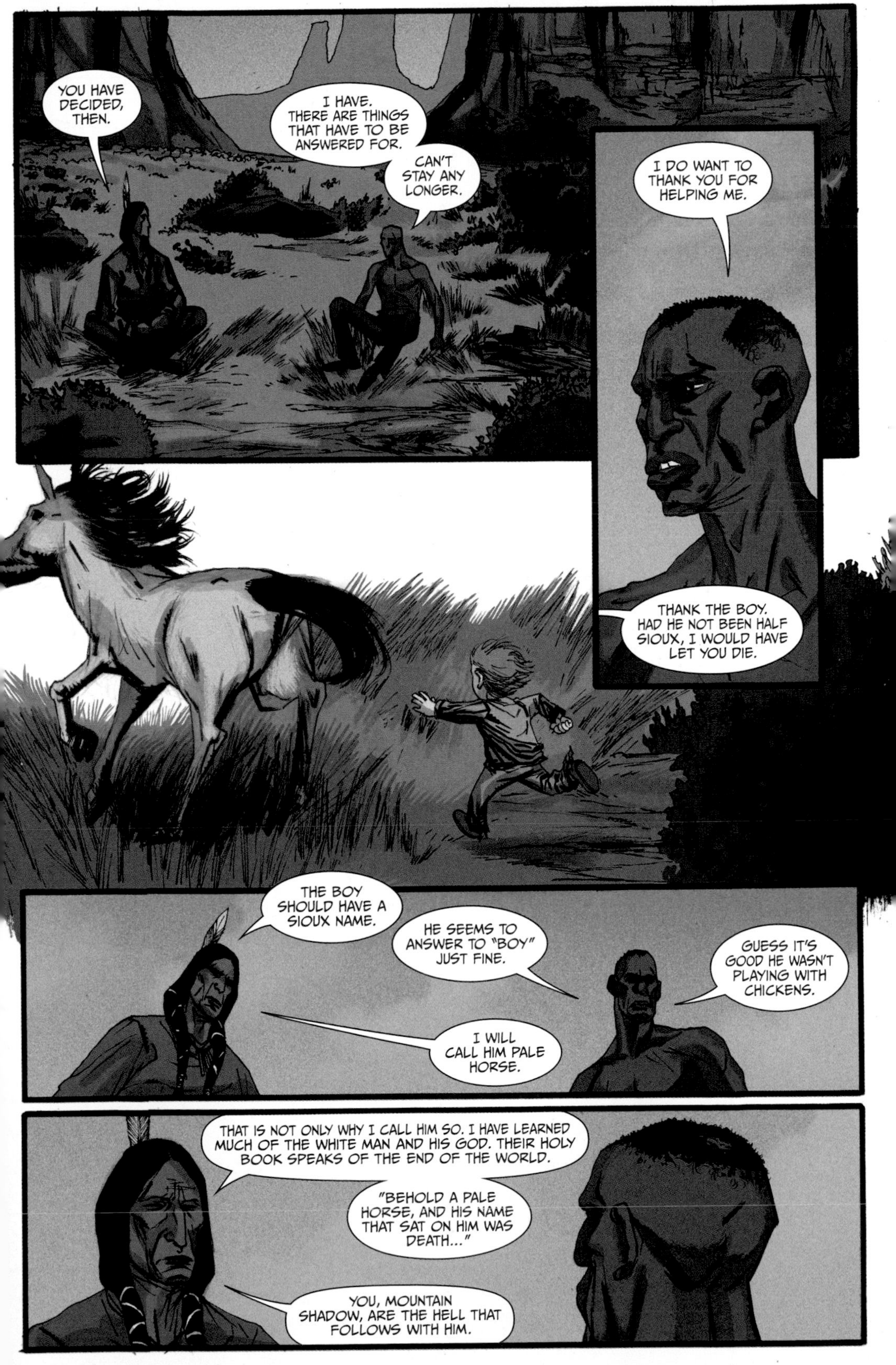
YOU HAVE DECIDED, THEN.
I HAVE. THERE ARE THINGS THAT HAVE TO BE ANSWERED FOR.
CAN'T STAY ANY LONGER.
I DO WANT TO THANK YOU FOR HELPING ME.
THANK THE BOY. HAD HE NOT BEEN HALF SIOUX, I WOULD HAVE LET YOU DIE.
THE BOY SHOULD HAVE A SIOUX NAME.
HE SEEMS TO ANSWER TO "BOY" JUST FINE.
GUESS IT'S GOOD HE WASN'T PLAYING WITH CHICKENS.
I WILL CALL HIM PALE HORSE.
THAT IS NOT ONLY WHY I CALL HIM SO. I HAVE LEARNED MUCH OF THE WHITE MAN AND HIS GOD. THEIR HOLY BOOK SPEAKS OF THE END OF THE WORLD.
"BEHOLD A PALE HORSE, AND HIS NAME THAT SAT ON HIM WAS DEATH..."
YOU, MOUNTAIN SHADOW, ARE THE HELL THAT FOLLOWS WITH HIM.

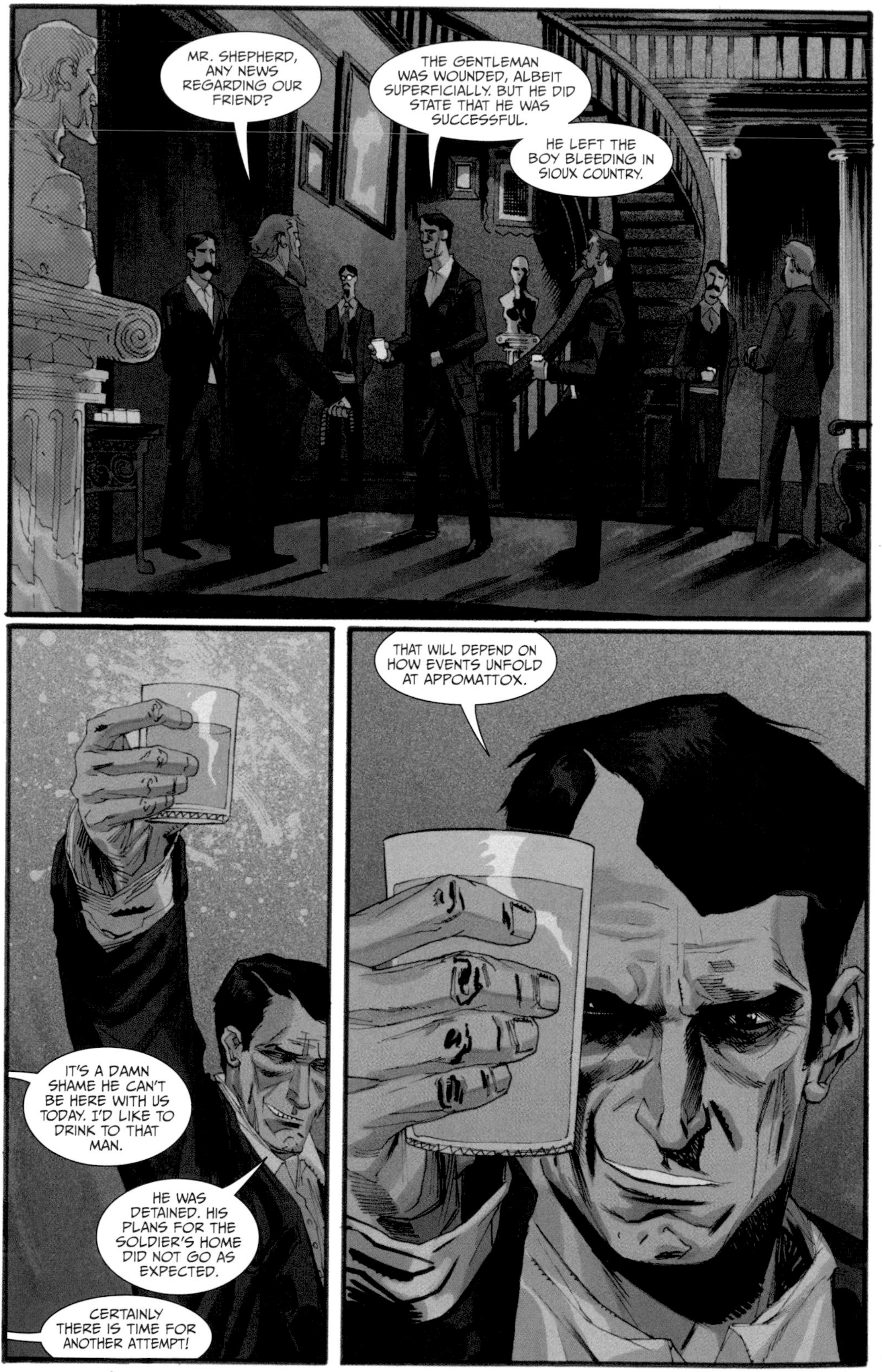
MR. SHEPHERD, ANY NEWS REGARDING OUR FRIEND?
THE GENTLEMAN WAS WOUNDED, ALBEIT SUPERFICIALLY. BUT HE DID STATE THAT HE WAS SUCCESSFUL.
HE LEFT THE BOY BLEEDING IN SIOUX COUNTRY.
IT'S A DAMN SHAME HE CAN'T BE HERE WITH US TODAY. I'D LIKE TO DRINK TO THAT MAN.
HE WAS DETAINED. HIS PLANS FOR THE SOLDIER'S HOME DID NOT GO AS EXPECTED.
CERTAINLY THERE IS TIME FOR ANOTHER ATTEMPT!
THAT WILL DEPEND ON HOW EVENTS UNFOLD AT APPOMATTOX.

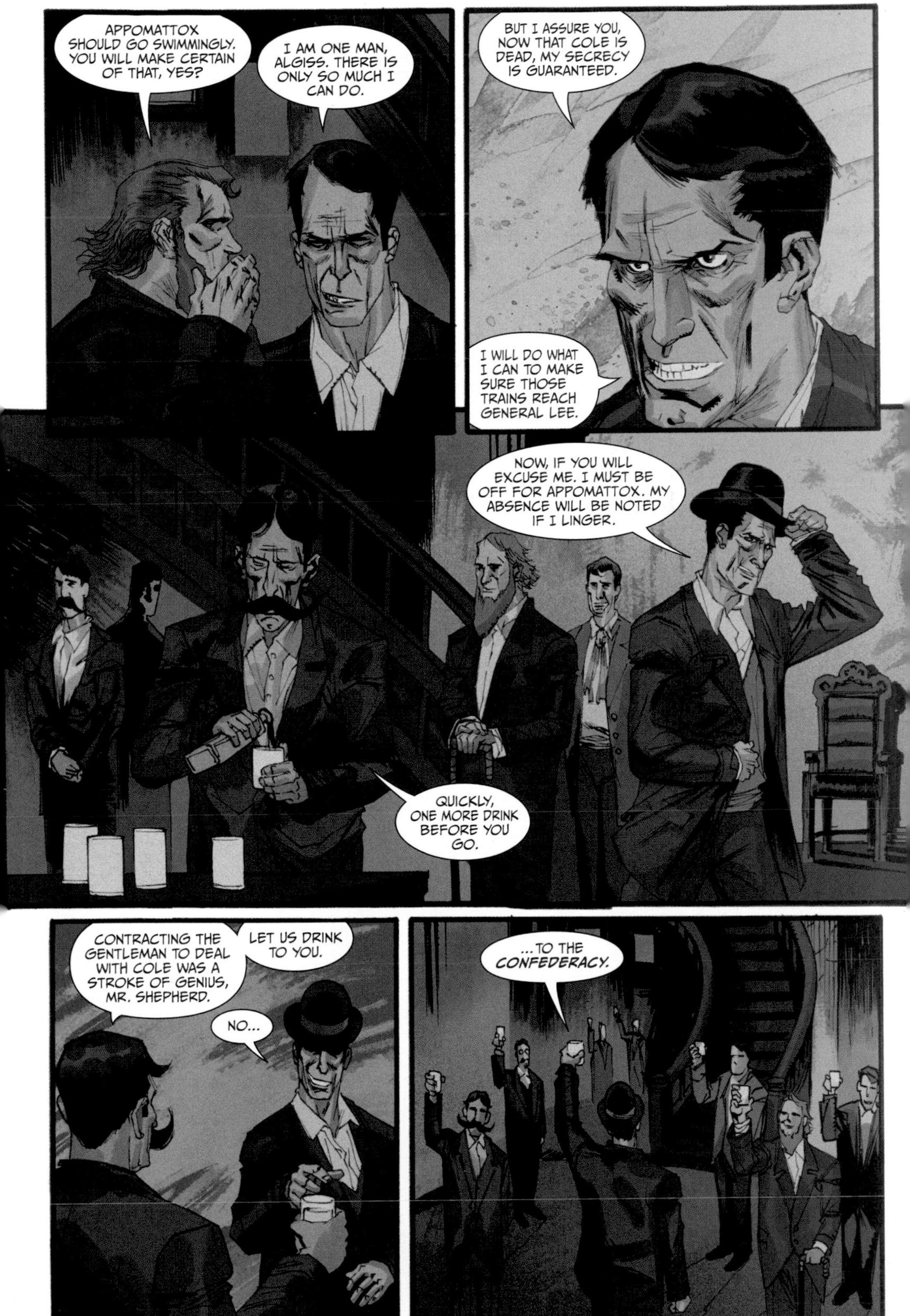
APPOMATTOX SHOULD GO SWIMMINGLY. YOU WILL MAKE CERTAIN OF THAT, YES?
I AM ONE MAN, ALGISS. THERE IS ONLY SO MUCH I CAN DO.
BUT I ASSURE YOU, NOW THAT COLE IS DEAD, MY SECRECY IS GUARANTEED.
I WILL DO WHAT I CAN TO MAKE SURE THOSE TRAINS REACH GENERAL LEE.
NOW, IF YOU WILL EXCUSE ME. I MUST BE OFF FOR APPOMATTOX. MY ABSENCE WILL BE NOTED IF I LINGER.
QUICKLY, ONE MORE DRINK BEFORE YOU GO.
CONTRACTING THE GENTLEMAN TO DEAL WITH COLE WAS A STROKE OF GENIUS, MR. SHEPHERD.
NO...
LET US DRINK TO YOU.
...TO THE *CONFEDERACY.*

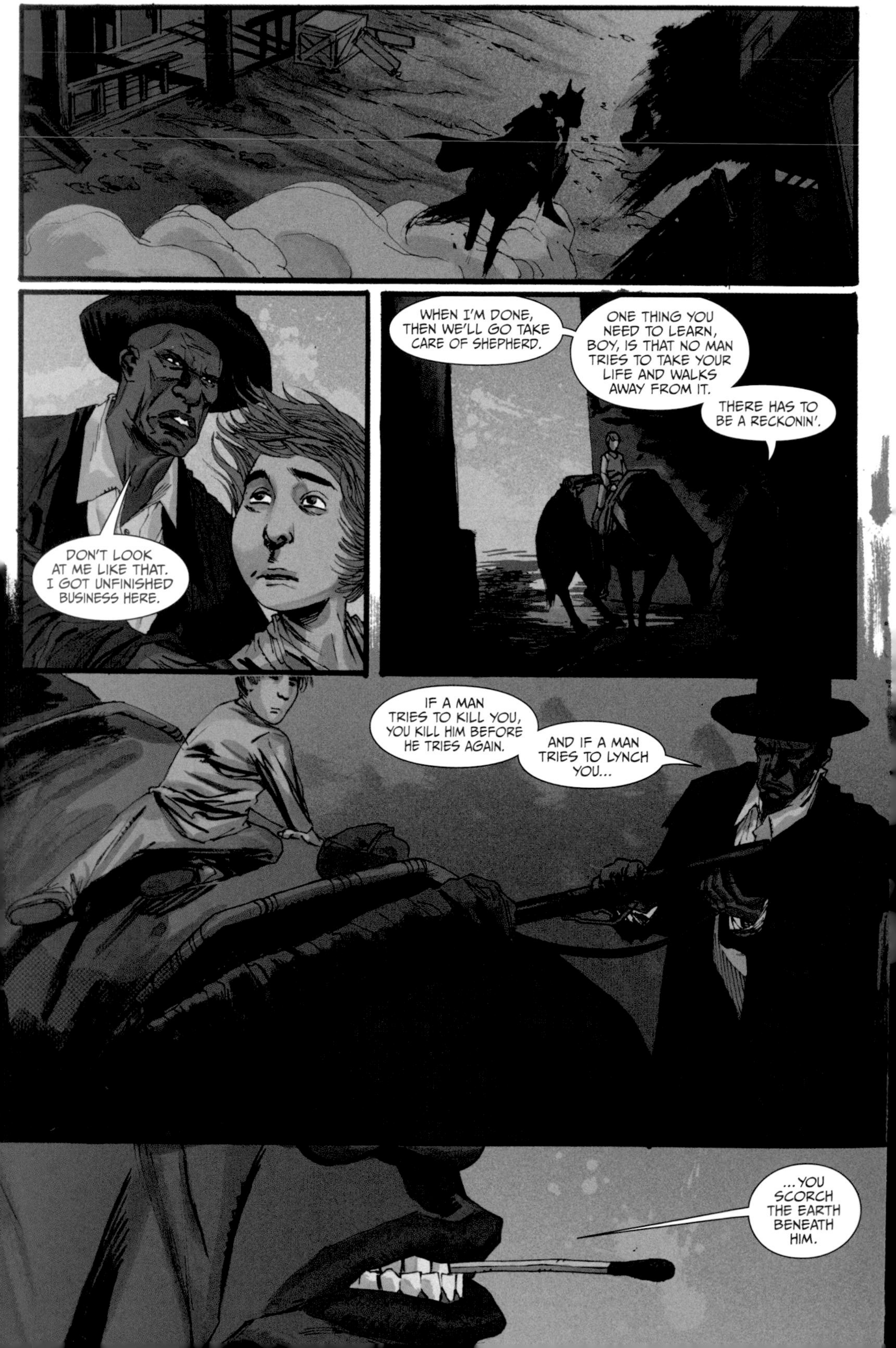
DON'T LOOK AT ME LIKE THAT. I GOT UNFINISHED BUSINESS HERE.
WHEN I'M DONE, THEN WE'LL GO TAKE CARE OF SHEPHERD.
ONE THING YOU NEED TO LEARN, BOY, IS THAT NO MAN TRIES TO TAKE YOUR LIFE AND WALKS AWAY FROM IT.
THERE HAS TO BE A RECKONIN'.
IF A MAN TRIES TO KILL YOU, YOU KILL HIM BEFORE HE TRIES AGAIN.
AND IF A MAN TRIES TO LYNCH YOU...
...YOU SCORCH THE EARTH BENEATH HIM.

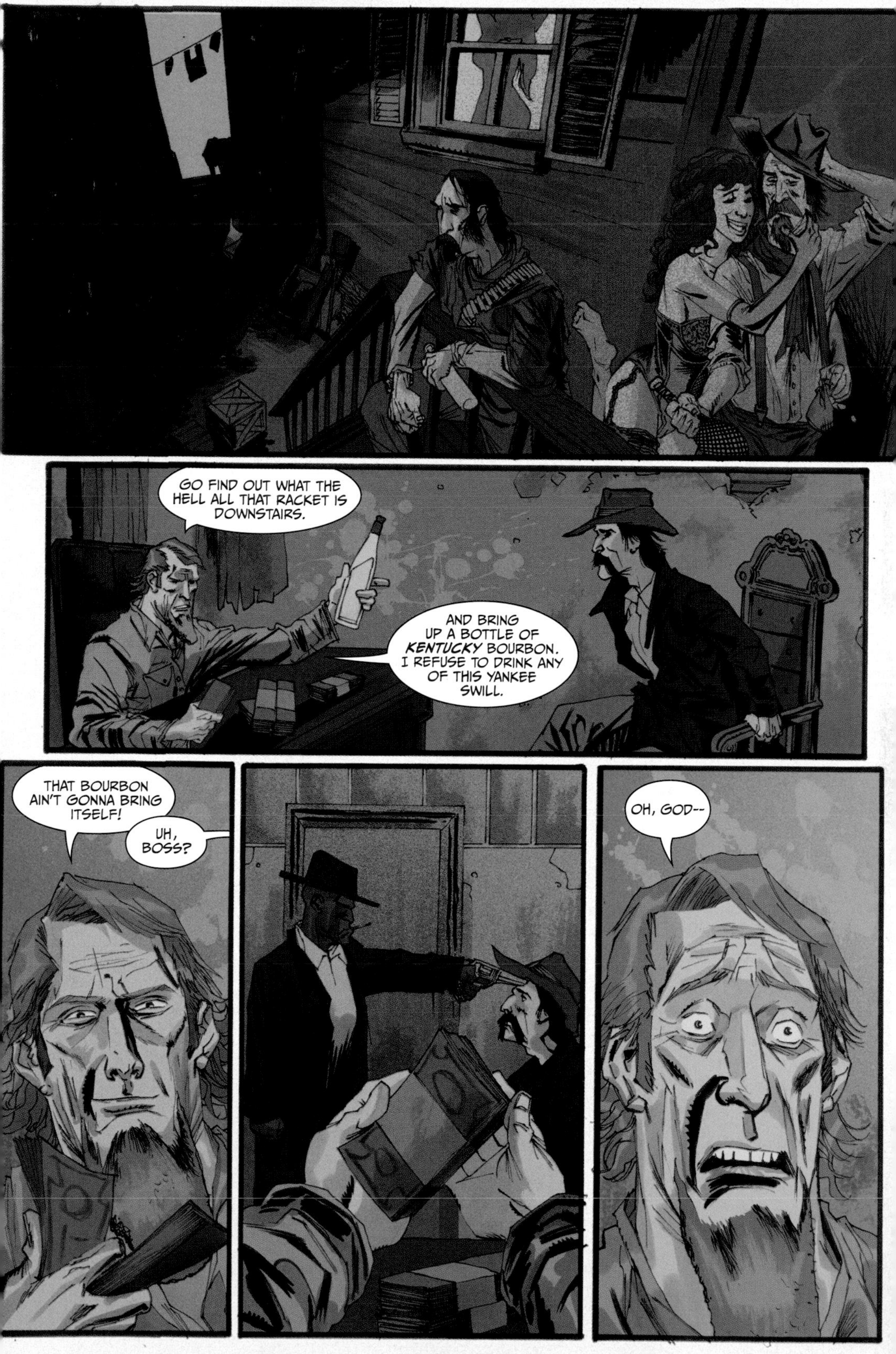
GO FIND OUT WHAT THE HELL ALL THAT RACKET IS DOWNSTAIRS.
AND BRING UP A BOTTLE OF *KENTUCKY* BOURBON. I REFUSE TO DRINK ANY OF THIS YANKEE SWILL.
THAT BOURBON AIN'T GONNA BRING ITSELF!
UH, BOSS?
OH, GOD--

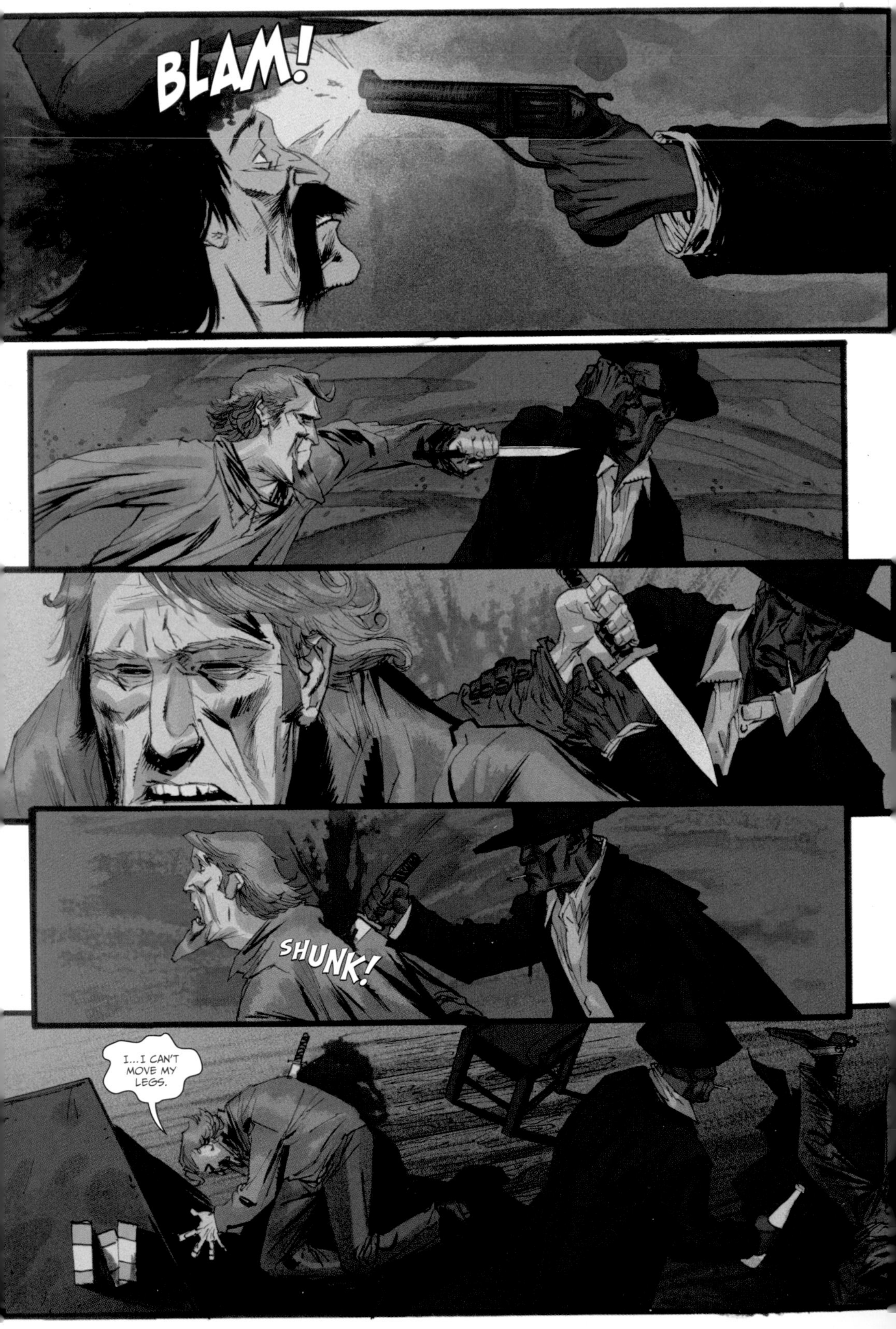
BLAM!
SHUNK!
I... I CAN'T MOVE MY LEGS.

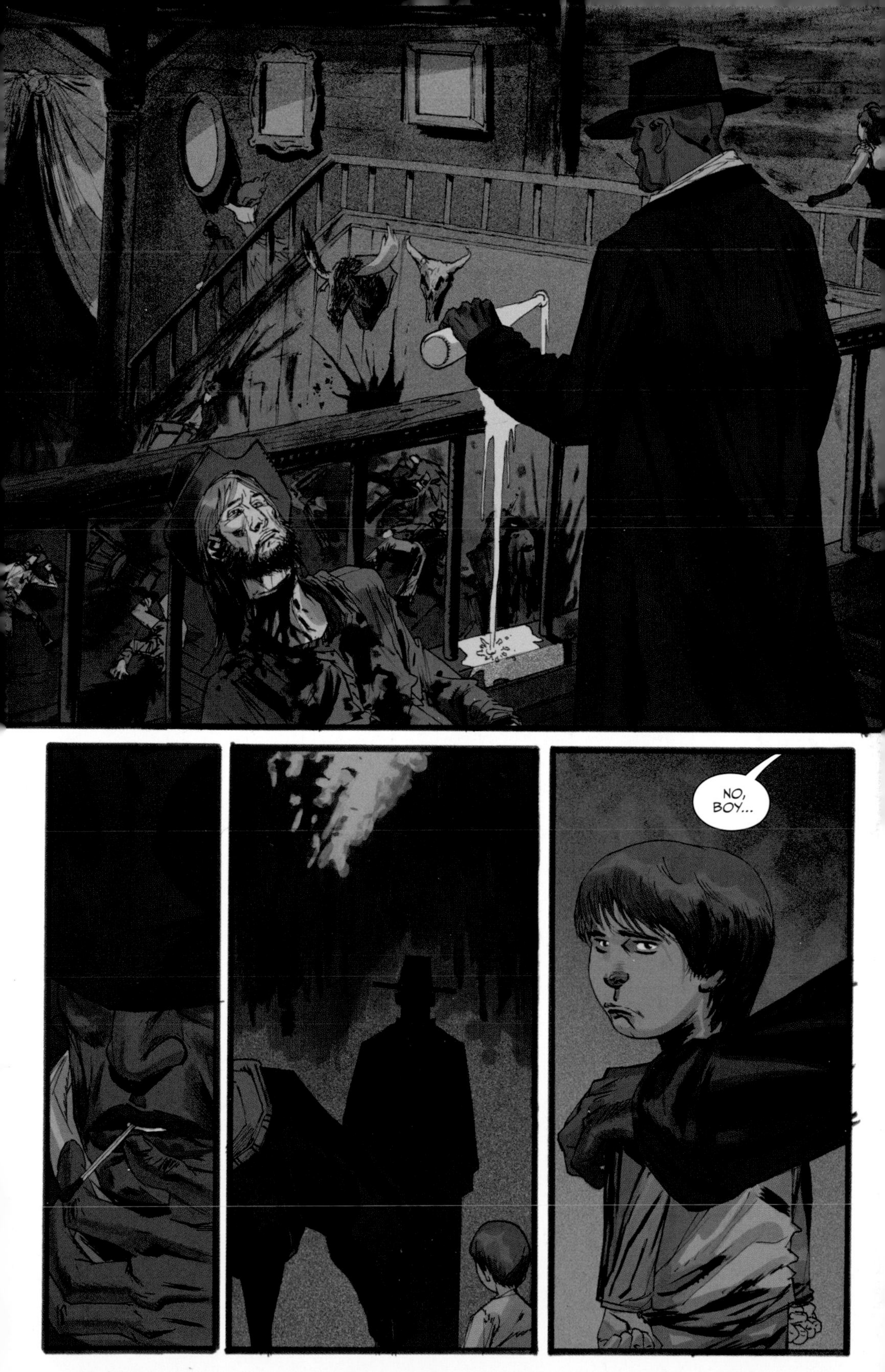
NO,
BOY...

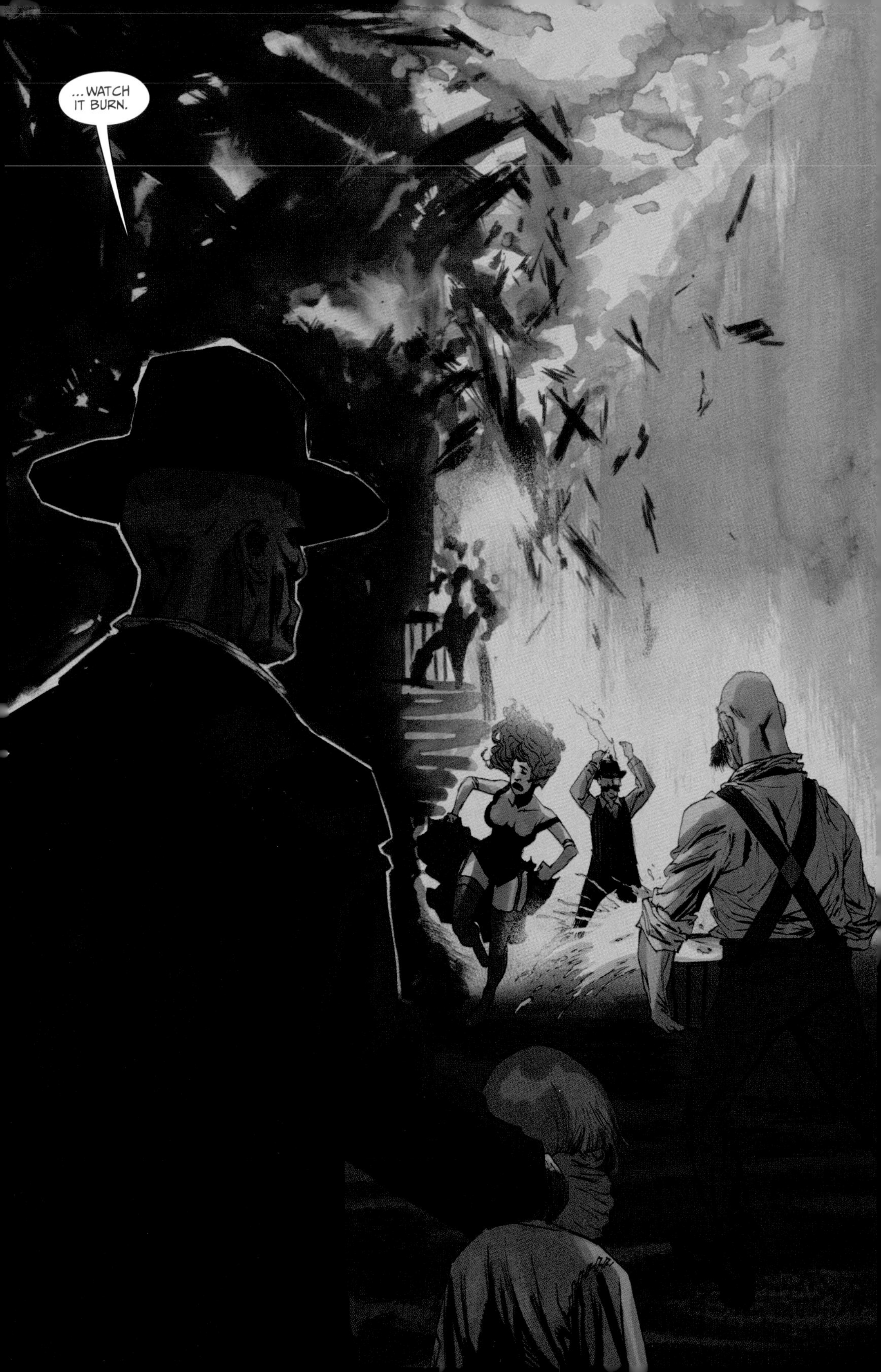
...WATCH IT BURN.

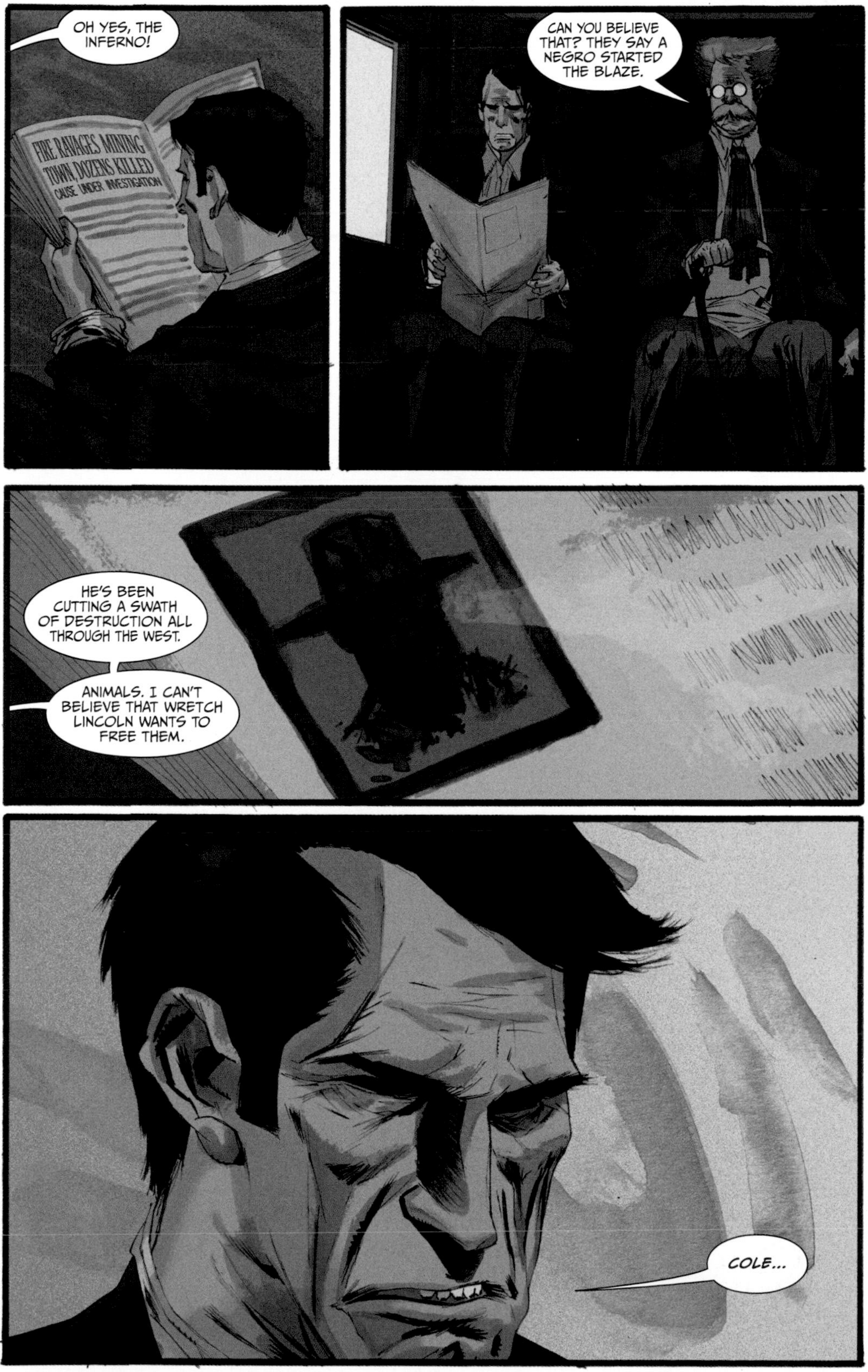
OH YES, THE INFERNO!
FIRE RAVAGES MINING TOWN DOZENS KILLED
CAUSE UNDER INVESTIGATION
CAN YOU BELIEVE THAT? THEY SAY A NEGRO STARTED THE BLAZE.
HE'S BEEN CUTTING A SWATH OF DESTRUCTION ALL THROUGH THE WEST.
ANIMALS. I CAN'T BELIEVE THAT WRETCH LINCOLN WANTS TO FREE THEM.
COLE...

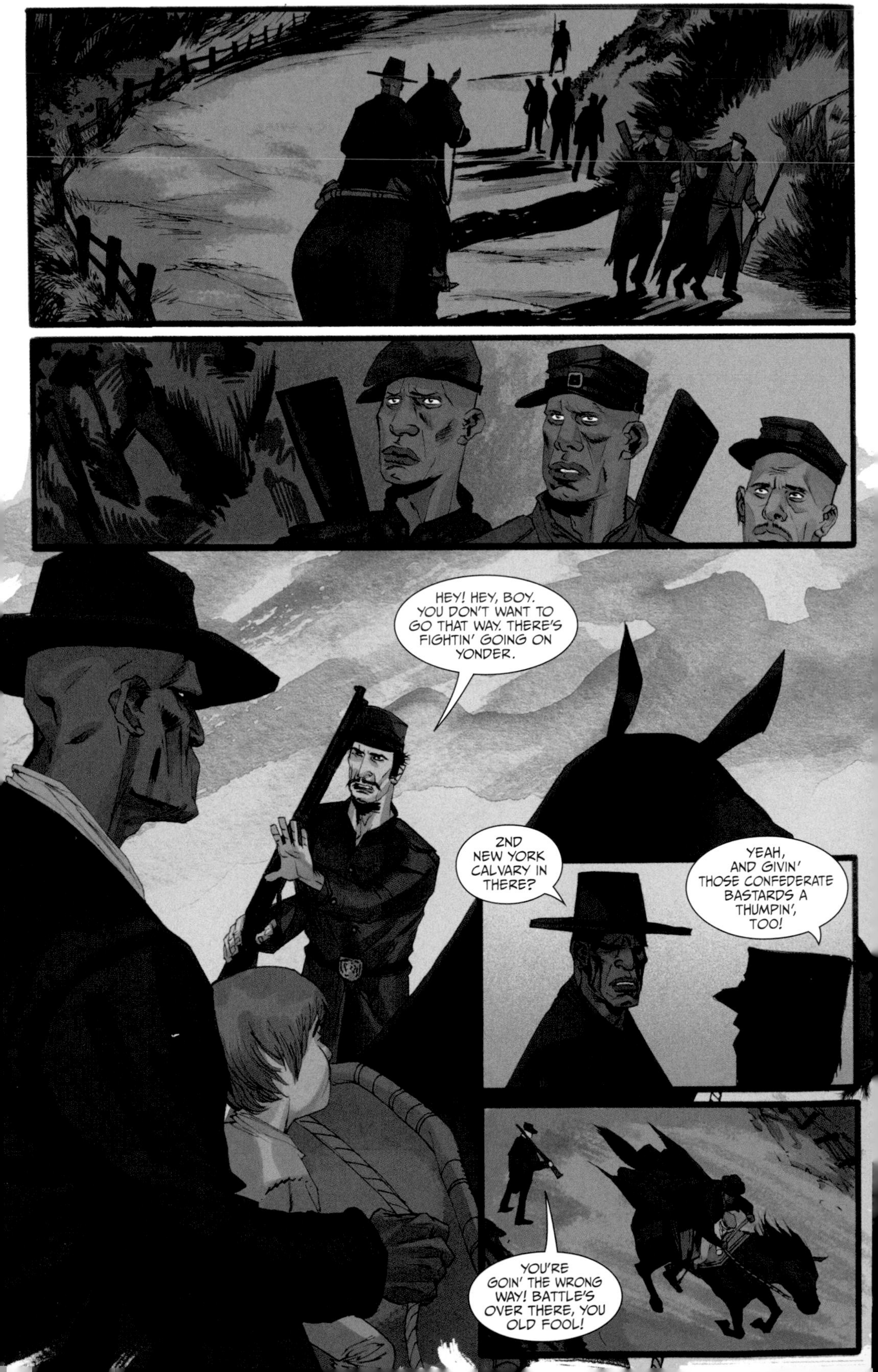
HEY! HEY, BOY. YOU DON'T WANT TO GO THAT WAY. THERE'S FIGHTIN' GOING ON YONDER.
2ND NEW YORK CALVARY IN THERE?
YEAH, AND GIVIN' THOSE CONFEDERATE BASTARDS A THUMPIN', TOO!
YOU'RE GOIN' THE WRONG WAY! BATTLE'S OVER THERE, YOU OLD FOOL!

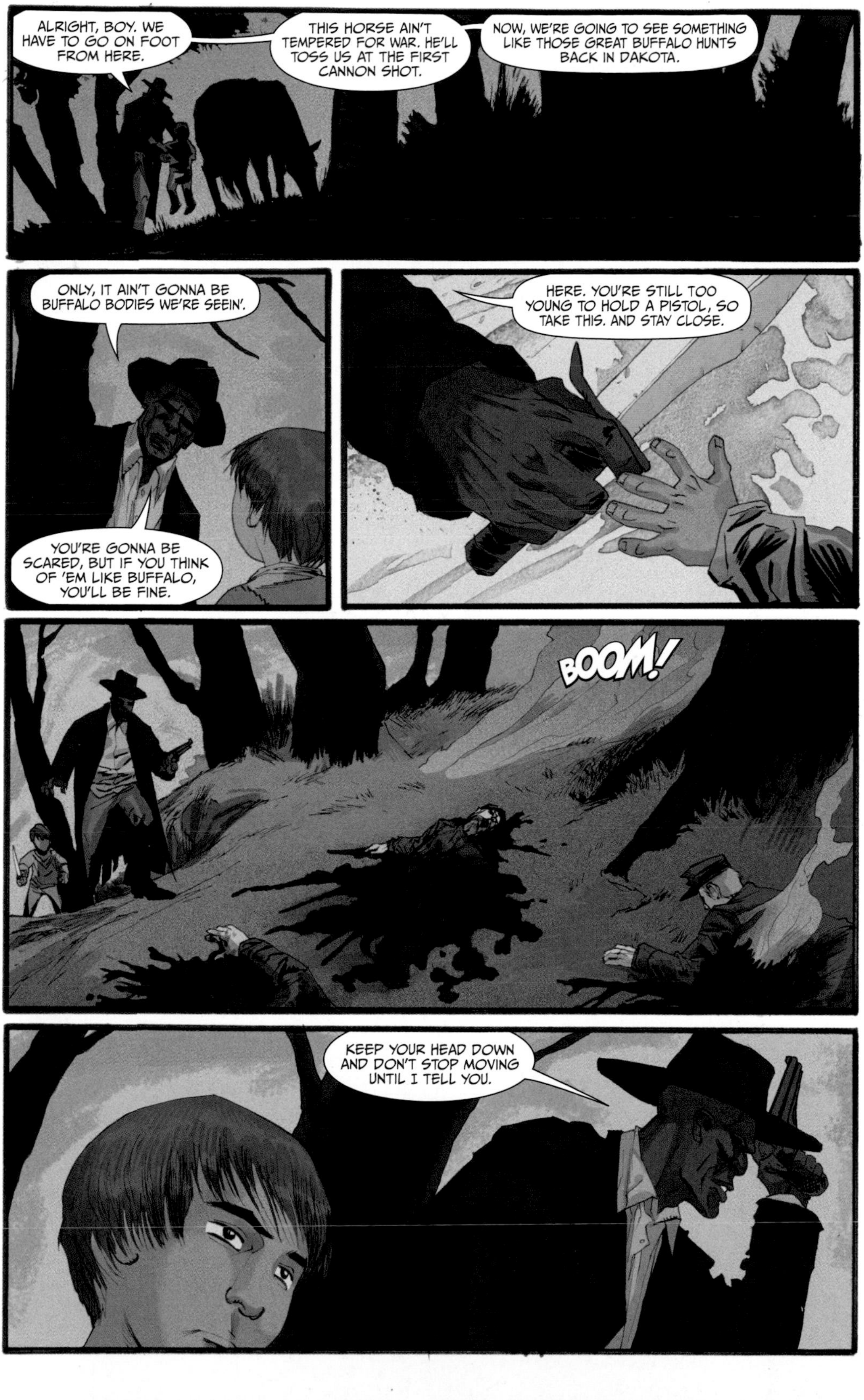
ALRIGHT, BOY. WE HAVE TO GO ON FOOT FROM HERE.
THIS HORSE AIN'T TEMPERED FOR WAR. HE'LL TOSS US AT THE FIRST CANNON SHOT.
NOW, WE'RE GOING TO SEE SOMETHING LIKE THOSE GREAT BUFFALO HUNTS BACK IN DAKOTA.
ONLY, IT AIN'T GONNA BE BUFFALO BODIES WE'RE SEEIN'.
YOU'RE GONNA BE SCARED, BUT IF YOU THINK OF 'EM LIKE BUFFALO, YOU'LL BE FINE.
HERE. YOU'RE STILL TOO YOUNG TO HOLD A PISTOL, SO TAKE THIS. AND STAY CLOSE.
BOOM!
KEEP YOUR HEAD DOWN AND DON'T STOP MOVING UNTIL I TELL YOU.

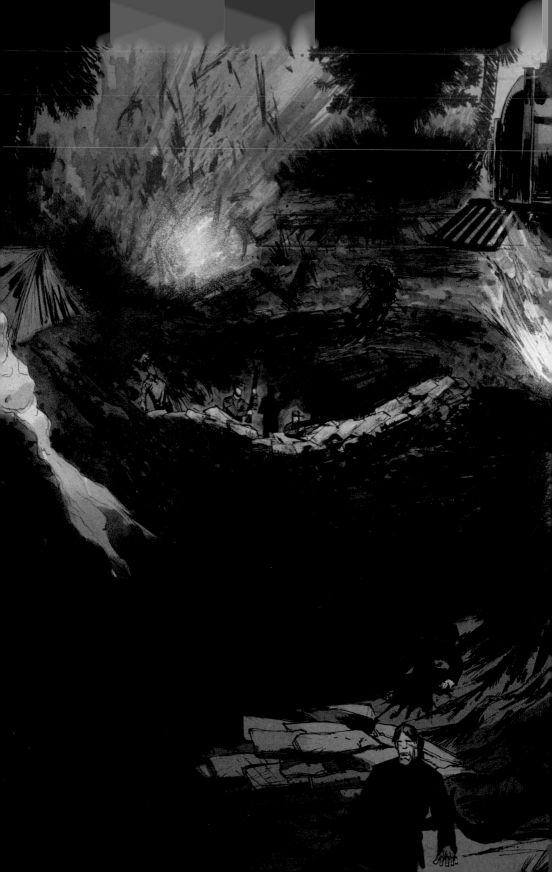

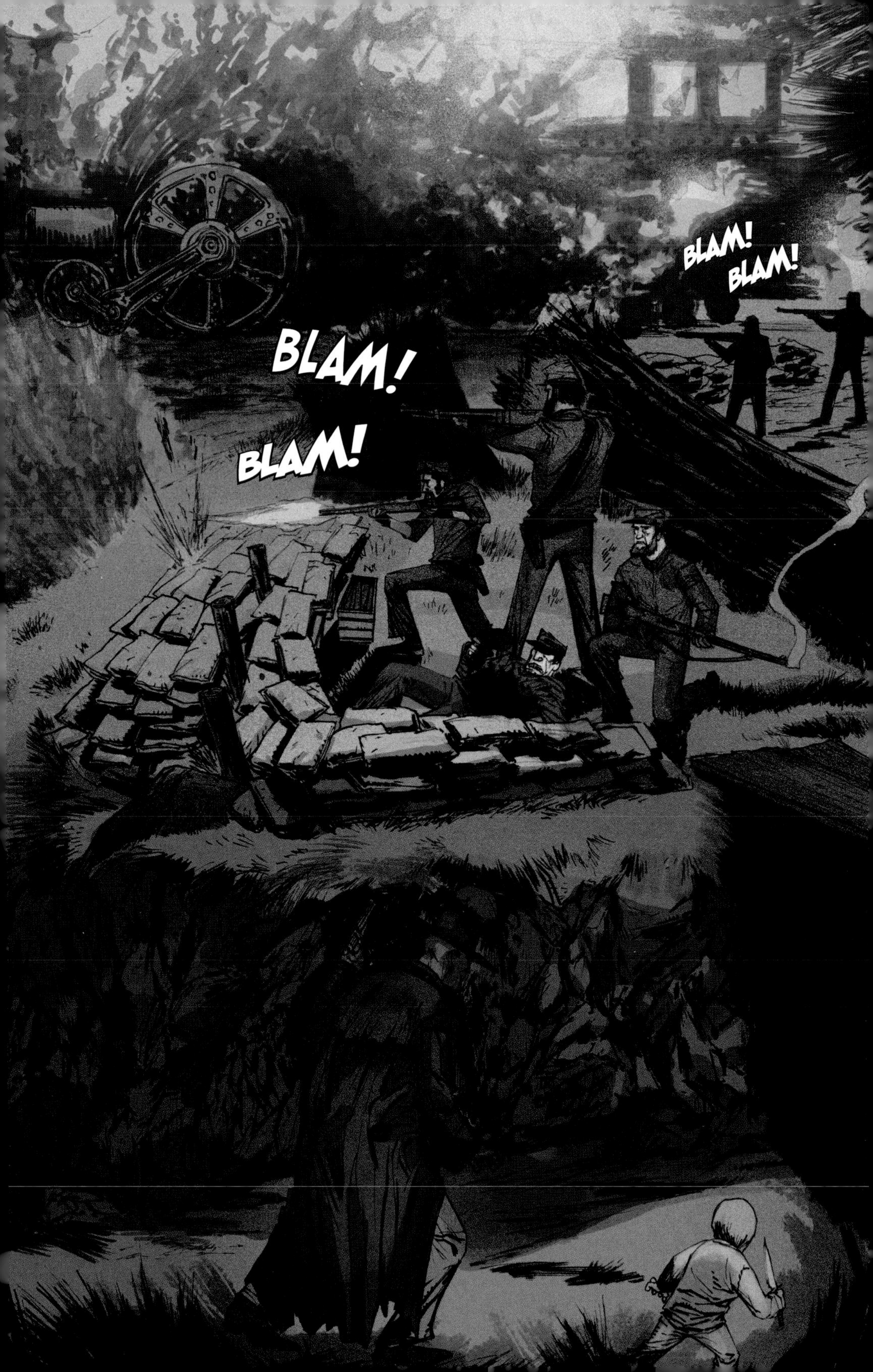
BLAM!
BLAM!
BLAM!
BLAM!

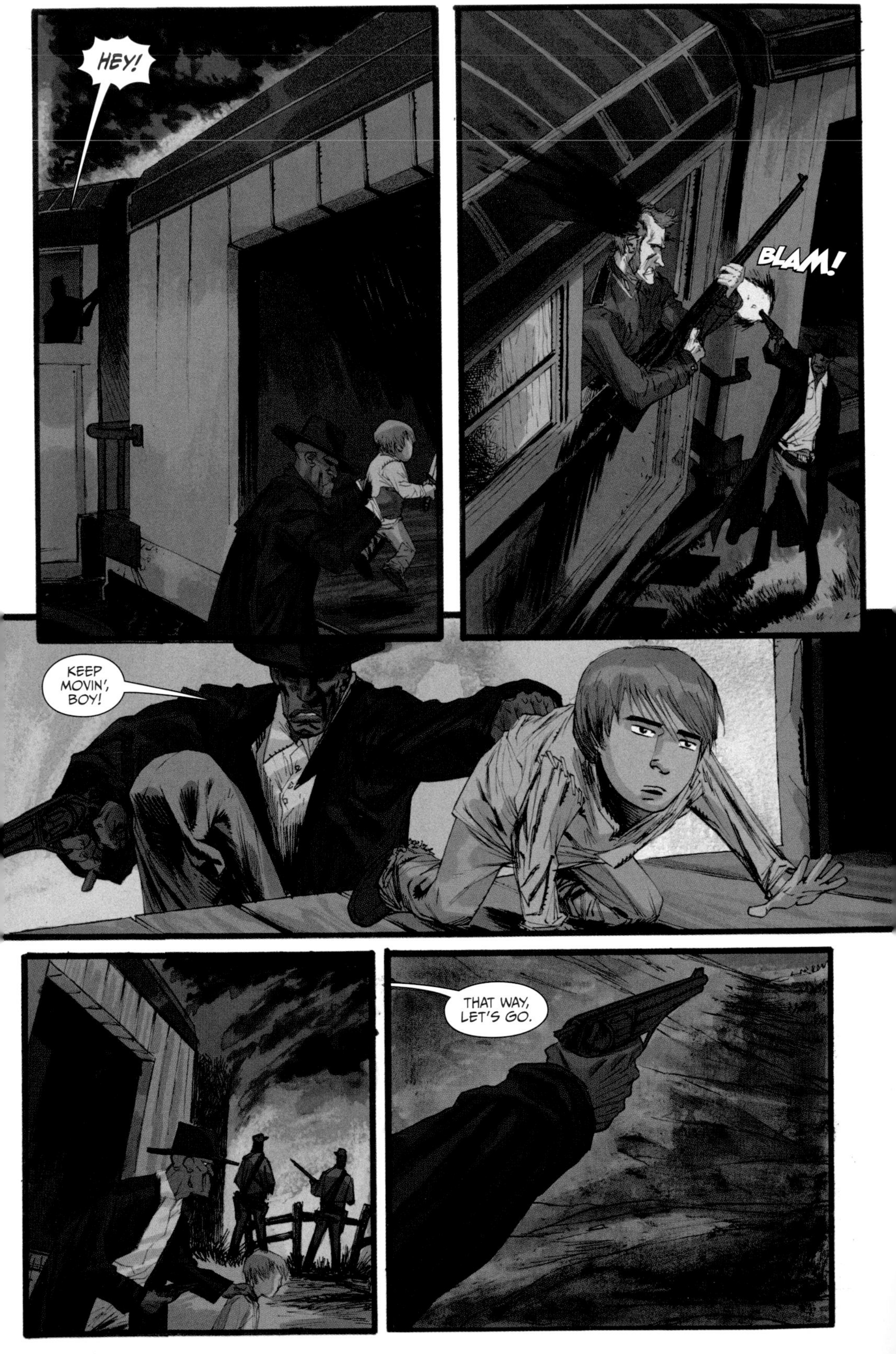
HEY!
BLAM!
KEEP MOVIN', BOY!
THAT WAY, LET'S GO.

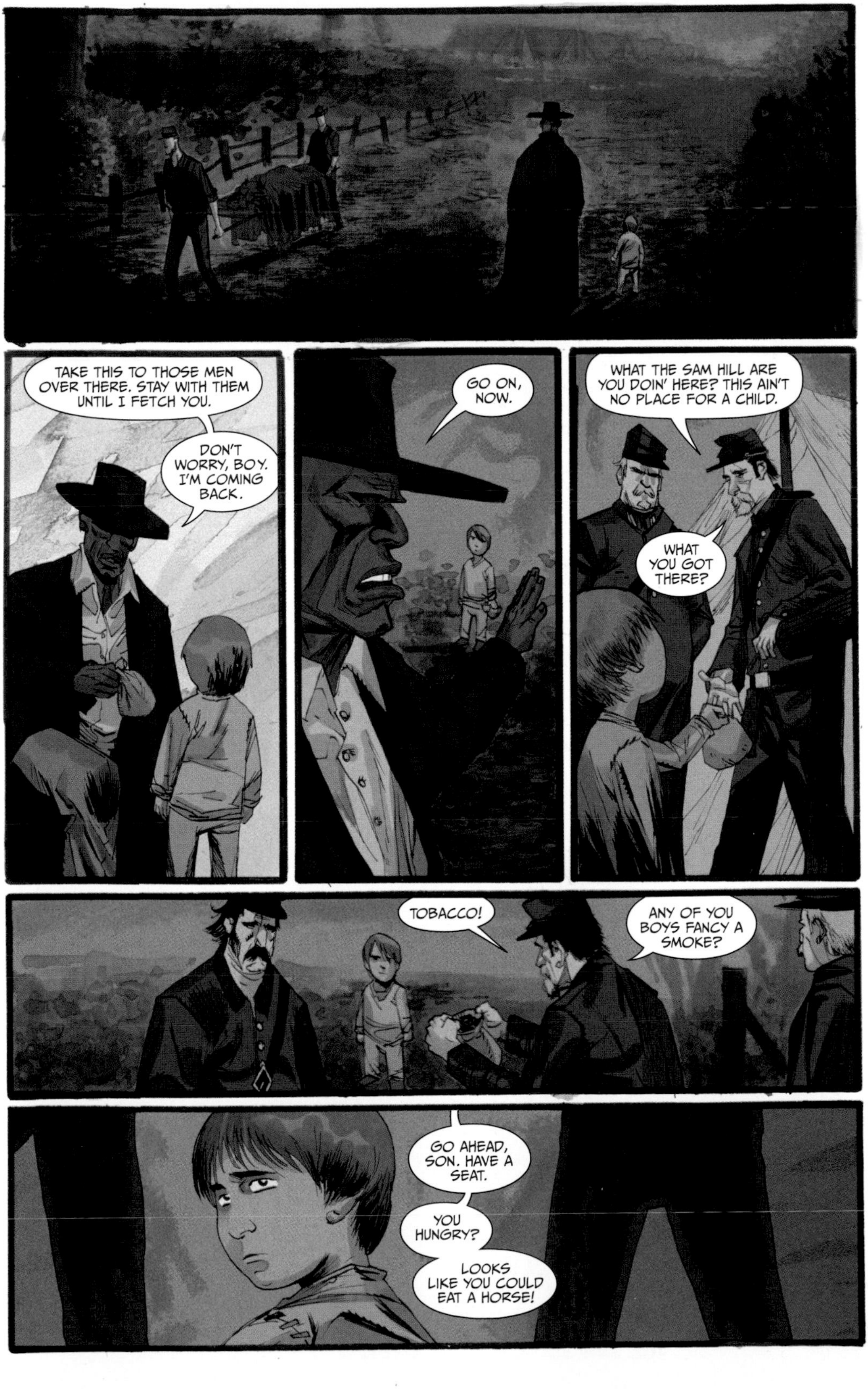
TAKE THIS TO THOSE MEN OVER THERE. STAY WITH THEM UNTIL I FETCH YOU.
DON'T WORRY, BOY. I'M COMING BACK.
GO ON, NOW.
WHAT THE SAM HILL ARE YOU DOIN' HERE? THIS AIN'T NO PLACE FOR A CHILD.
WHAT YOU GOT THERE?
TOBACCO!
ANY OF YOU BOYS FANCY A SMOKE?
GO AHEAD, SON. HAVE A SEAT.
YOU HUNGRY?
LOOKS LIKE YOU COULD EAT A HORSE!

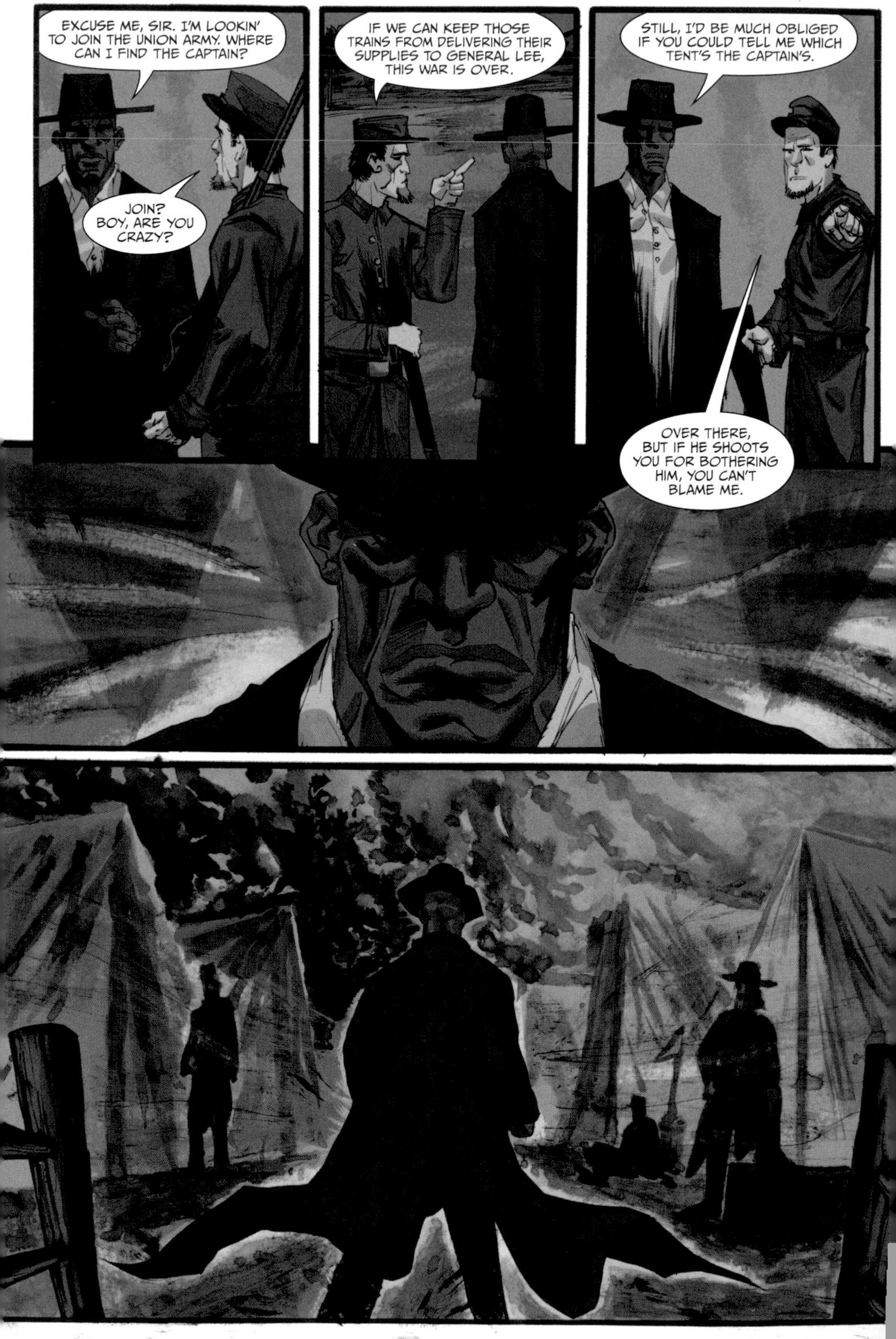
EXCUSE ME, SIR. I'M LOOKIN' TO JOIN THE UNION ARMY. WHERE CAN I FIND THE CAPTAIN?
JOIN? BOY, ARE YOU CRAZY?
IF WE CAN KEEP THOSE TRAINS FROM DELIVERING THEIR SUPPLIES TO GENERAL LEE, THIS WAR IS OVER.
STILL, I'D BE MUCH OBLIGED IF YOU COULD TELL ME WHICH TENT'S THE CAPTAIN'S.
OVER THERE, BUT IF HE SHOOTS YOU FOR BOTHERING HIM, YOU CAN'T BLAME ME.

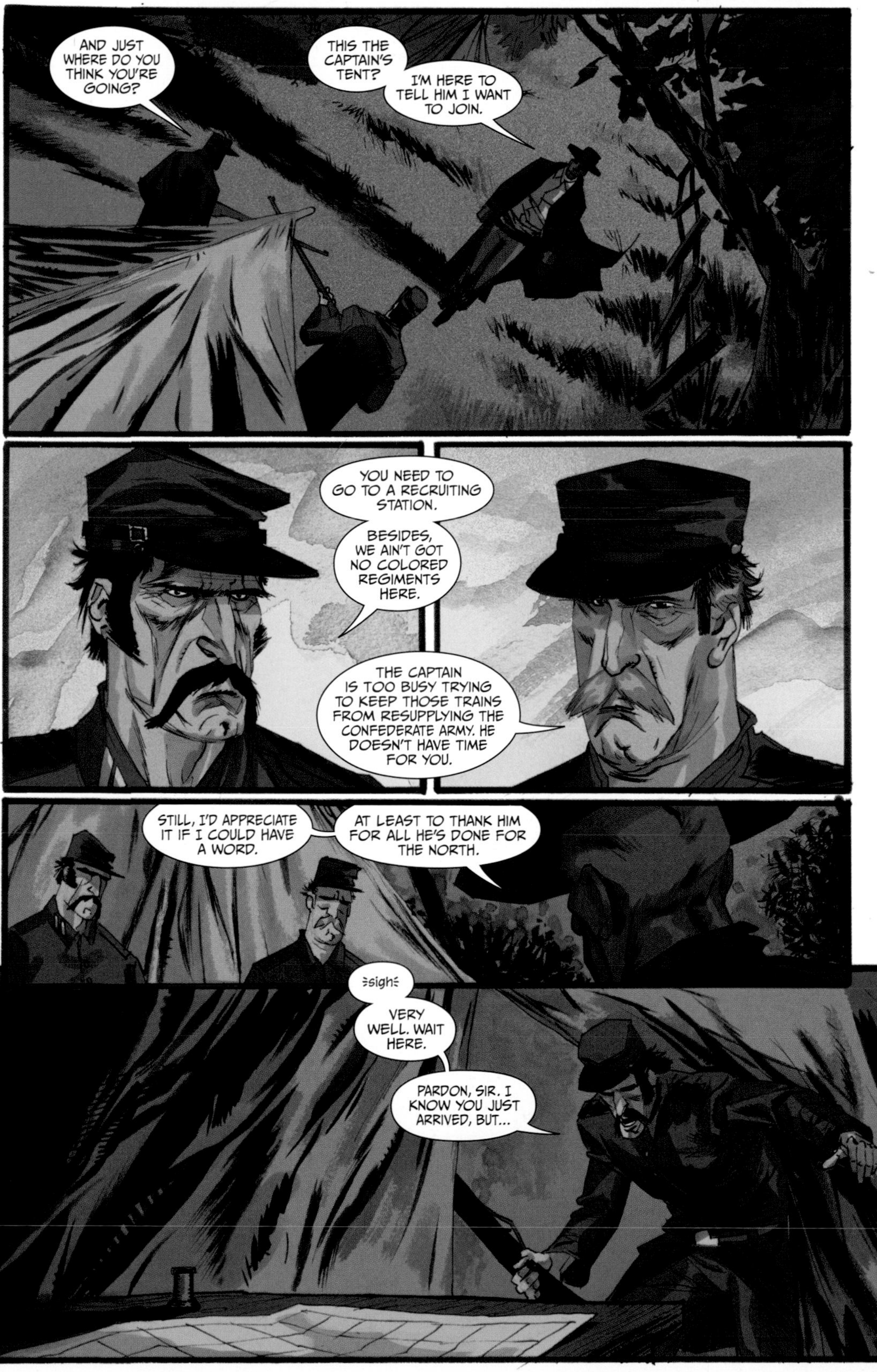
AND JUST WHERE DO YOU THINK YOU'RE GOING?
THIS THE CAPTAIN'S TENT?
I'M HERE TO TELL HIM I WANT TO JOIN.
YOU NEED TO GO TO A RECRUITING STATION.
BESIDES, WE AIN'T GOT NO COLORED REGIMENTS HERE.
THE CAPTAIN IS TOO BUSY TRYING TO KEEP THOSE TRAINS FROM RESUPPLYING THE CONFEDERATE ARMY. HE DOESN'T HAVE TIME FOR YOU.
STILL, I'D APPRECIATE IT IF I COULD HAVE A WORD.
AT LEAST TO THANK HIM FOR ALL HE'S DONE FOR THE NORTH.
sigh
VERY WELL. WAIT HERE.
PARDON, SIR. I KNOW YOU JUST ARRIVED, BUT...

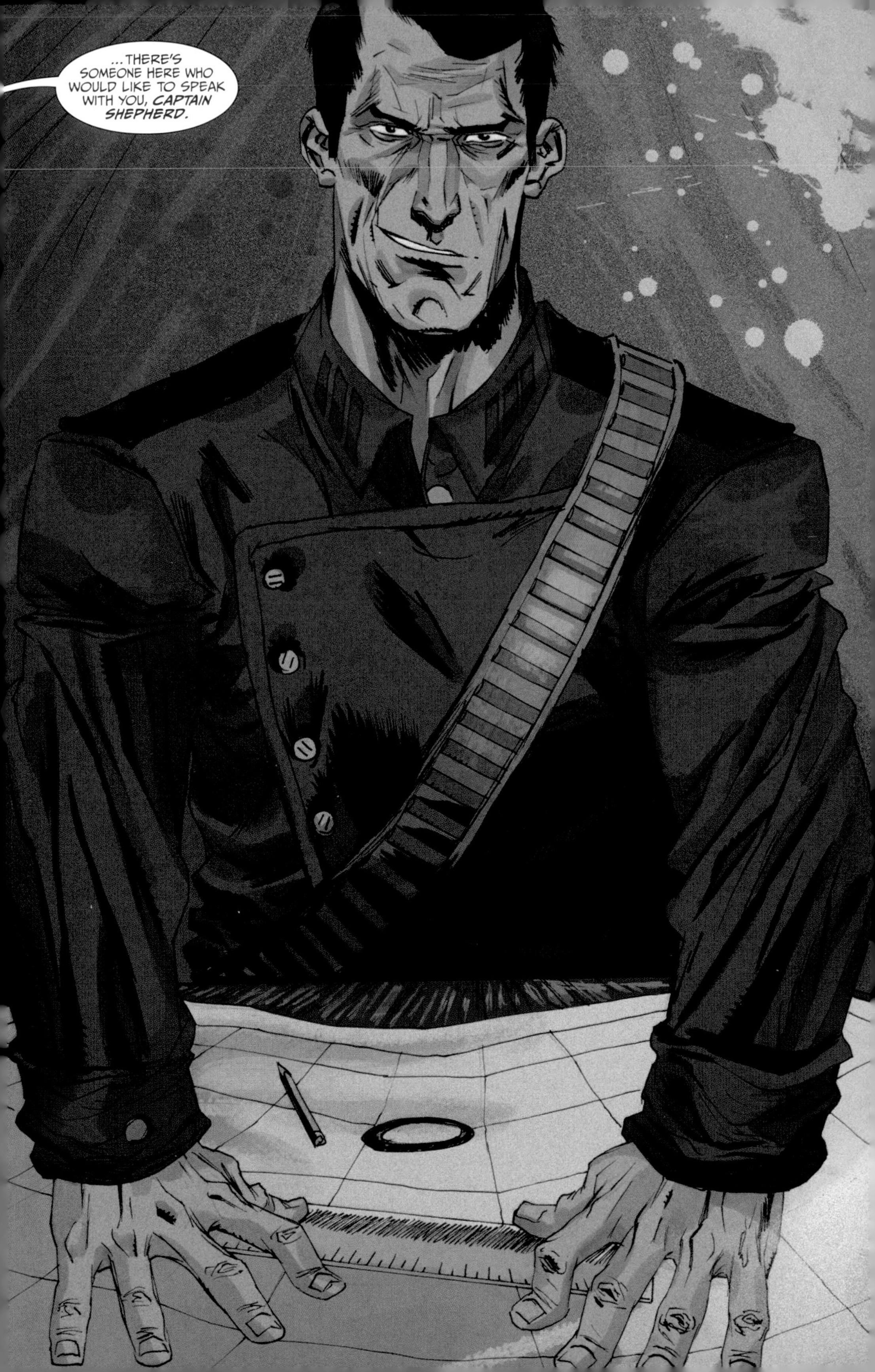
...THERE'S SOMEONE HERE WHO WOULD LIKE TO SPEAK WITH YOU, *CAPTAIN SHEPHERD.*

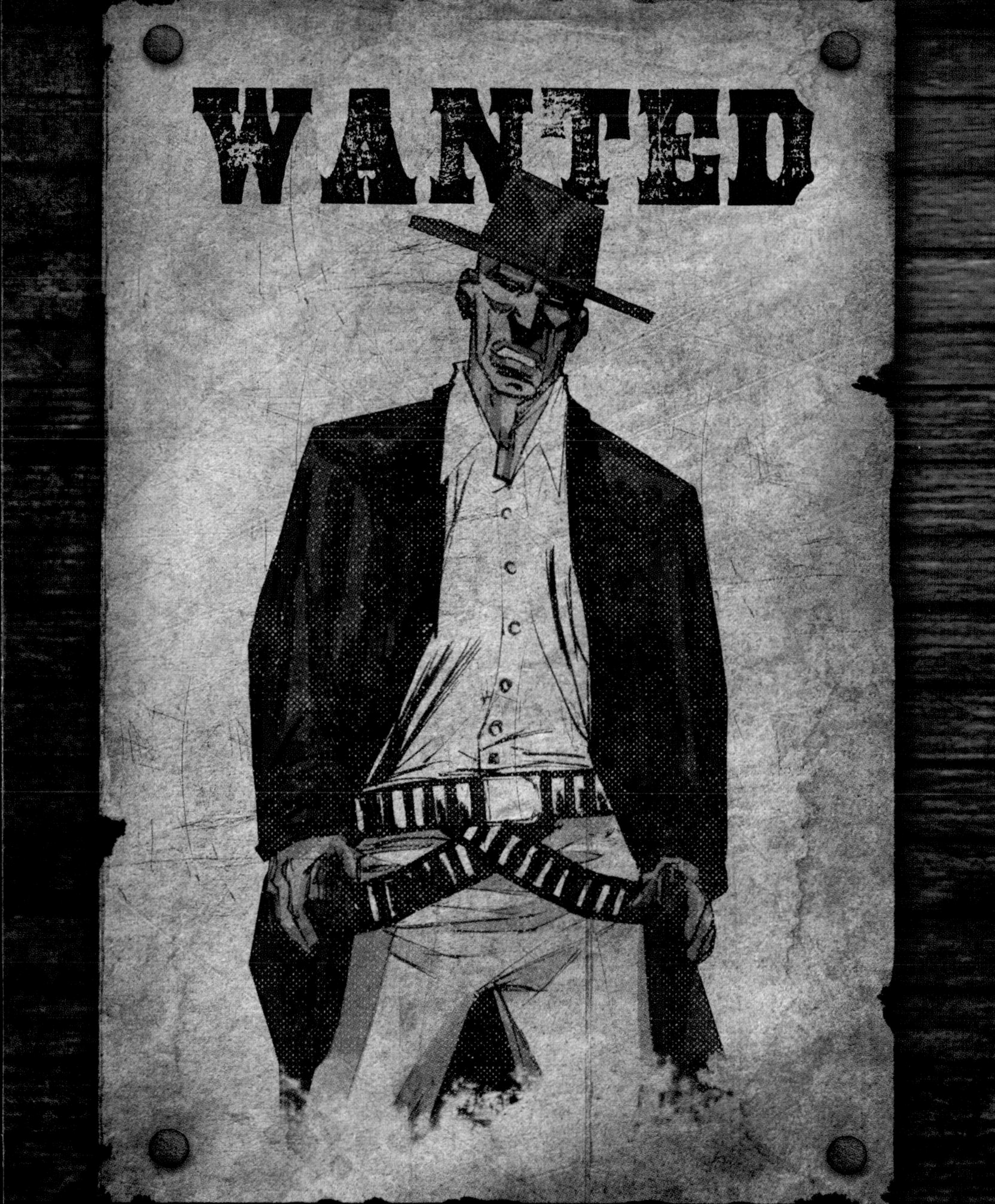
WANTED

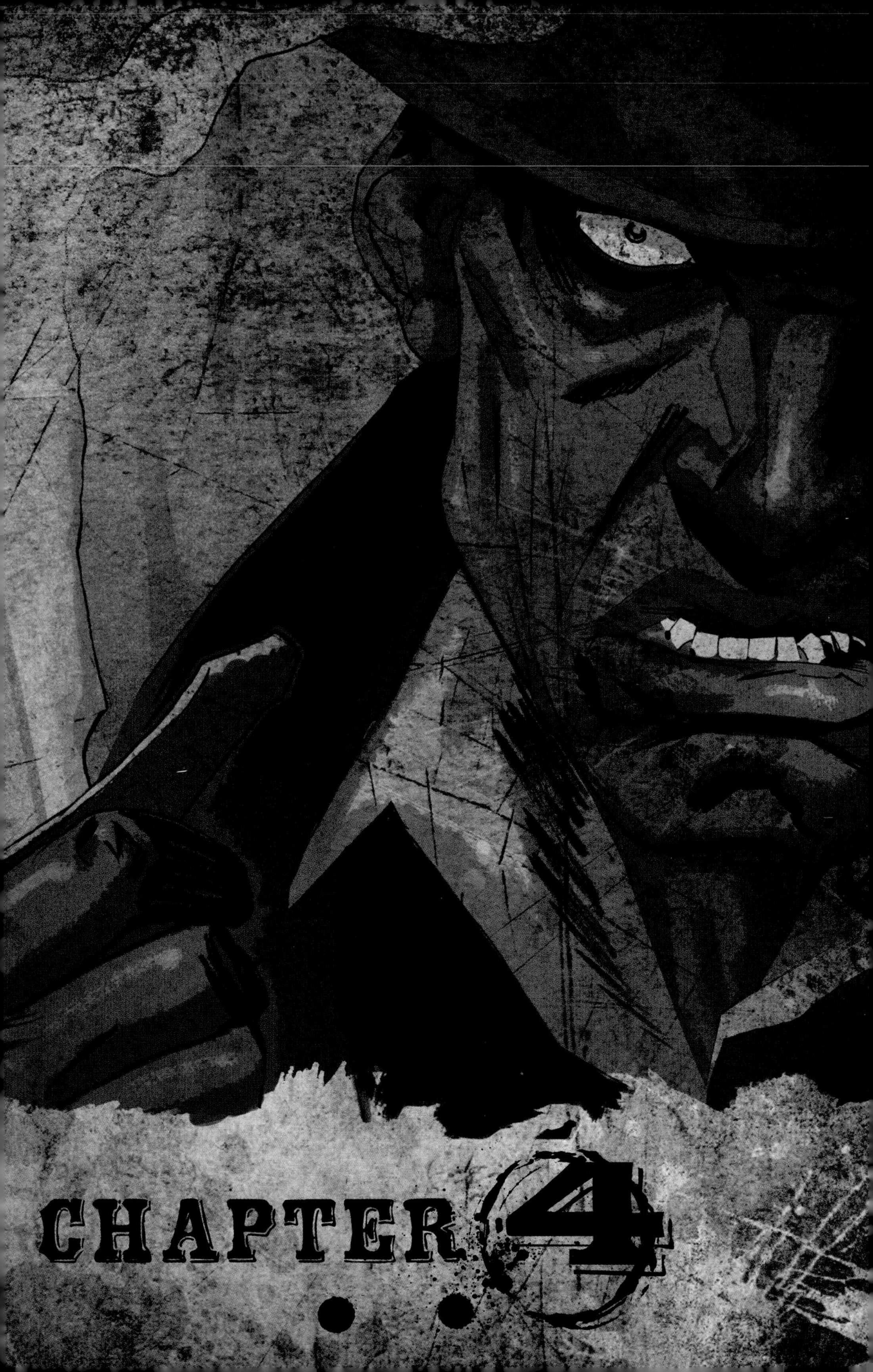
CHAPTER 4

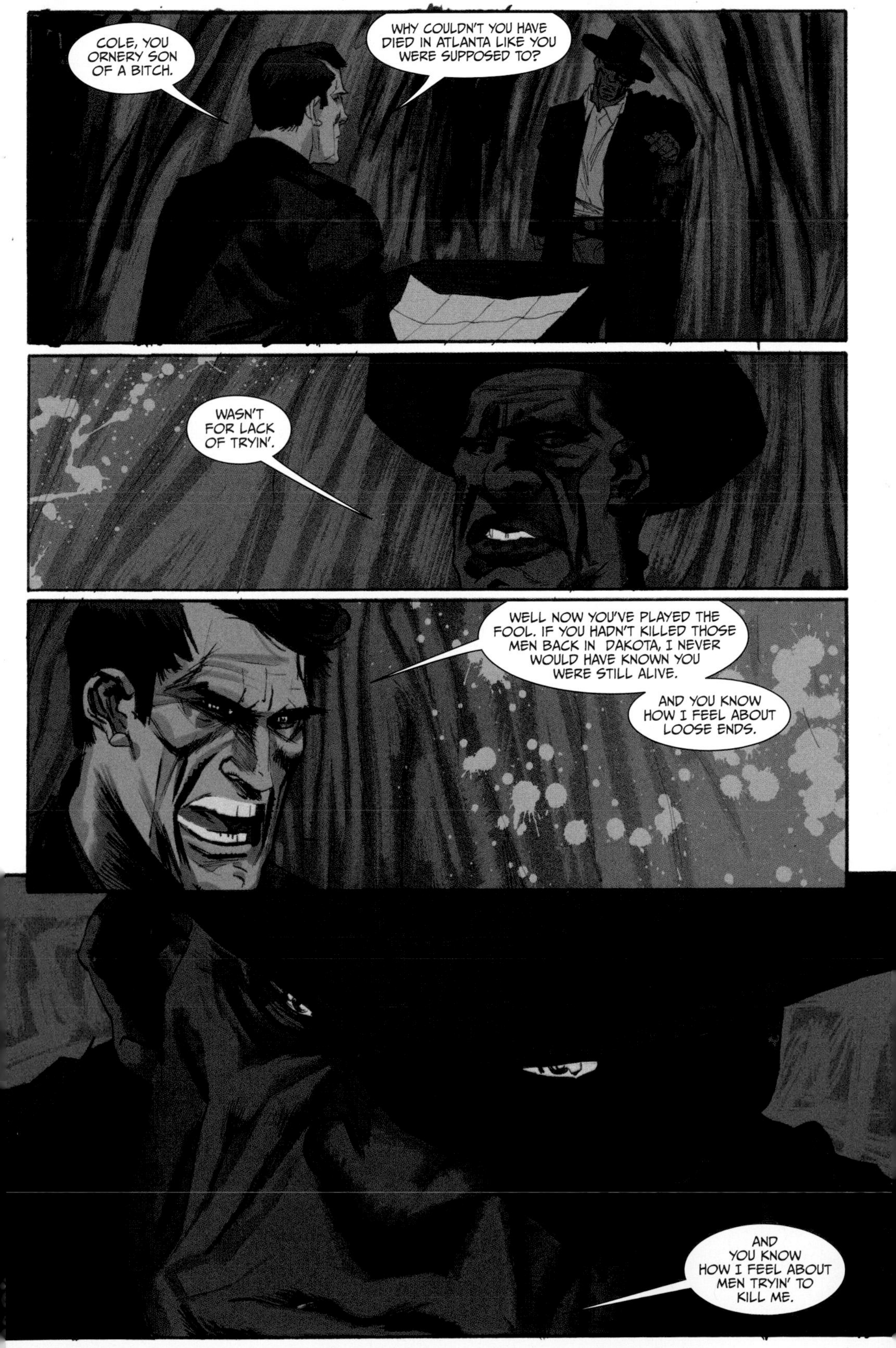
COLE, YOU ORNERY SON OF A BITCH.
WHY COULDN'T YOU HAVE DIED IN ATLANTA LIKE YOU WERE SUPPOSED TO?
WASN'T FOR LACK OF TRYIN'.
WELL NOW YOU'VE PLAYED THE FOOL. IF YOU HADN'T KILLED THOSE MEN BACK IN DAKOTA, I NEVER WOULD HAVE KNOWN YOU WERE STILL ALIVE.
AND YOU KNOW HOW I FEEL ABOUT LOOSE ENDS.
AND YOU KNOW HOW I FEEL ABOUT MEN TRYIN' TO KILL ME.

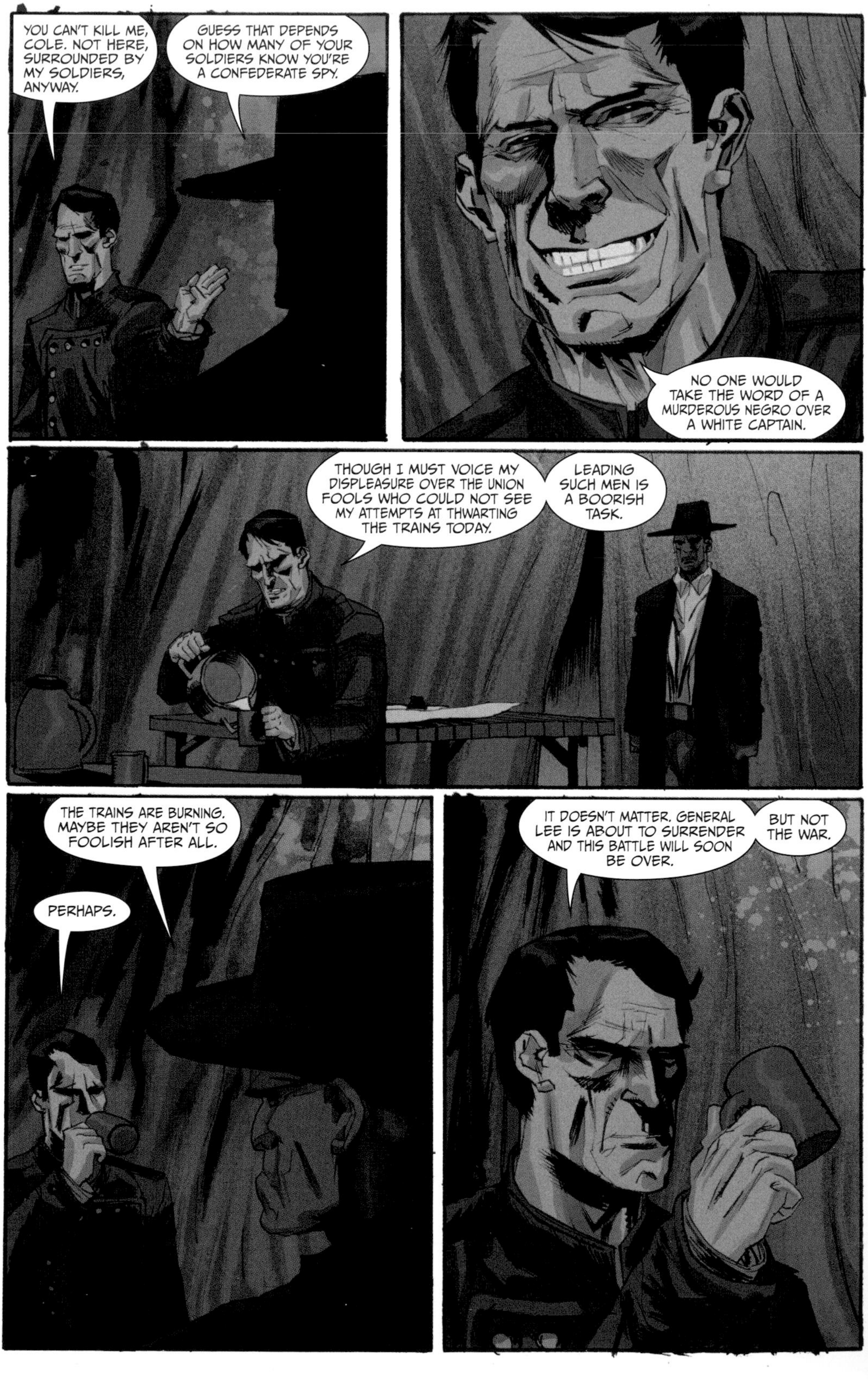
YOU CAN'T KILL ME, COLE. NOT HERE, SURROUNDED BY MY SOLDIERS, ANYWAY.
GUESS THAT DEPENDS ON HOW MANY OF YOUR SOLDIERS KNOW YOU'RE A CONFEDERATE SPY.
NO ONE WOULD TAKE THE WORD OF A MURDEROUS NEGRO OVER A WHITE CAPTAIN.
THOUGH I MUST VOICE MY DISPLEASURE OVER THE UNION FOOLS WHO COULD NOT SEE MY ATTEMPTS AT THWARTING THE TRAINS TODAY.
LEADING SUCH MEN IS A BOORISH TASK.
THE TRAINS ARE BURNING. MAYBE THEY AREN'T SO FOOLISH AFTER ALL.
PERHAPS.
IT DOESN'T MATTER. GENERAL LEE IS ABOUT TO SURRENDER AND THIS BATTLE WILL SOON BE OVER.
BUT NOT THE WAR.

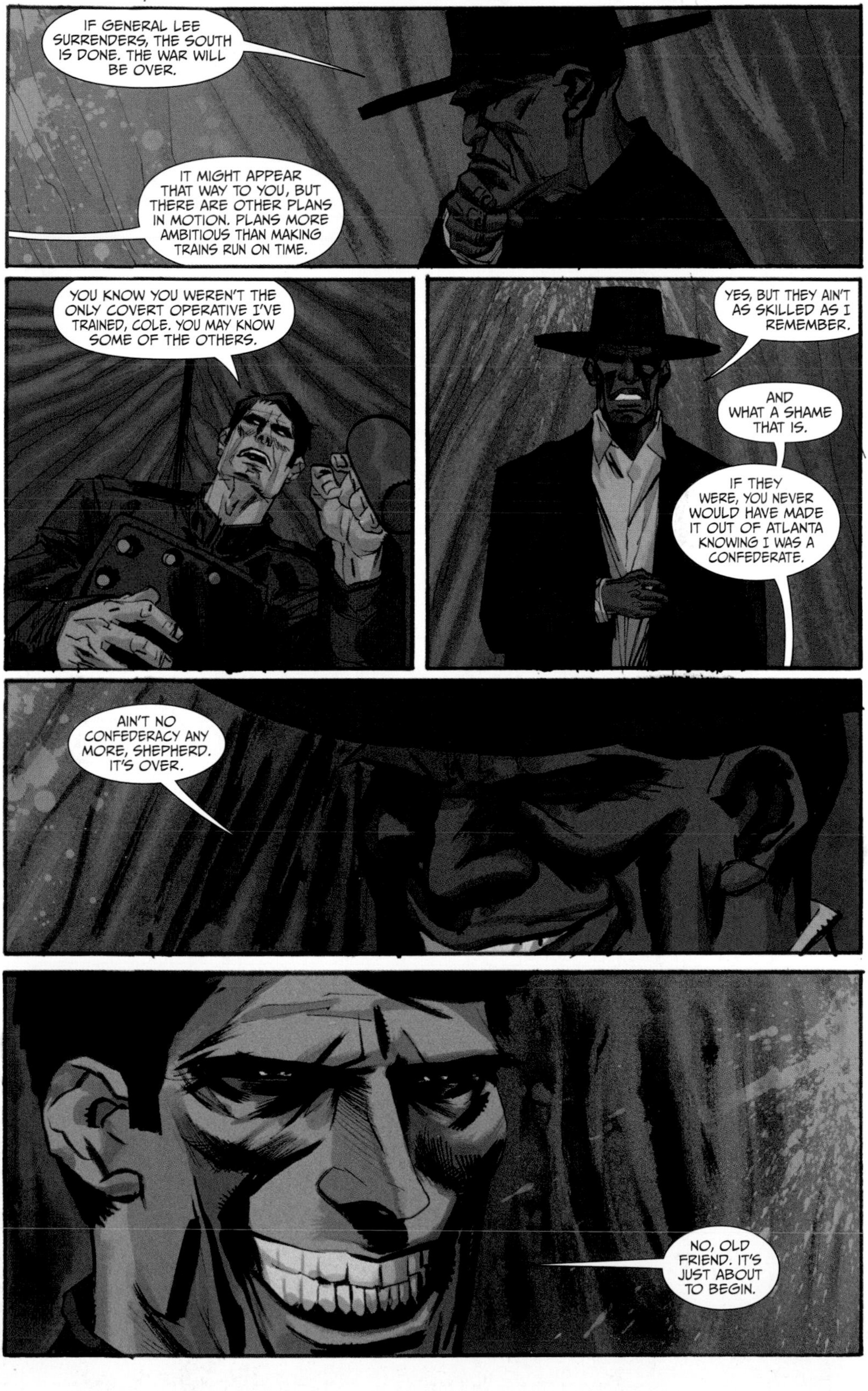
IF GENERAL LEE SURRENDERS, THE SOUTH IS DONE. THE WAR WILL BE OVER.
IT MIGHT APPEAR THAT WAY TO YOU, BUT THERE ARE OTHER PLANS IN MOTION. PLANS MORE AMBITIOUS THAN MAKING TRAINS RUN ON TIME.
YOU KNOW YOU WEREN'T THE ONLY COVERT OPERATIVE I'VE TRAINED, COLE. YOU MAY KNOW SOME OF THE OTHERS.
YES, BUT THEY AIN'T AS SKILLED AS I REMEMBER.
AND WHAT A SHAME THAT IS.
IF THEY WERE, YOU NEVER WOULD HAVE MADE IT OUT OF ATLANTA KNOWING I WAS A CONFEDERATE.
AIN'T NO CONFEDERACY ANY MORE, SHEPHERD. IT'S OVER.
NO, OLD FRIEND. IT'S JUST ABOUT TO BEGIN.

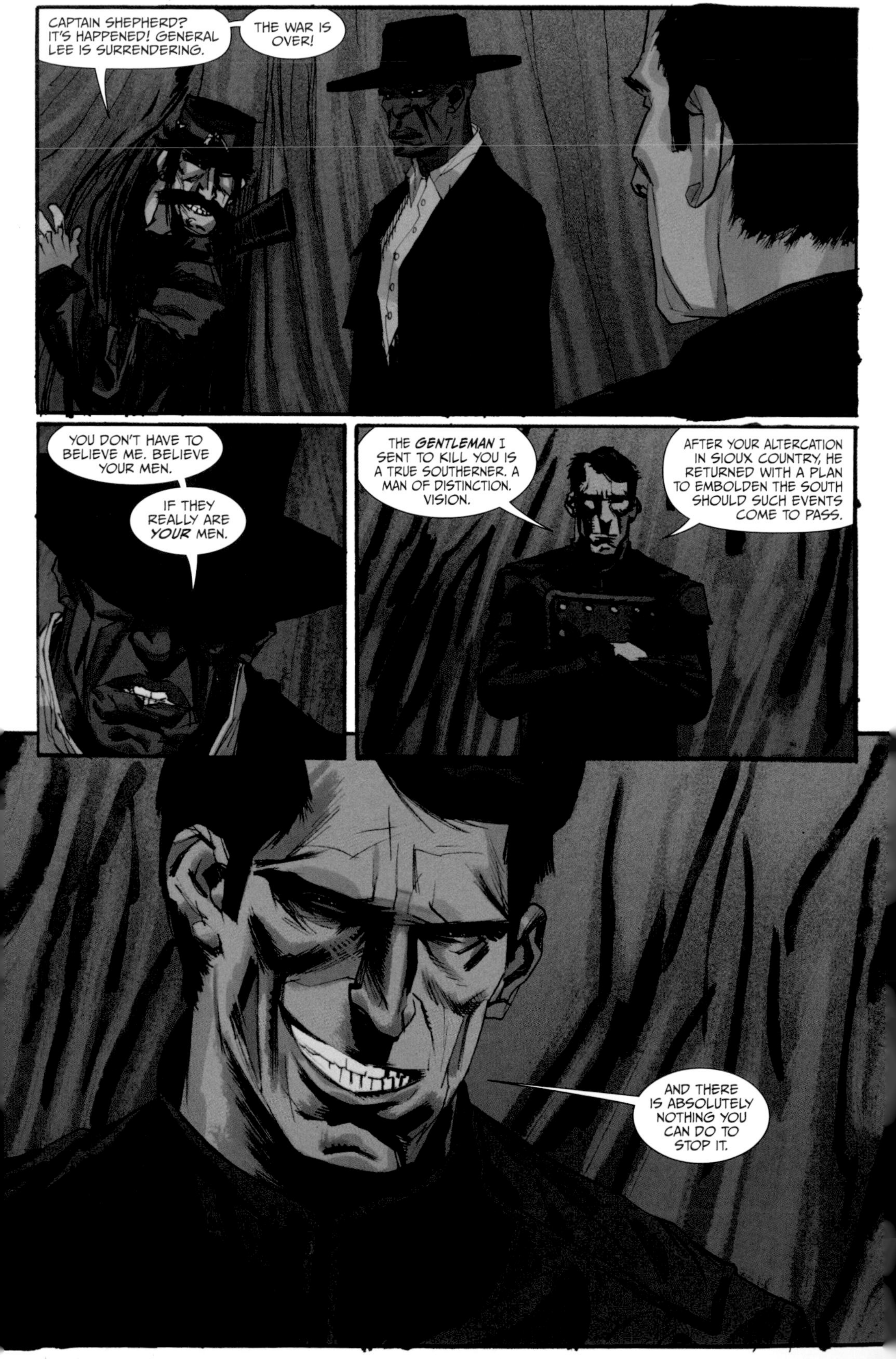
CAPTAIN SHEPHERD? IT'S HAPPENED! GENERAL LEE IS SURRENDERING.
THE WAR IS OVER!
YOU DON'T HAVE TO BELIEVE ME. BELIEVE YOUR MEN.
IF THEY REALLY ARE *YOUR* MEN.
THE *GENTLEMAN* I SENT TO KILL YOU IS A TRUE SOUTHERNER. A MAN OF DISTINCTION. VISION.
AFTER YOUR ALTERCATION IN SIOUX COUNTRY, HE RETURNED WITH A PLAN TO EMBOLDEN THE SOUTH SHOULD SUCH EVENTS COME TO PASS.
AND THERE IS ABSOLUTELY NOTHING YOU CAN DO TO STOP IT.

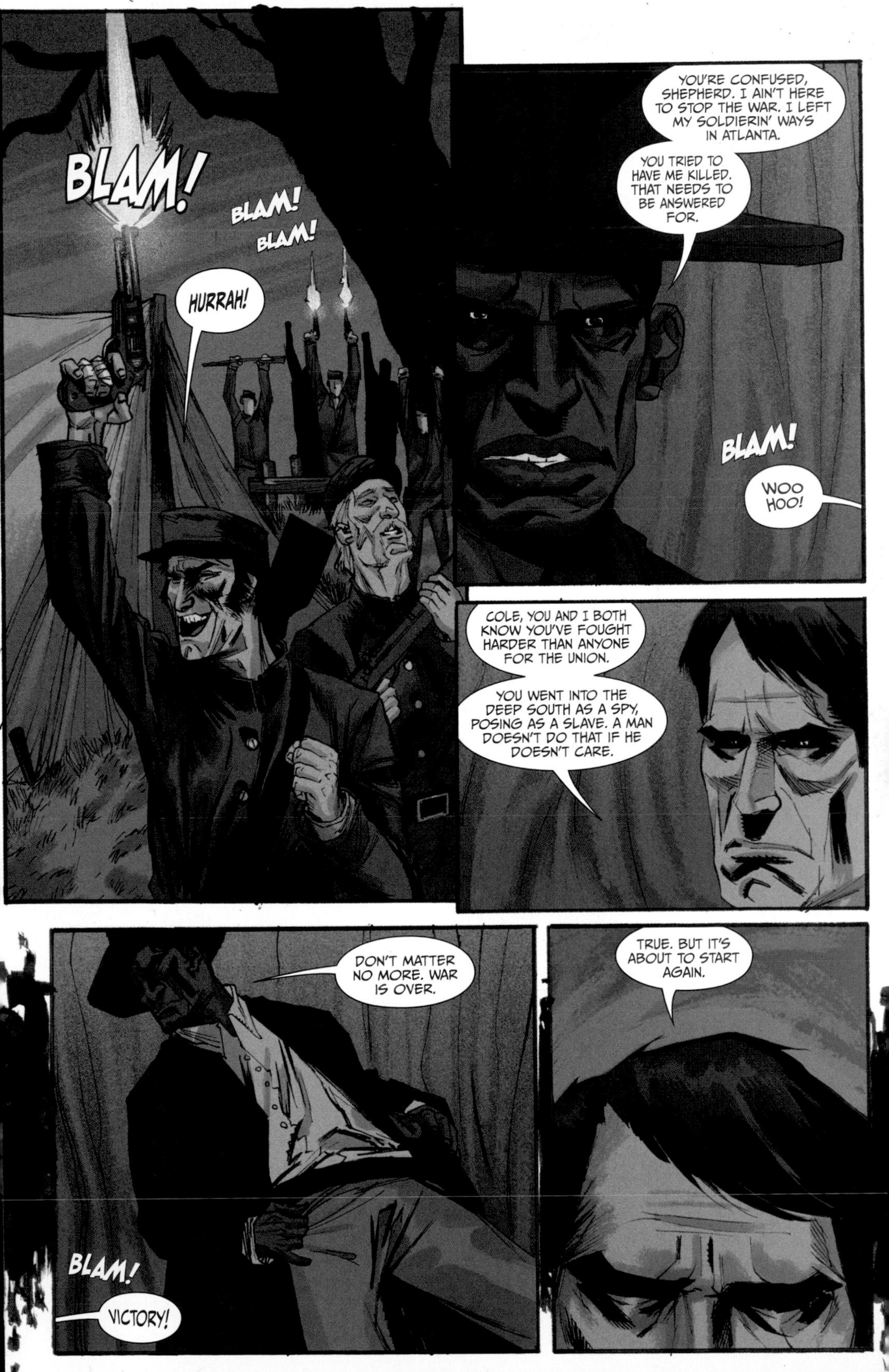
BLAM!
BLAM!
BLAM!
HURRAH!
YOU'RE CONFUSED, SHEPHERD. I AIN'T HERE TO STOP THE WAR. I LEFT MY SOLDIERIN' WAYS IN ATLANTA.
YOU TRIED TO HAVE ME KILLED. THAT NEEDS TO BE ANSWERED FOR.
BLAM!
WOO HOO!
COLE, YOU AND I BOTH KNOW YOU'VE FOUGHT HARDER THAN ANYONE FOR THE UNION.
YOU WENT INTO THE DEEP SOUTH AS A SPY, POSING AS A SLAVE. A MAN DOESN'T DO THAT IF HE DOESN'T CARE.
DON'T MATTER NO MORE. WAR IS OVER.
BLAM!
VICTORY!
TRUE. BUT IT'S ABOUT TO START AGAIN.

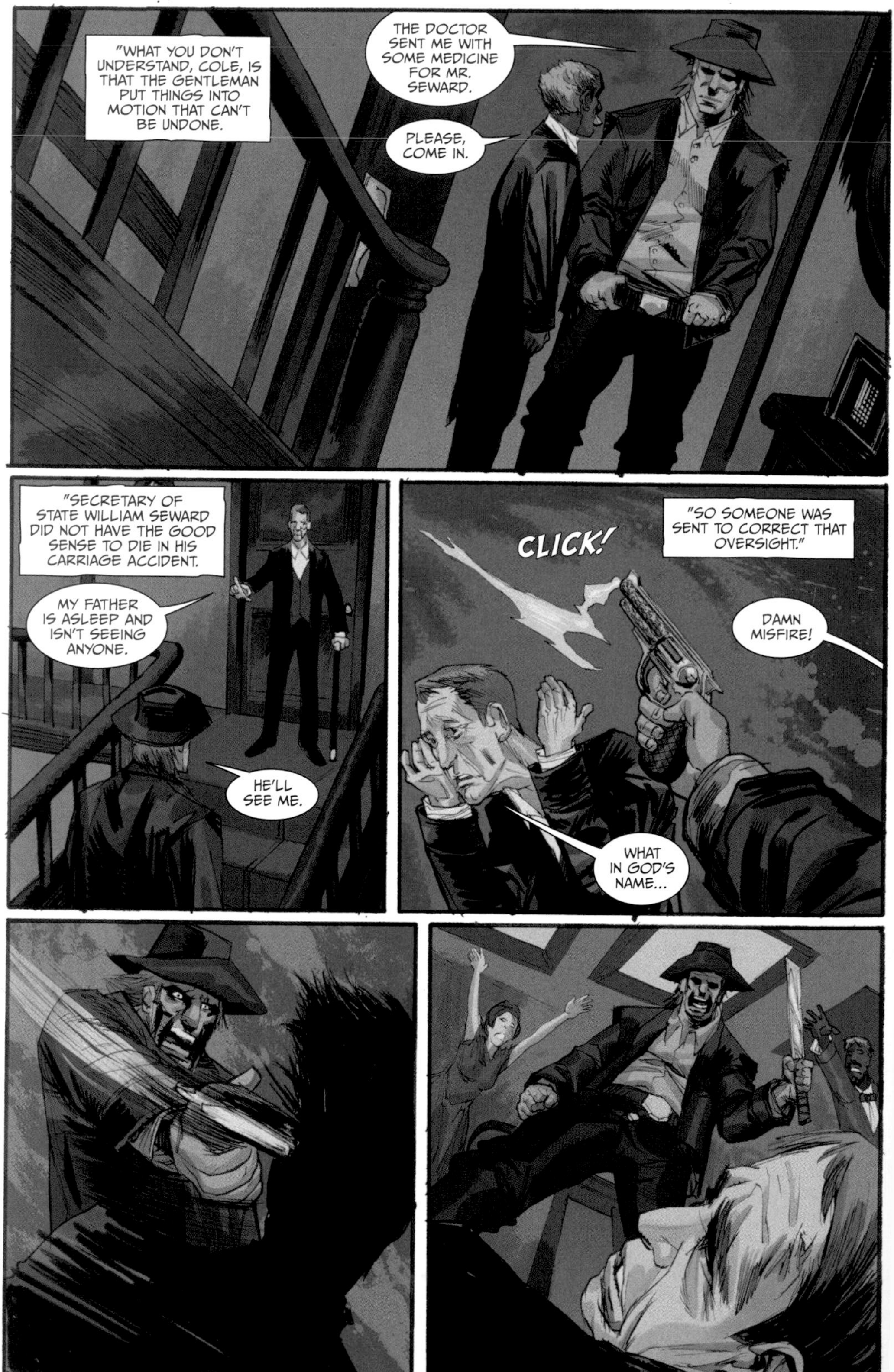
"WHAT YOU DON'T UNDERSTAND, COLE, IS THAT THE GENTLEMAN PUT THINGS INTO MOTION THAT CAN'T BE UNDONE.
THE DOCTOR SENT ME WITH SOME MEDICINE FOR MR. SEWARD.
PLEASE, COME IN.
"SECRETARY OF STATE WILLIAM SEWARD DID NOT HAVE THE GOOD SENSE TO DIE IN HIS CARRIAGE ACCIDENT.
MY FATHER IS ASLEEP AND ISN'T SEEING ANYONE.
HE'LL SEE ME.
"SO SOMEONE WAS SENT TO CORRECT THAT OVERSIGHT."
CLICK!
DAMN MISFIRE!
WHAT IN GOD'S NAME...

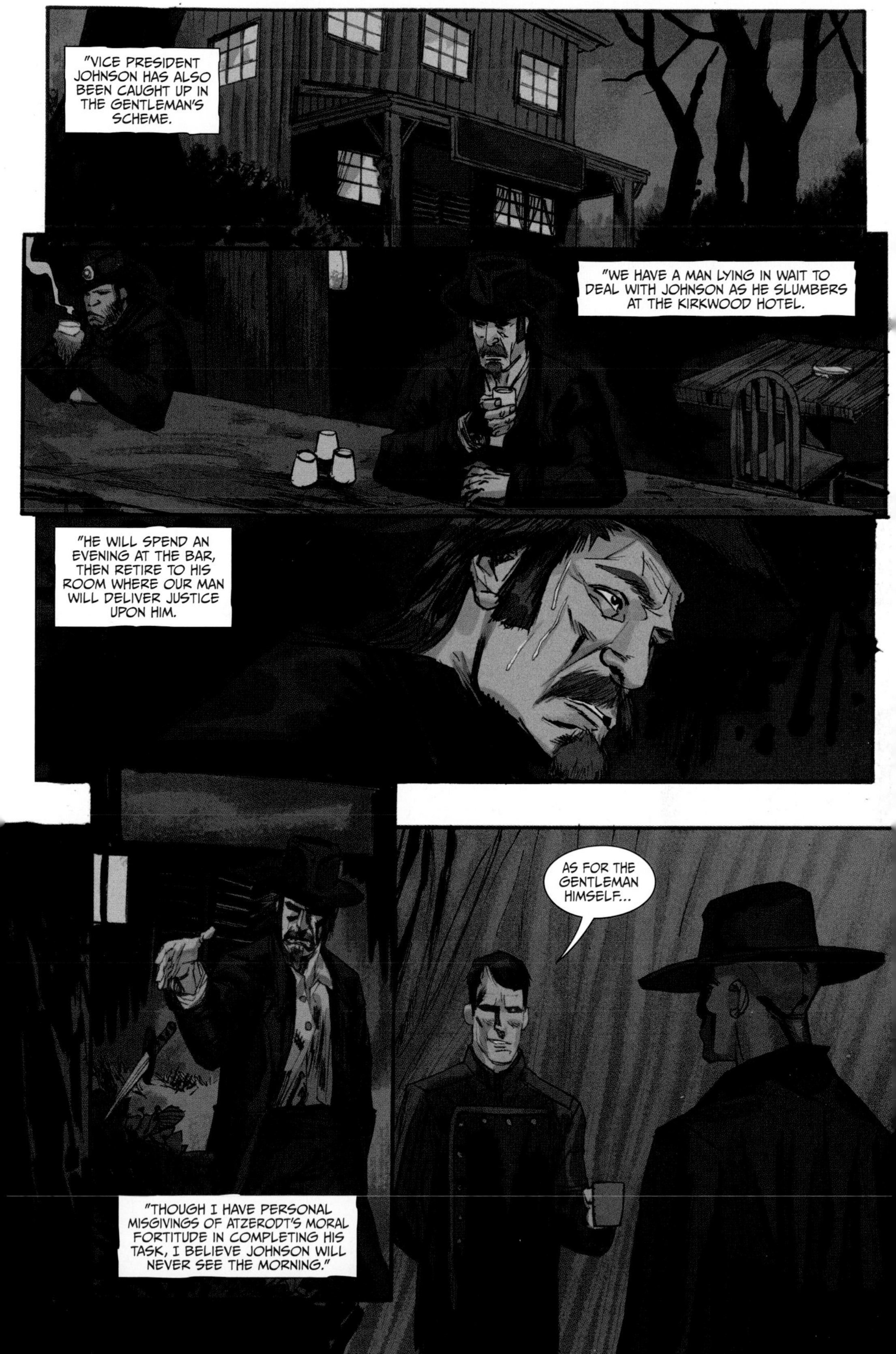
"VICE PRESIDENT JOHNSON HAS ALSO BEEN CAUGHT UP IN THE GENTLEMAN'S SCHEME.
"WE HAVE A MAN LYING IN WAIT TO DEAL WITH JOHNSON AS HE SLUMBERS AT THE KIRKWOOD HOTEL.
"HE WILL SPEND AN EVENING AT THE BAR, THEN RETIRE TO HIS ROOM WHERE OUR MAN WILL DELIVER JUSTICE UPON HIM.
AS FOR THE GENTLEMAN HIMSELF...
"THOUGH I HAVE PERSONAL MISGIVINGS OF ATZERODT'S MORAL FORTITUDE IN COMPLETING HIS TASK, I BELIEVE JOHNSON WILL NEVER SEE THE MORNING."

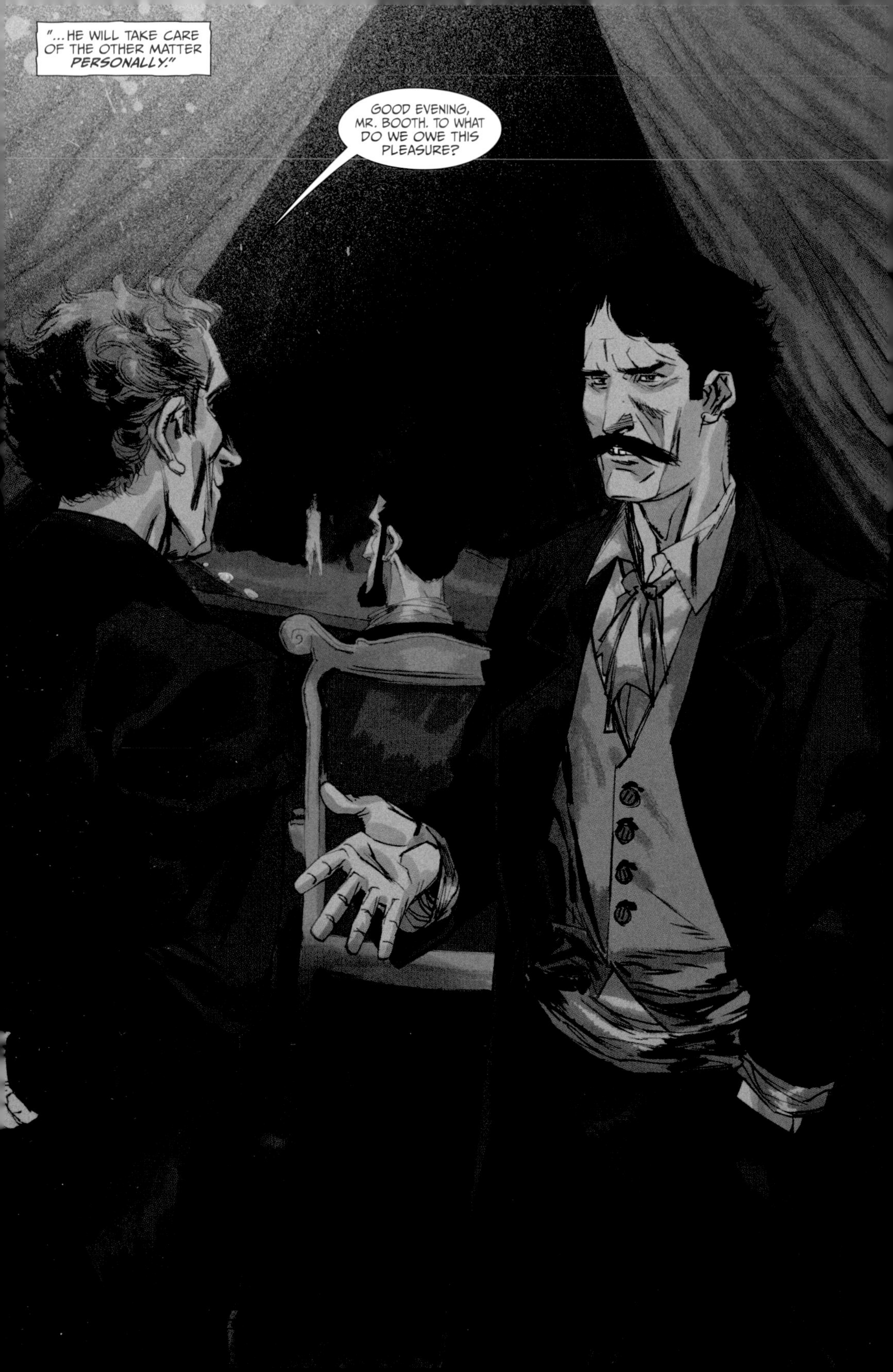
"...HE WILL TAKE CARE OF THE OTHER MATTER *PERSONALLY.*"
GOOD EVENING, MR. BOOTH. TO WHAT DO WE OWE THIS PLEASURE?

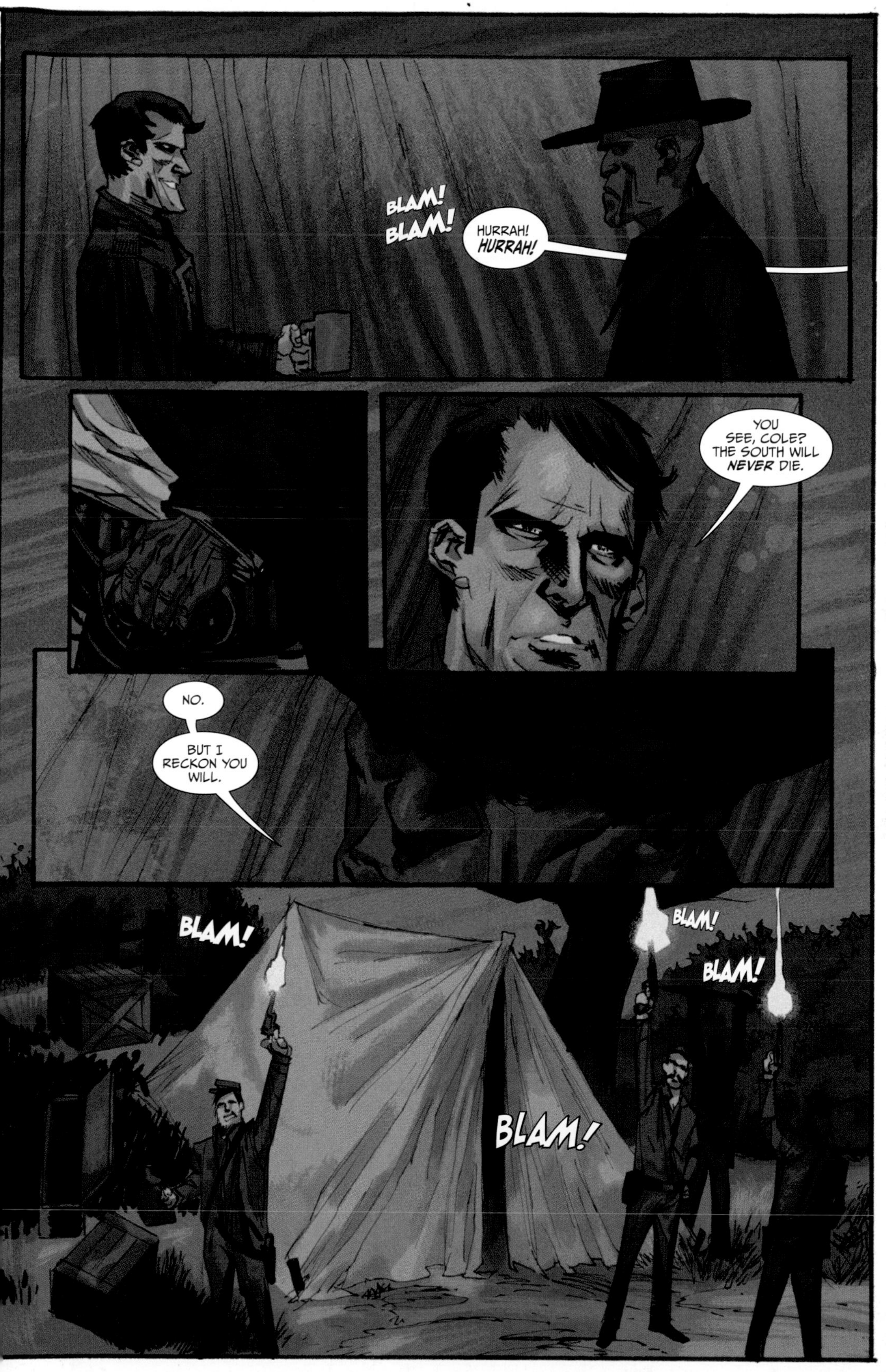
BLAM!
BLAM!
HURRAH! HURRAH!
YOU SEE, COLE? THE SOUTH WILL NEVER DIE.
NO.
BUT I RECKON YOU WILL.
BLAM!
BLAM!
BLAM!
BLAM!

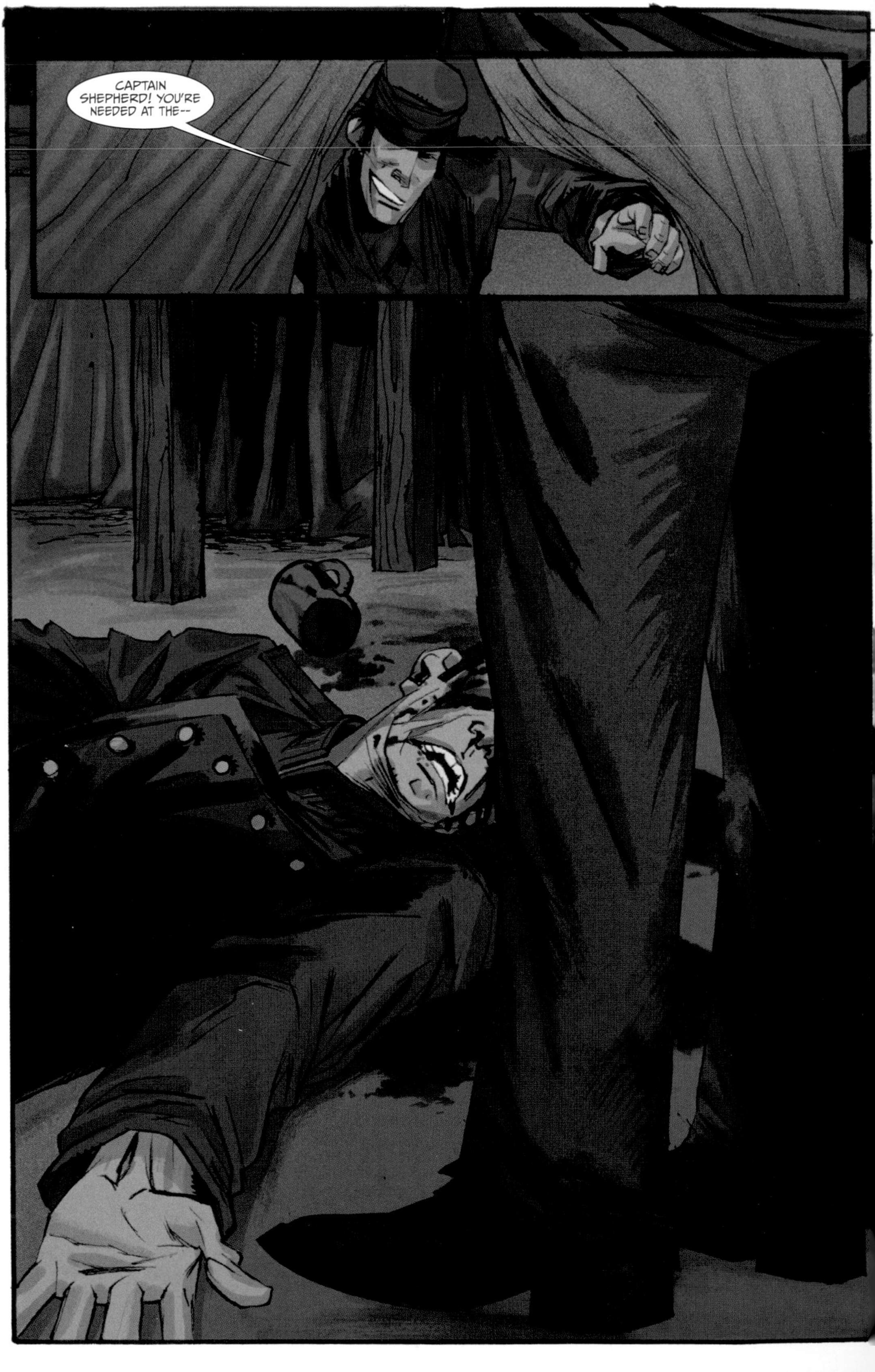
CAPTAIN SHEPHERD! YOU'RE NEEDED AT THE--

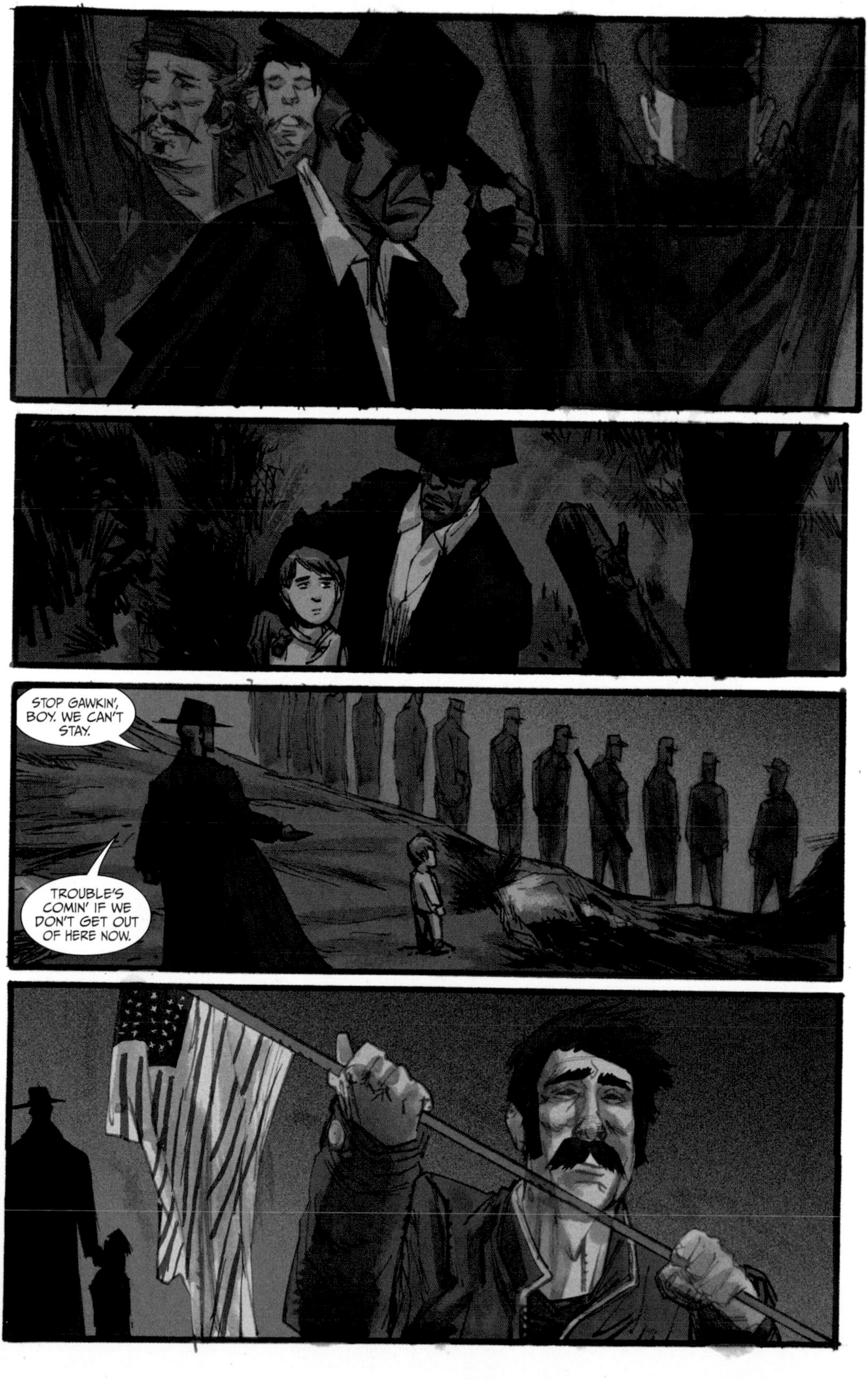
STOP GAWKIN', BOY. WE CAN'T STAY.
TROUBLE'S COMIN' IF WE DON'T GET OUT OF HERE NOW.

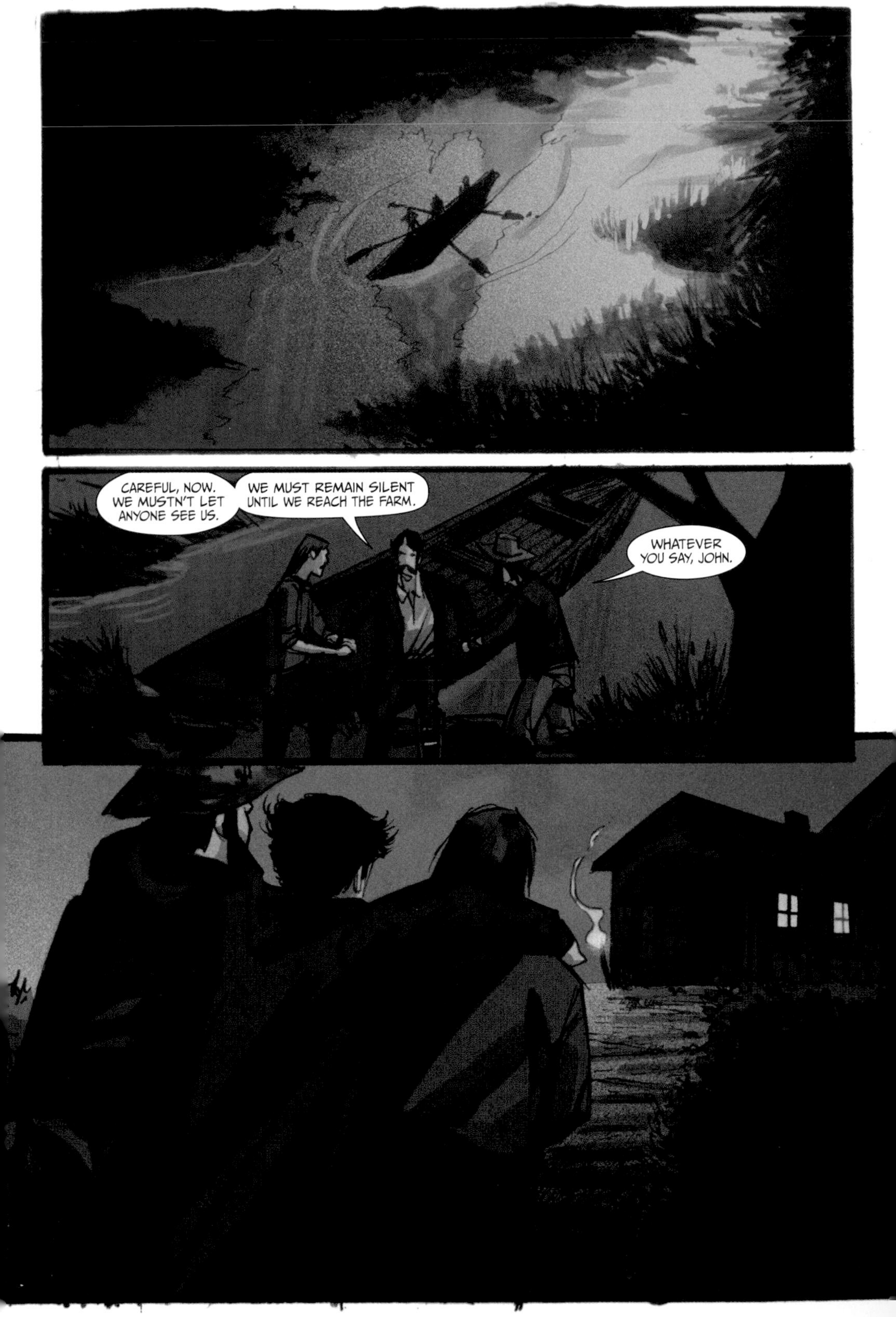
CAREFUL, NOW. WE MUSTN'T LET ANYONE SEE US.
WE MUST REMAIN SILENT UNTIL WE REACH THE FARM.
WHATEVER YOU SAY, JOHN.

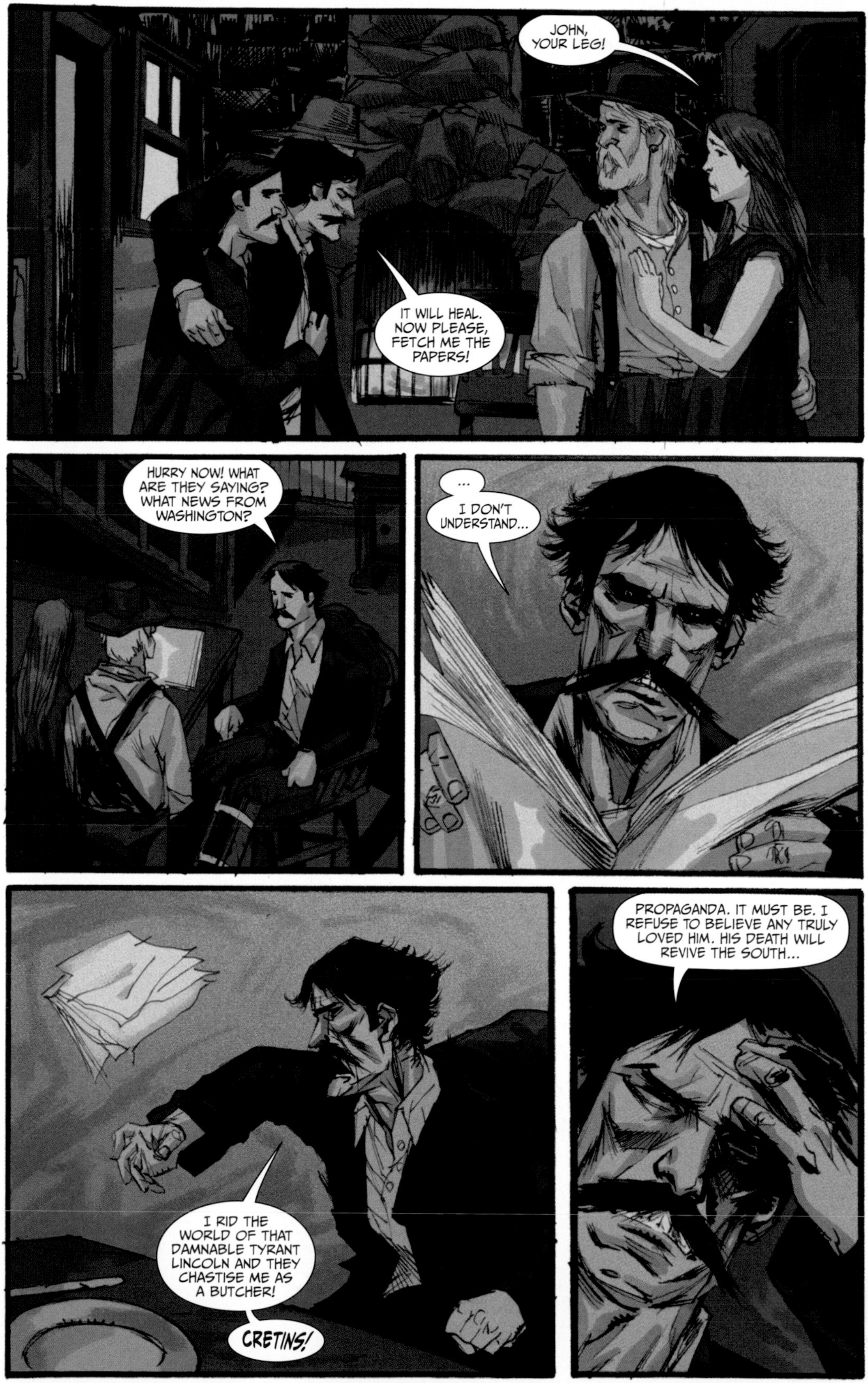
JOHN, YOUR LEG!
IT WILL HEAL. NOW PLEASE, FETCH ME THE PAPERS!
HURRY NOW! WHAT ARE THEY SAYING? WHAT NEWS FROM WASHINGTON?
...
I DON'T UNDERSTAND...
I RID THE WORLD OF THAT DAMNABLE TYRANT LINCOLN AND THEY CHASTISE ME AS A BUTCHER!
CRETINS!
PROPAGANDA. IT MUST BE. I REFUSE TO BELIEVE ANY TRULY LOVED HIM. HIS DEATH WILL REVIVE THE SOUTH...

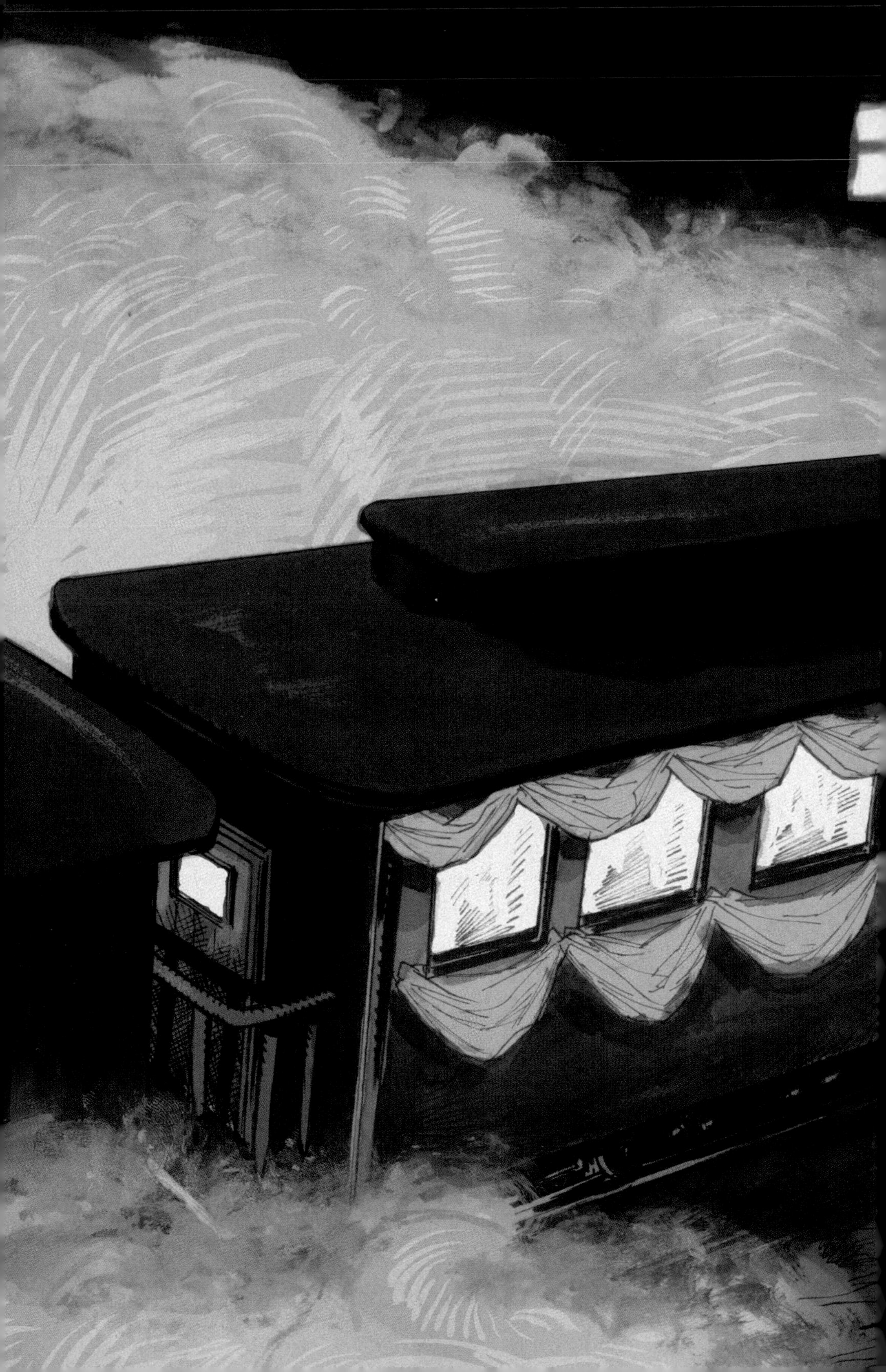

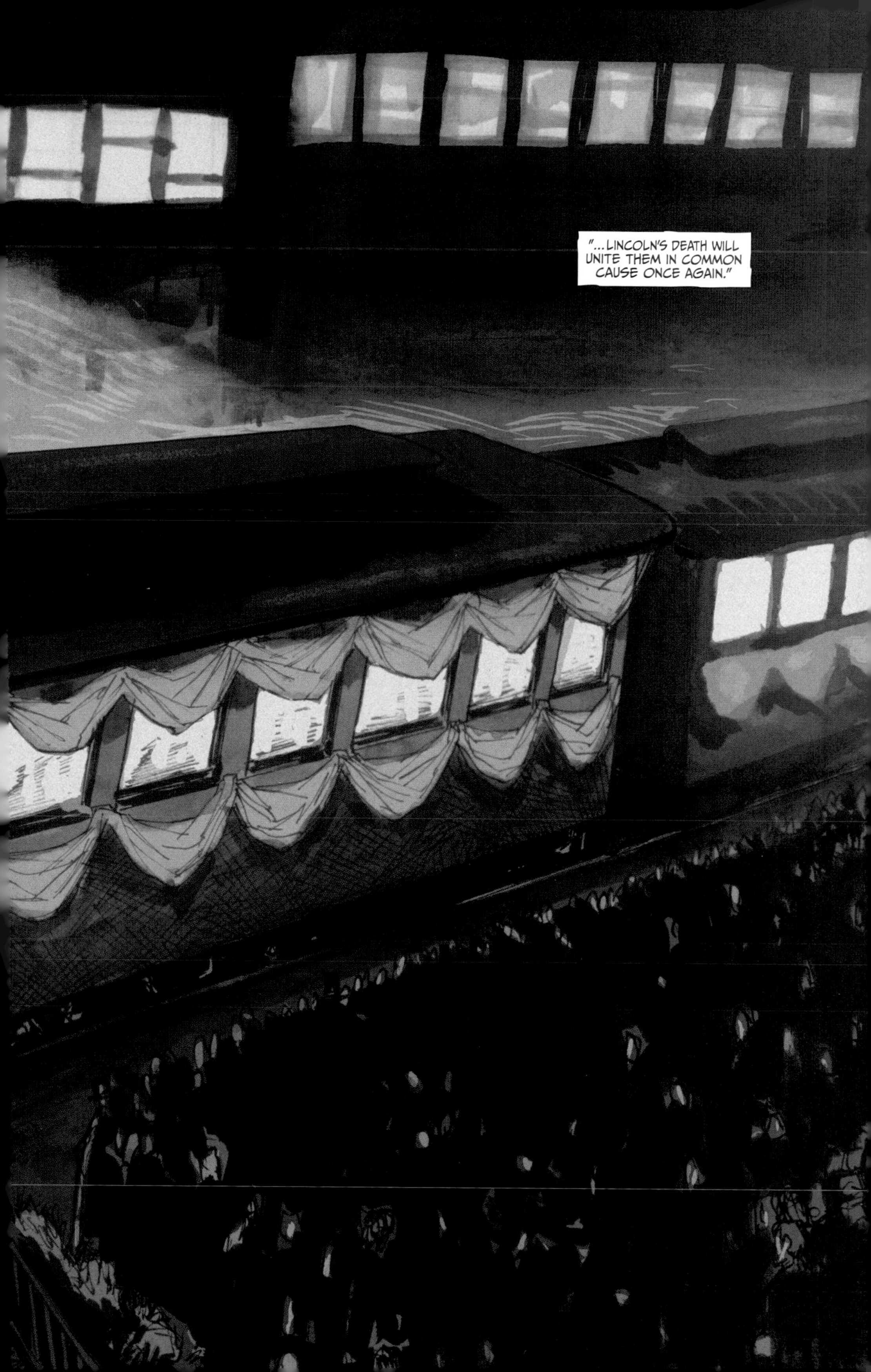
"...LINCOLN'S DEATH WILL UNITE THEM IN COMMON CAUSE ONCE AGAIN."

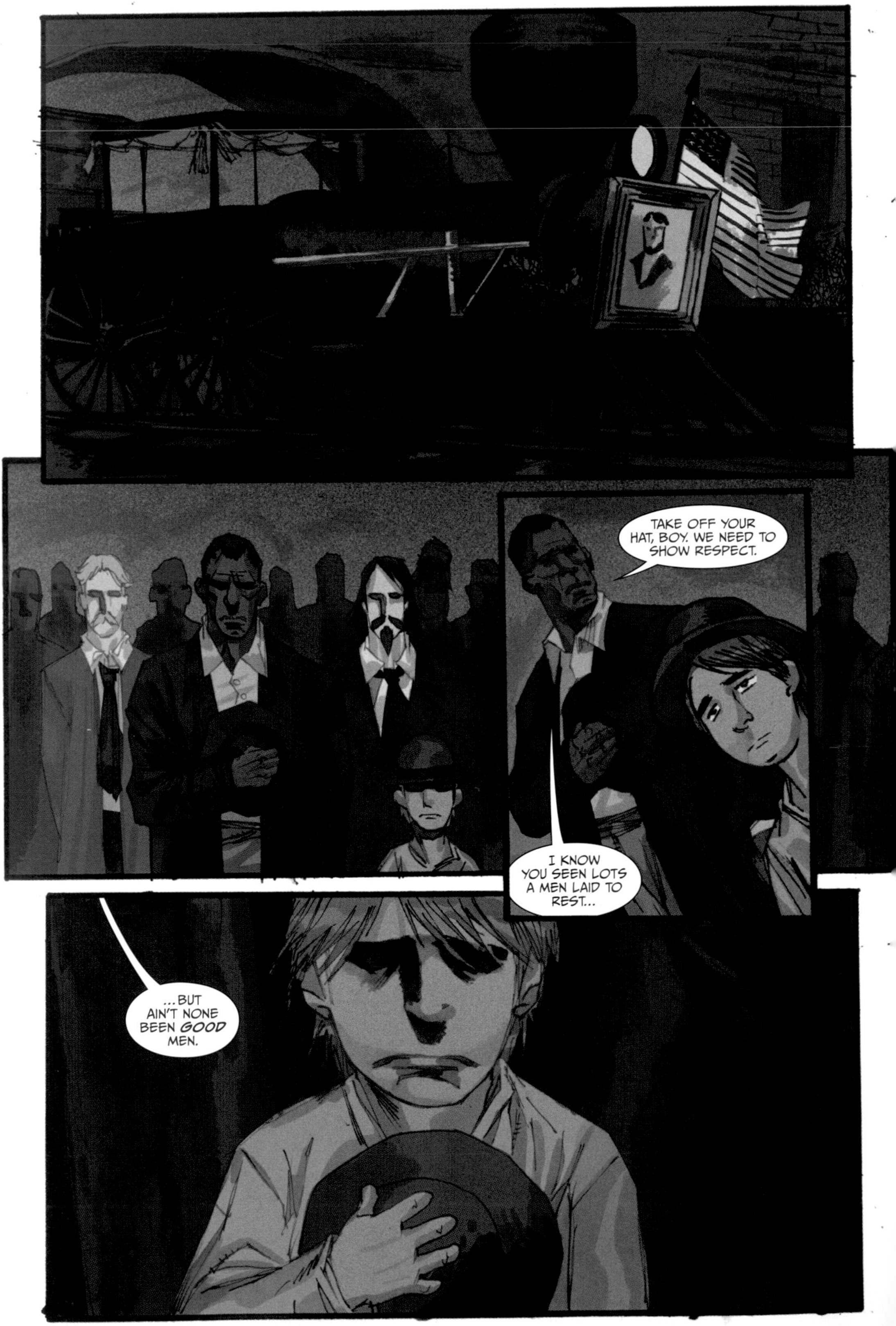
TAKE OFF YOUR HAT, BOY. WE NEED TO SHOW RESPECT.
I KNOW YOU SEEN LOTS A MEN LAID TO REST...
...BUT AIN'T NONE BEEN GOOD MEN.

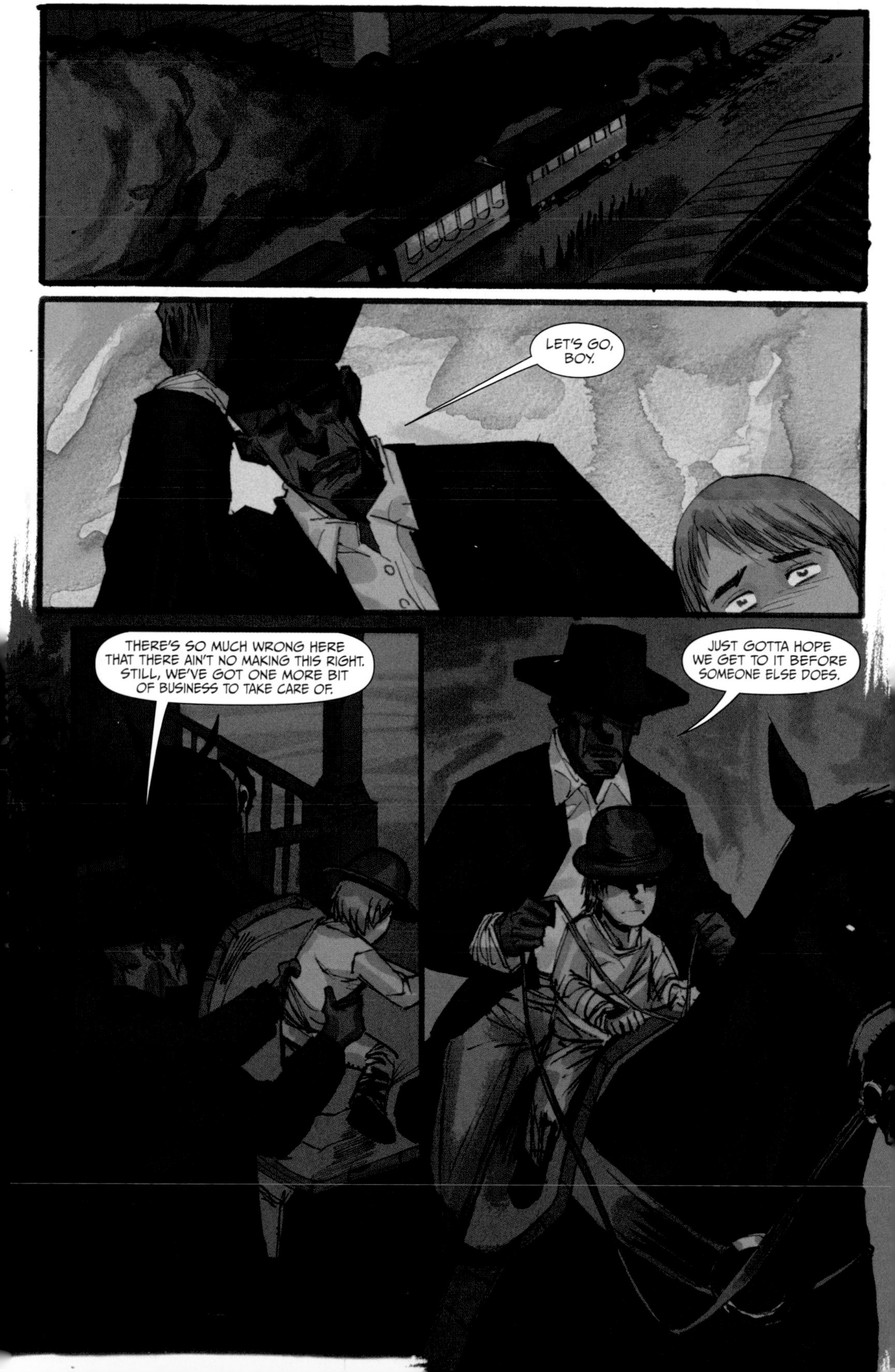
LET'S GO, BOY.
THERE'S SO MUCH WRONG HERE THAT THERE AIN'T NO MAKING THIS RIGHT. STILL, WE'VE GOT ONE MORE BIT OF BUSINESS TO TAKE CARE OF.
JUST GOTTA HOPE WE GET TO IT BEFORE SOMEONE ELSE DOES.

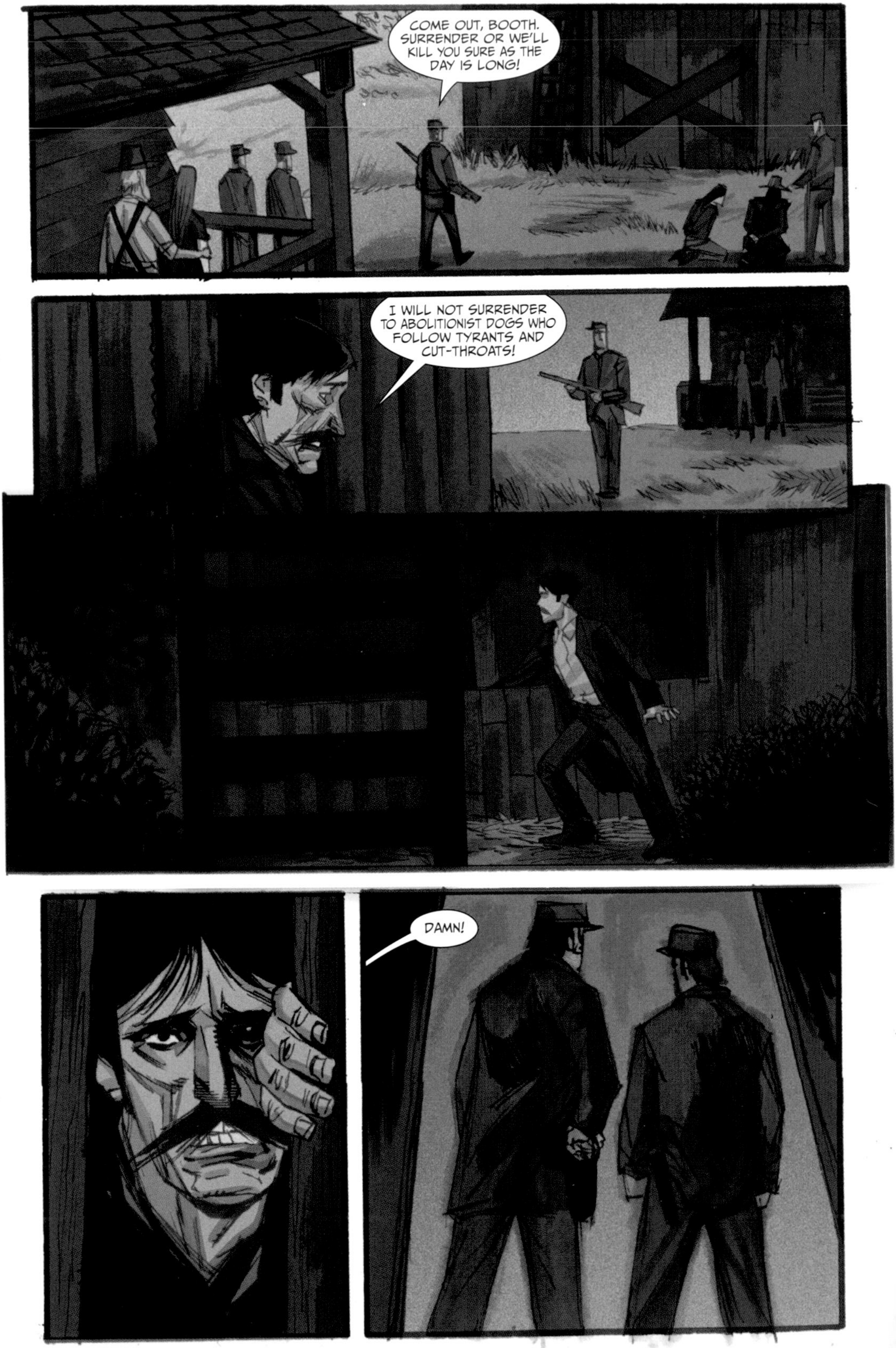
COME OUT, BOOTH. SURRENDER OR WE'LL KILL YOU SURE AS THE DAY IS LONG!
I WILL NOT SURRENDER TO ABOLITIONIST DOGS WHO FOLLOW TYRANTS AND CUT-THROATS!
DAMN!

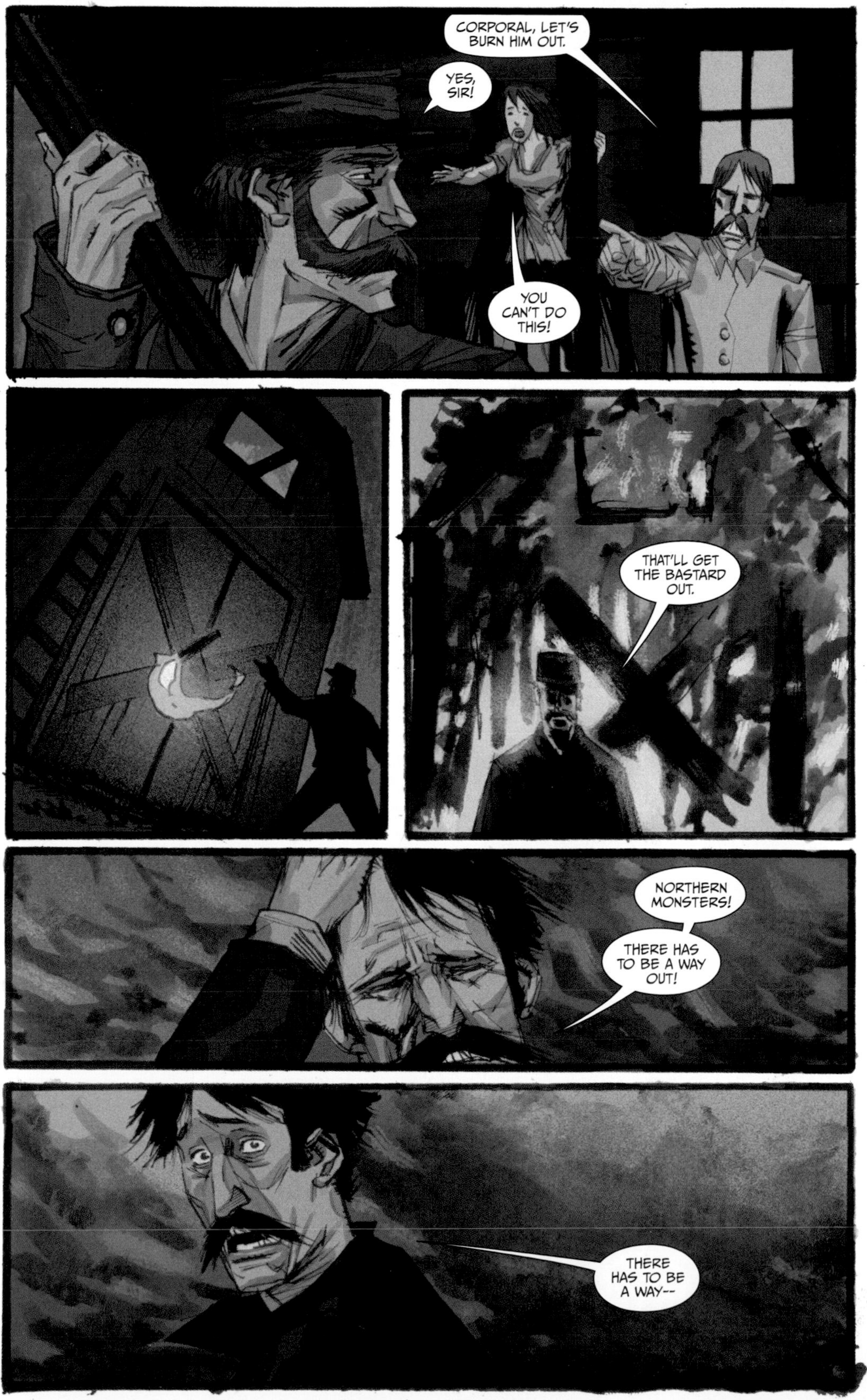
CORPORAL, LET'S BURN HIM OUT.
YES, SIR!
YOU CAN'T DO THIS!
THAT'LL GET THE BASTARD OUT.
NORTHERN MONSTERS!
THERE HAS TO BE A WAY OUT!
THERE HAS TO BE A WAY--

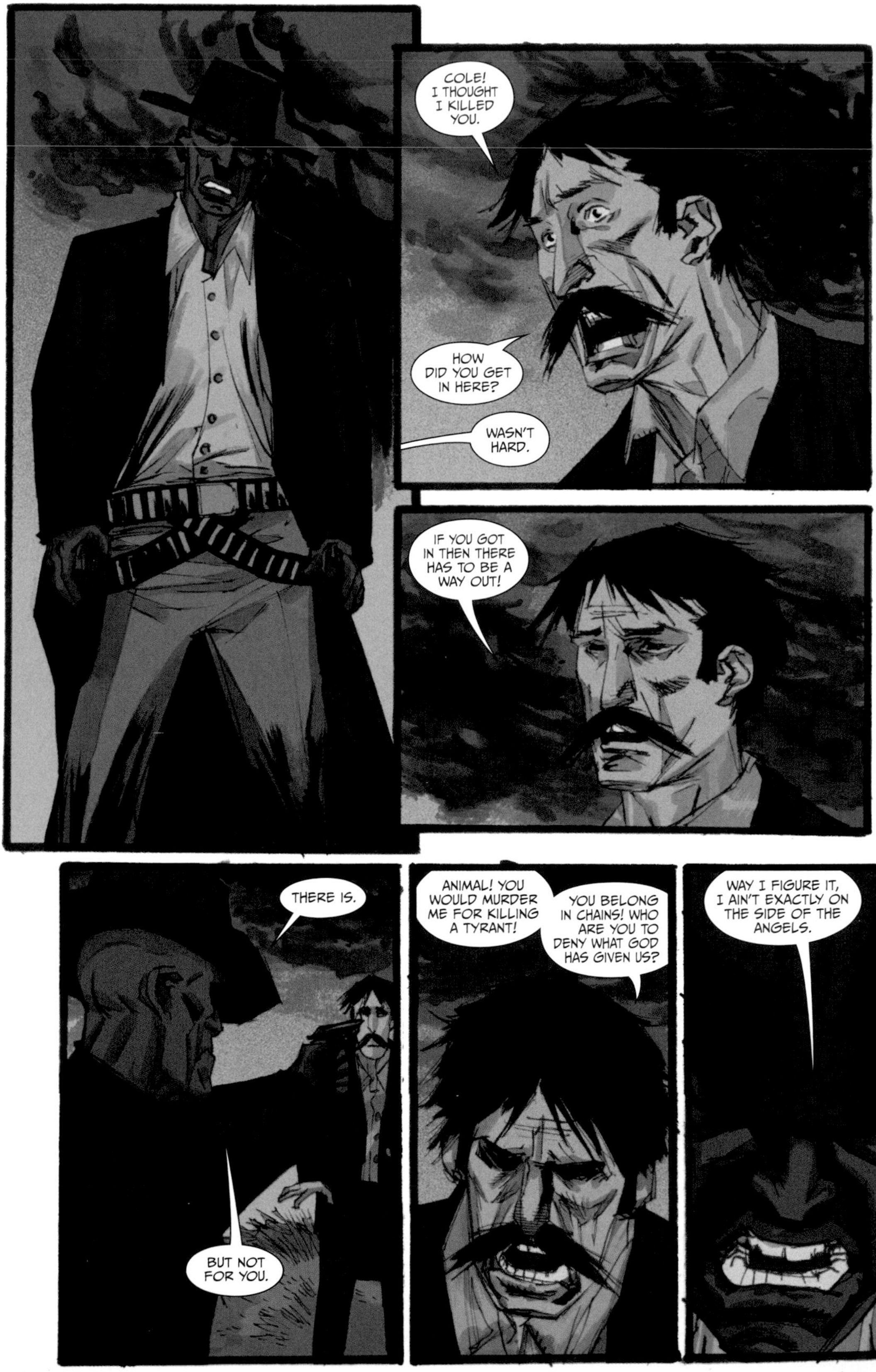
COLE! I THOUGHT I KILLED YOU.
HOW DID YOU GET IN HERE?
WASN'T HARD.
IF YOU GOT IN THEN THERE HAS TO BE A WAY OUT!
THERE IS.
BUT NOT FOR YOU.
ANIMAL! YOU WOULD MURDER ME FOR KILLING A TYRANT!
YOU BELONG IN CHAINS! WHO ARE YOU TO DENY WHAT GOD HAS GIVEN US?
WAY I FIGURE IT, I AIN'T EXACTLY ON THE SIDE OF THE ANGELS.

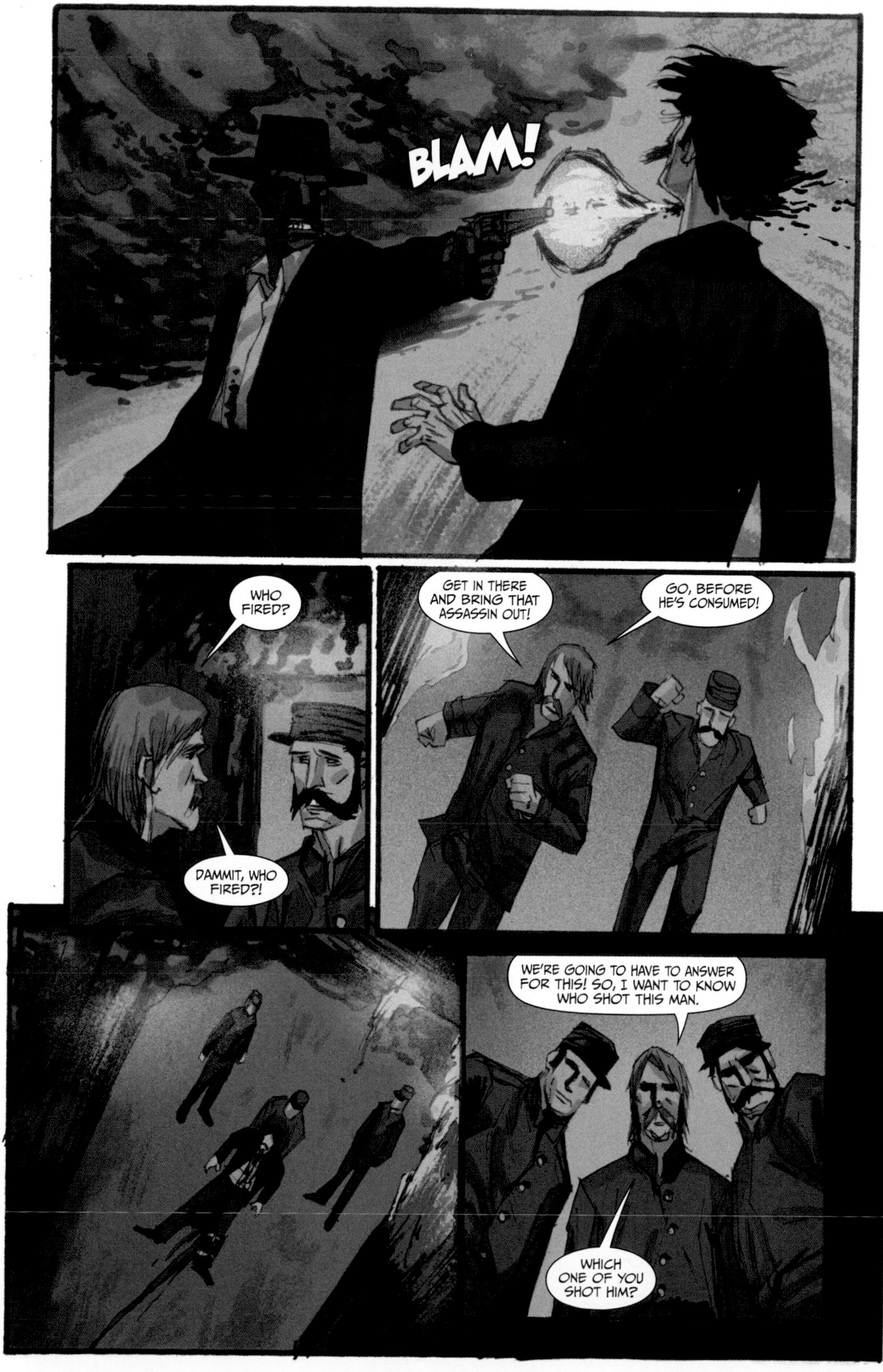
BLAM!
WHO FIRED?
DAMMIT, WHO FIRED?!
GET IN THERE AND BRING THAT ASSASSIN OUT!
GO, BEFORE HE'S CONSUMED!
WE'RE GOING TO HAVE TO ANSWER FOR THIS! SO, I WANT TO KNOW WHO SHOT THIS MAN.
WHICH ONE OF YOU SHOT HIM?

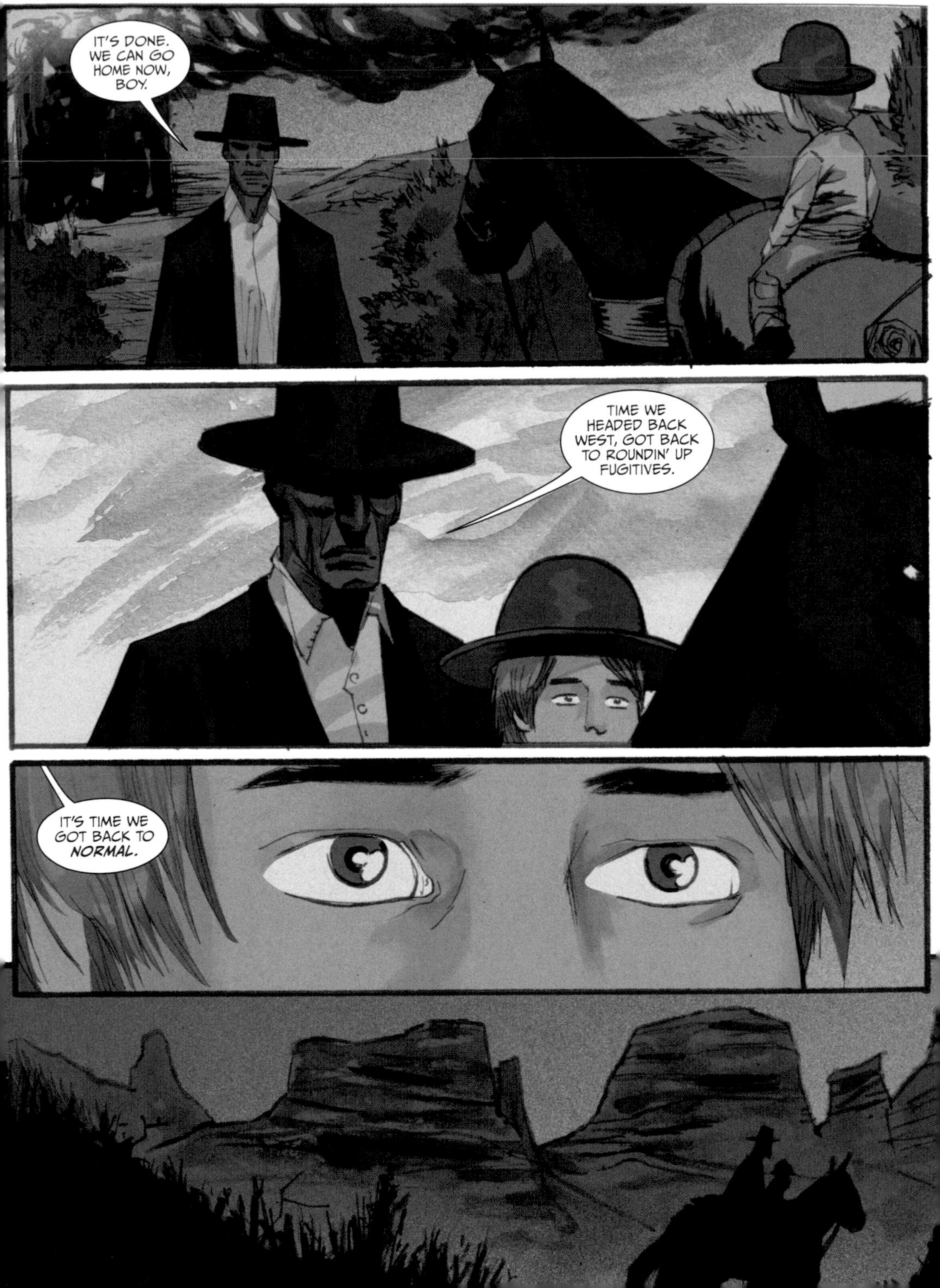
IT'S DONE. WE CAN GO HOME NOW, BOY.
TIME WE HEADED BACK WEST, GOT BACK TO ROUNDIN' UP FUGITIVES.
IT'S TIME WE GOT BACK TO *NORMAL.*

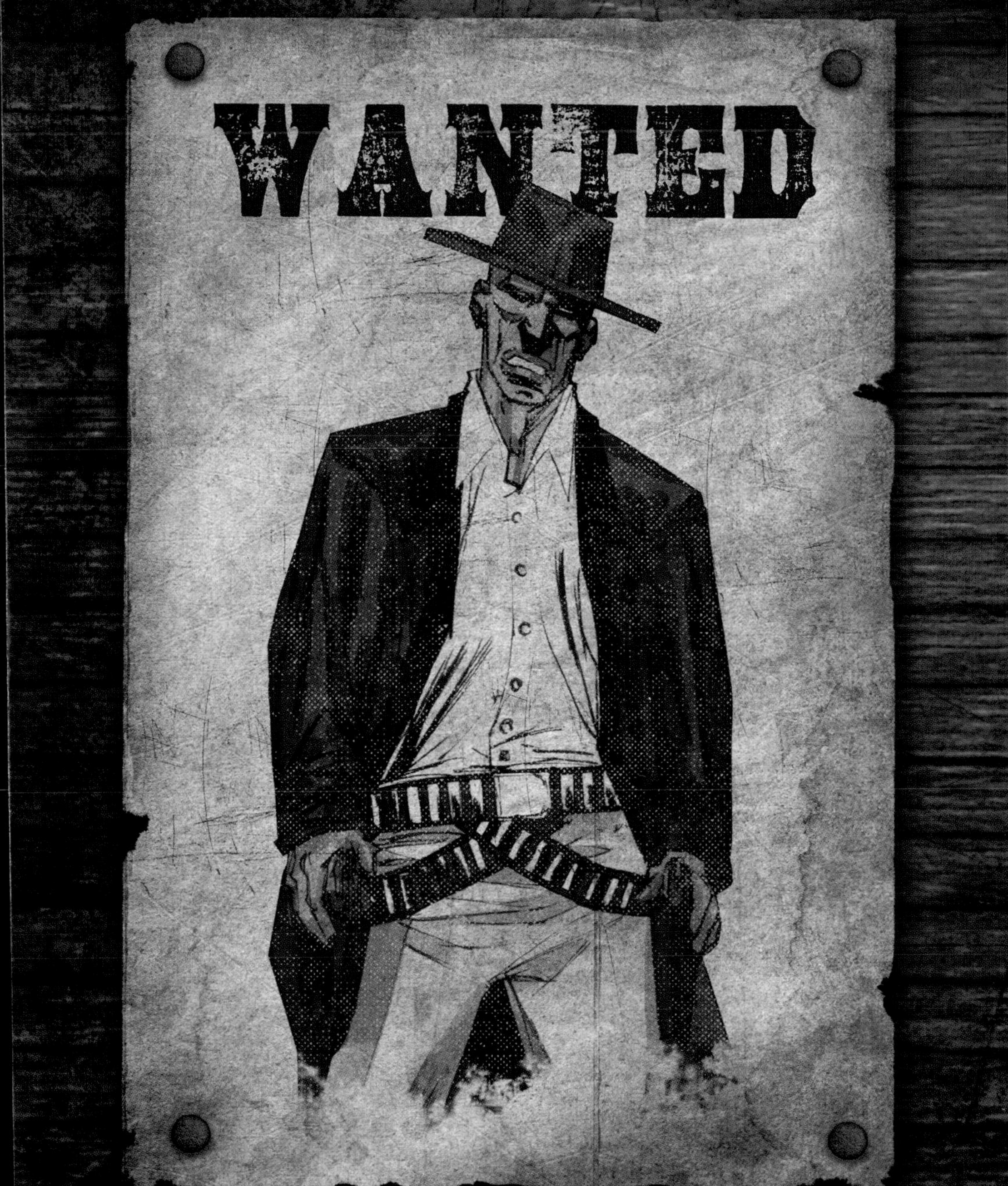
WANTED

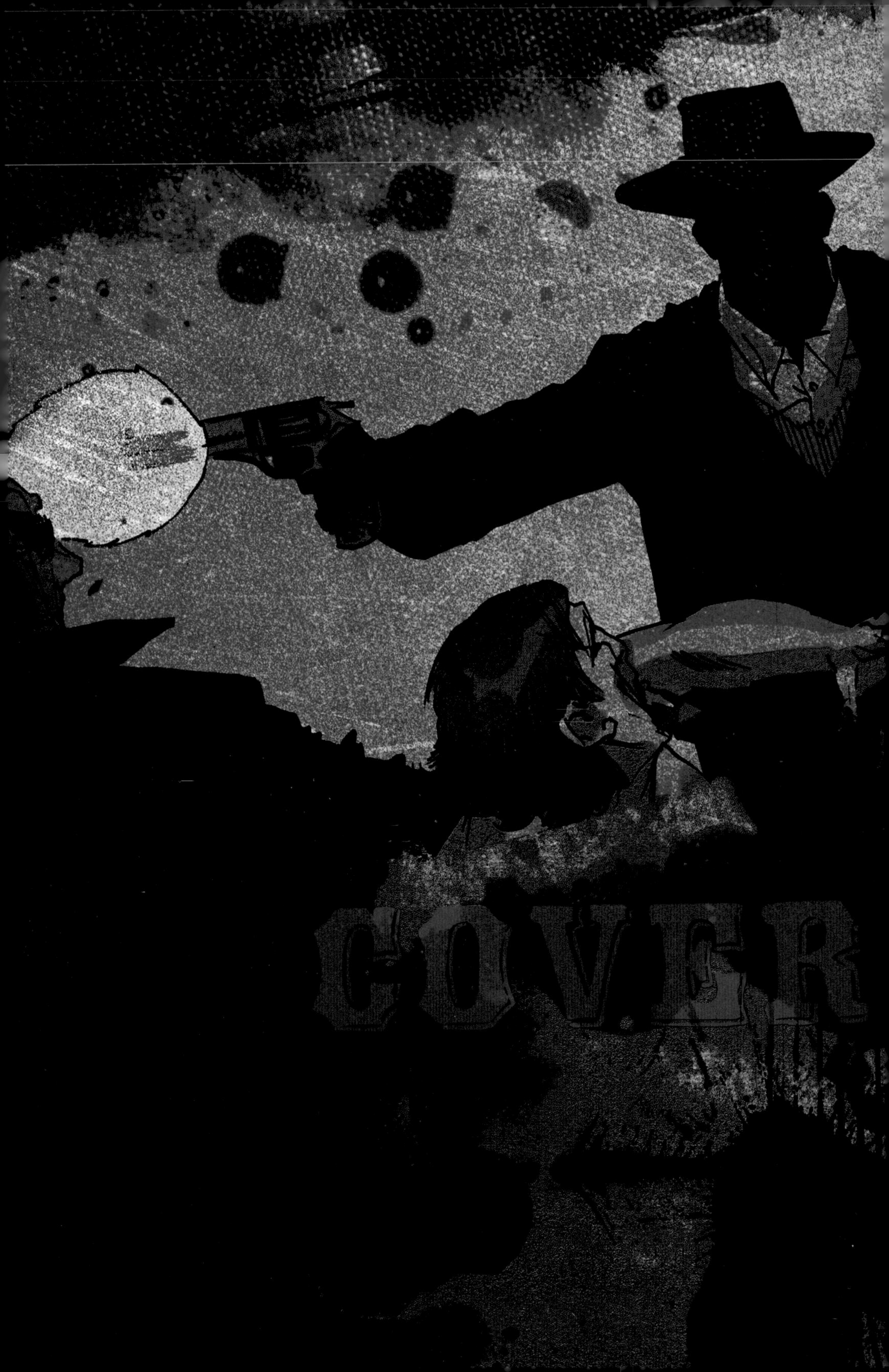
COVER

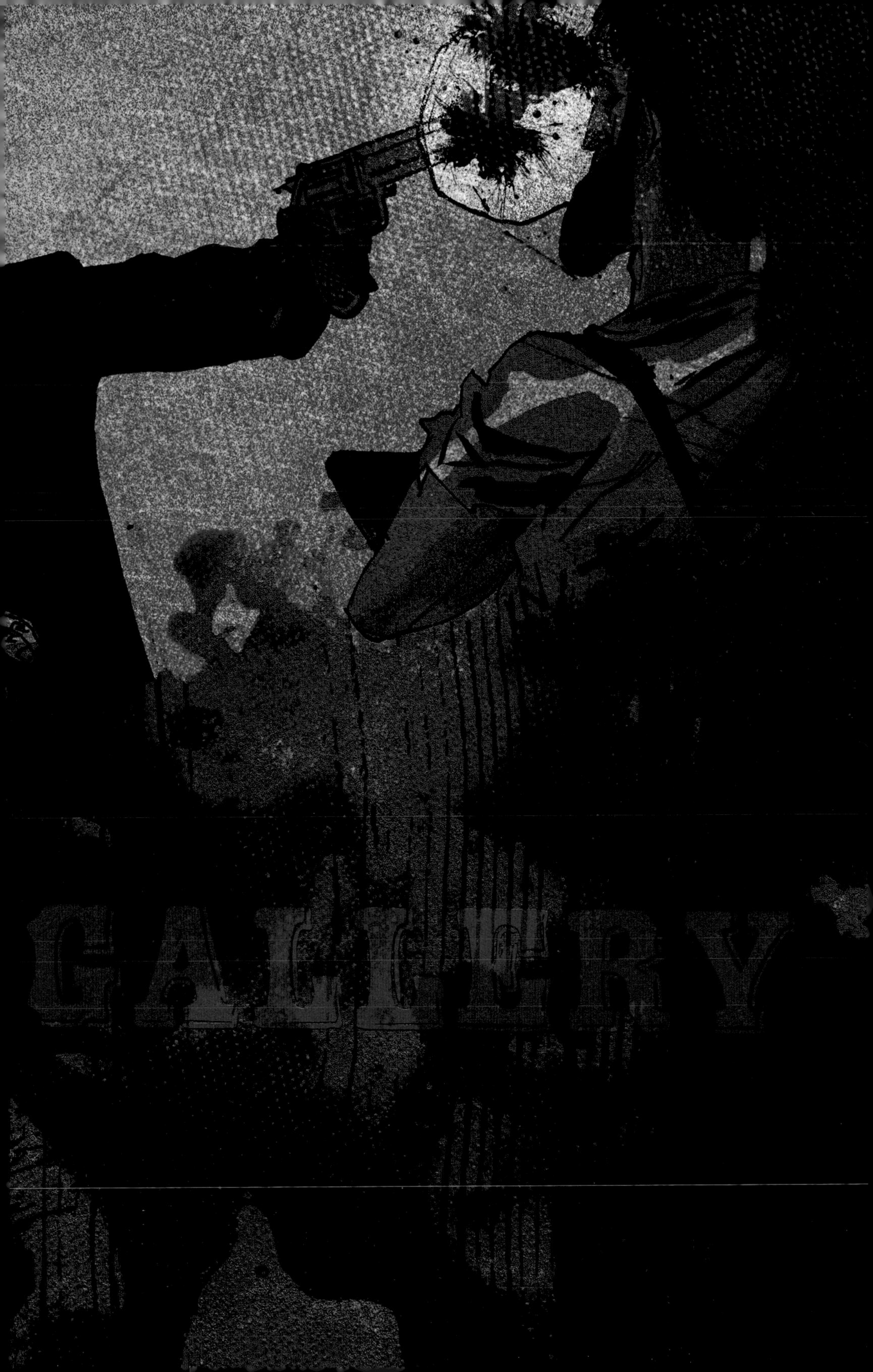
GALLERY

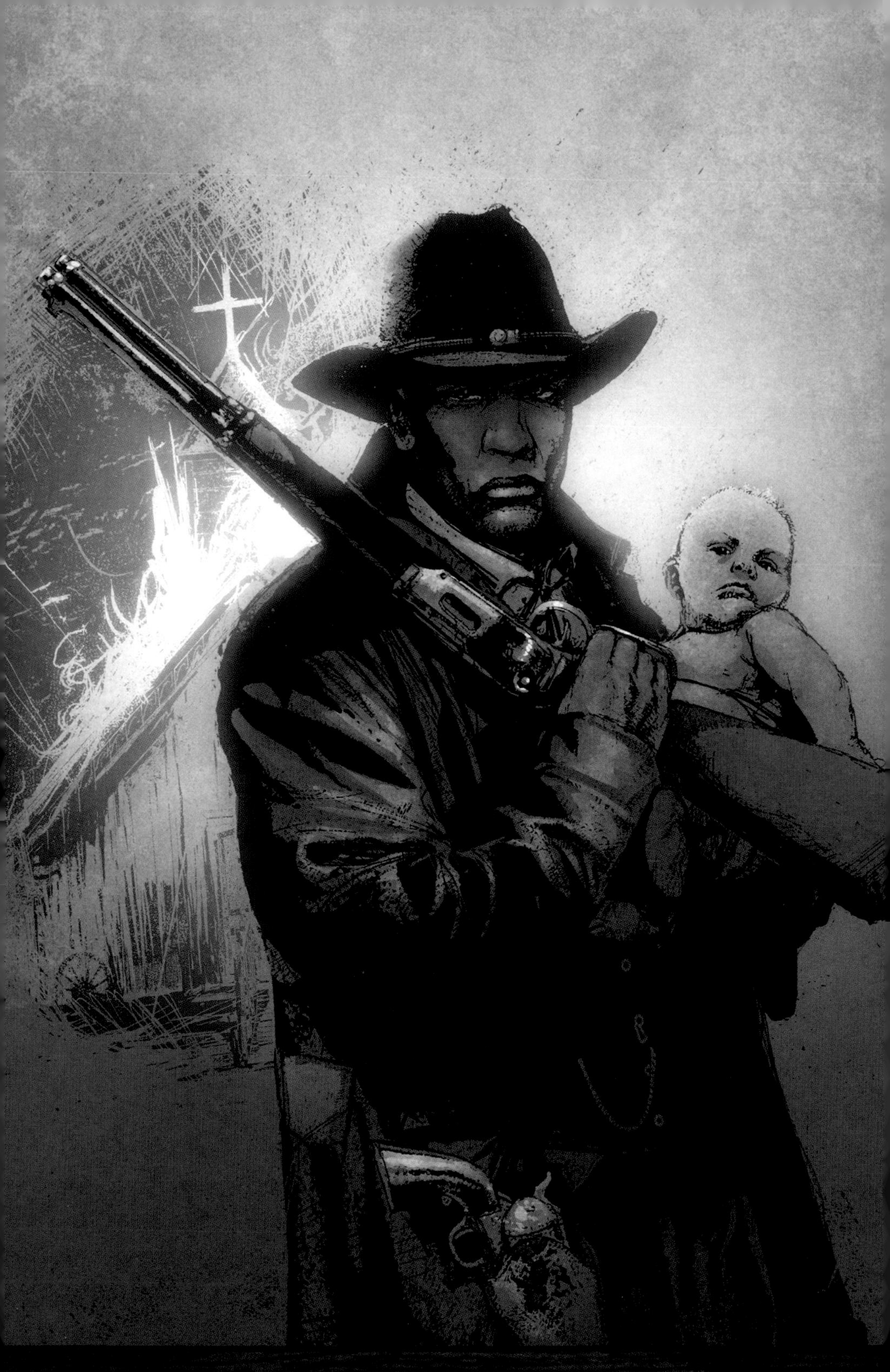

COVER 1A: LEONARDO MANCO COLORS BY: NICK FILARDI

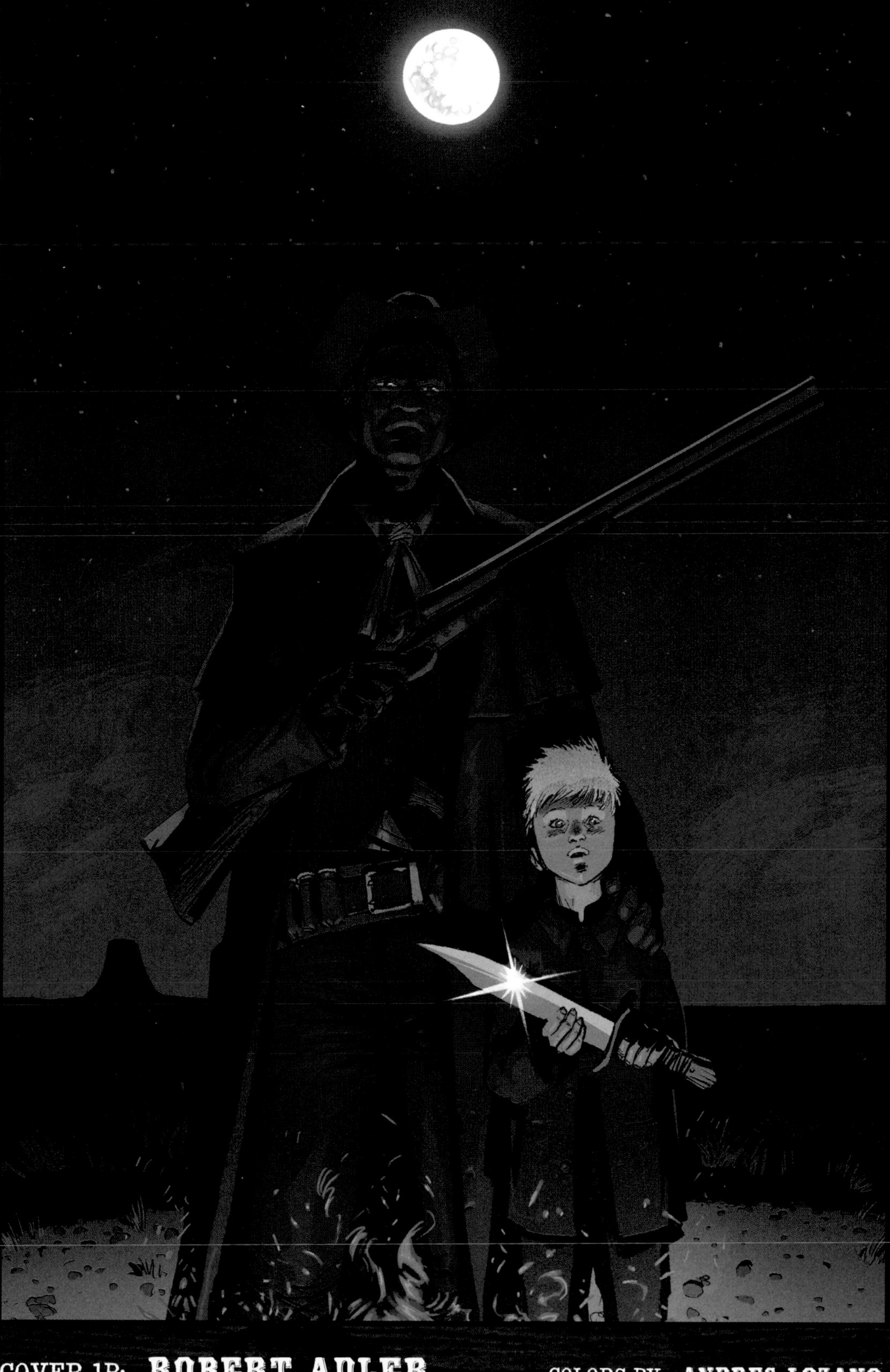

COVER 1B: **ROBERT ADLER** COLORS BY: **ANDRES LOZANO**

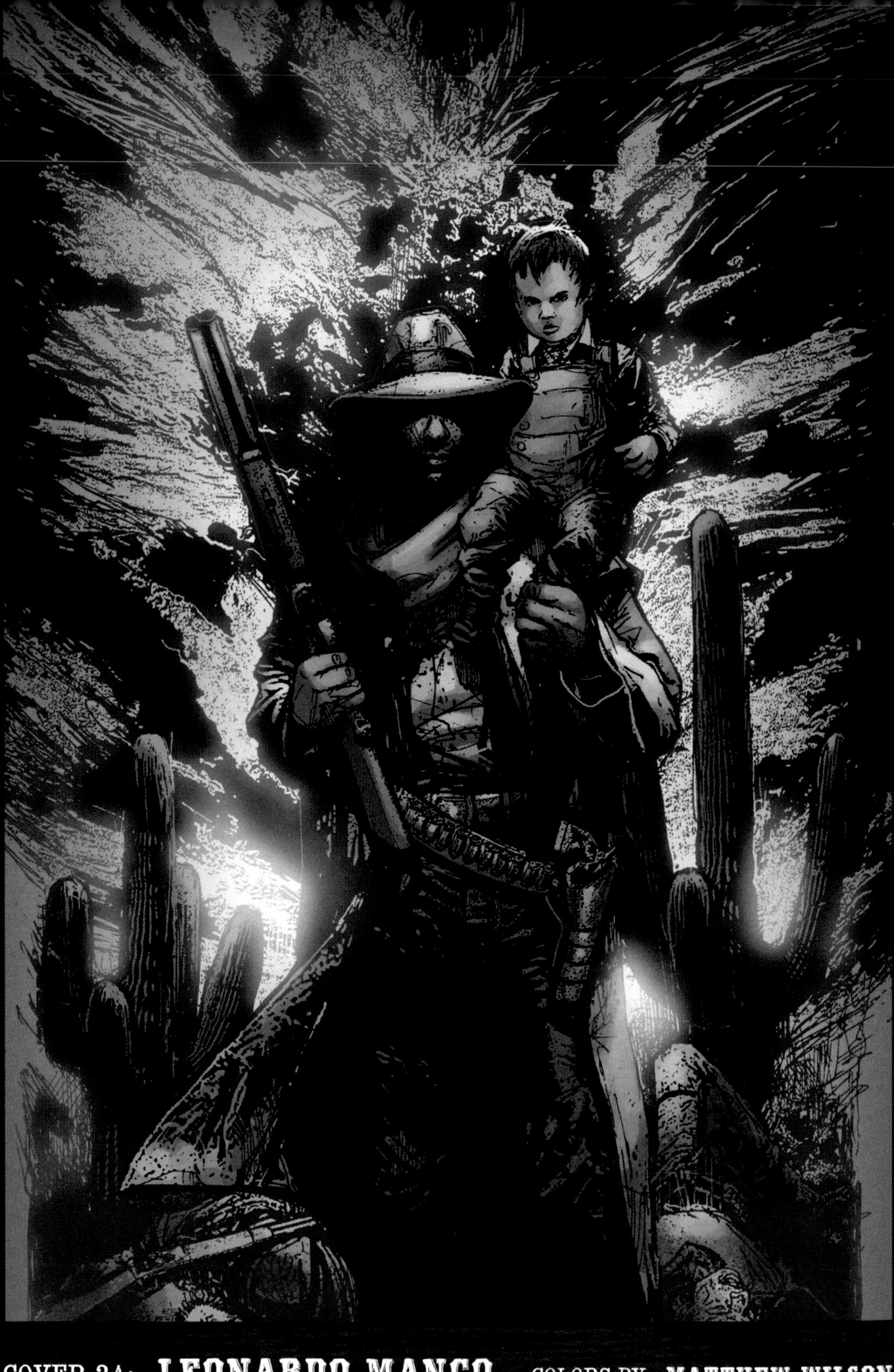

COVER 2A: **LEONARDO MANCO** COLORS BY: **MATTHEW WILSON**

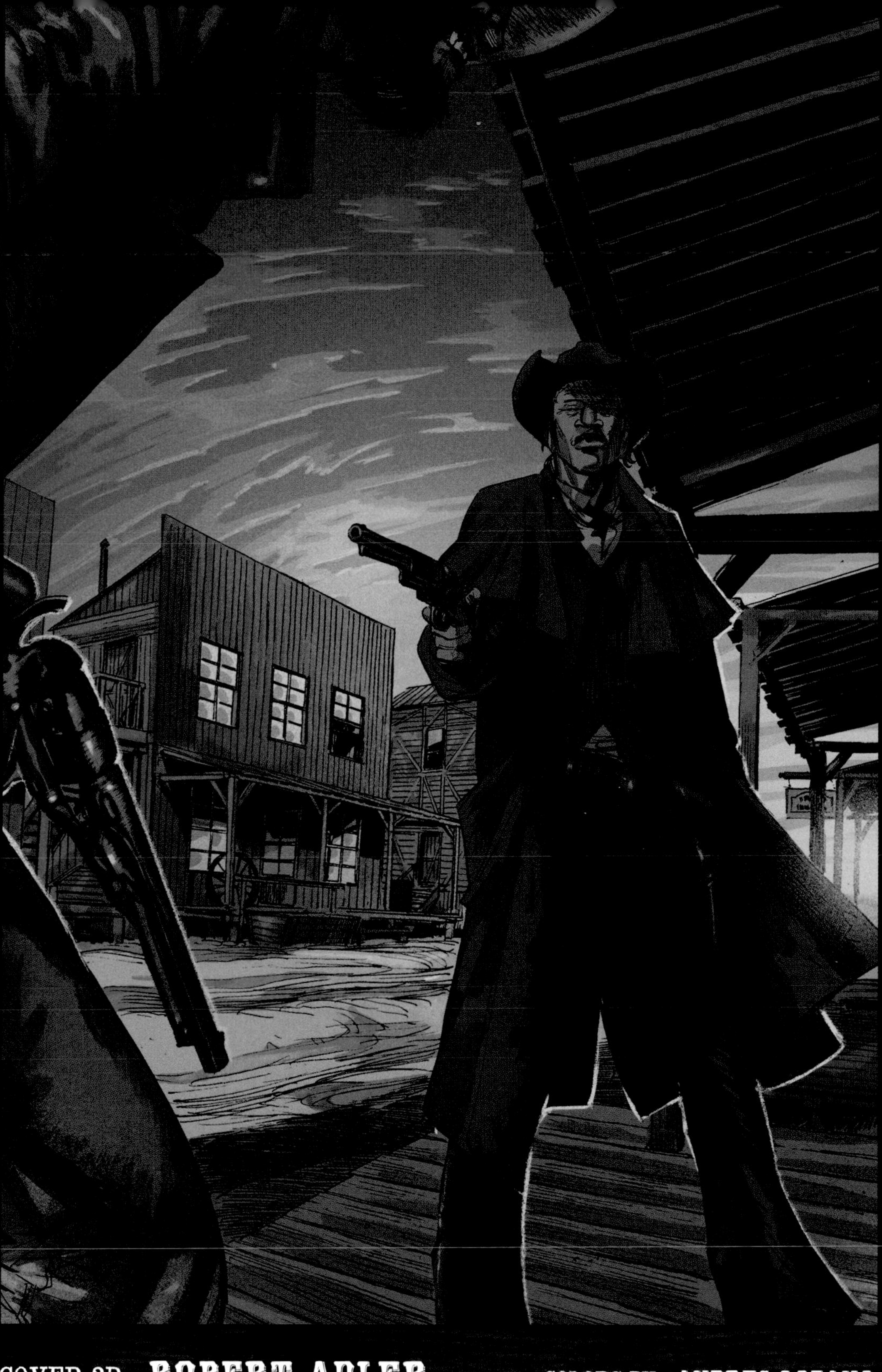

COVER 2B: **ROBERT ADLER** COLORS BY: **ANDRES LOZANO**

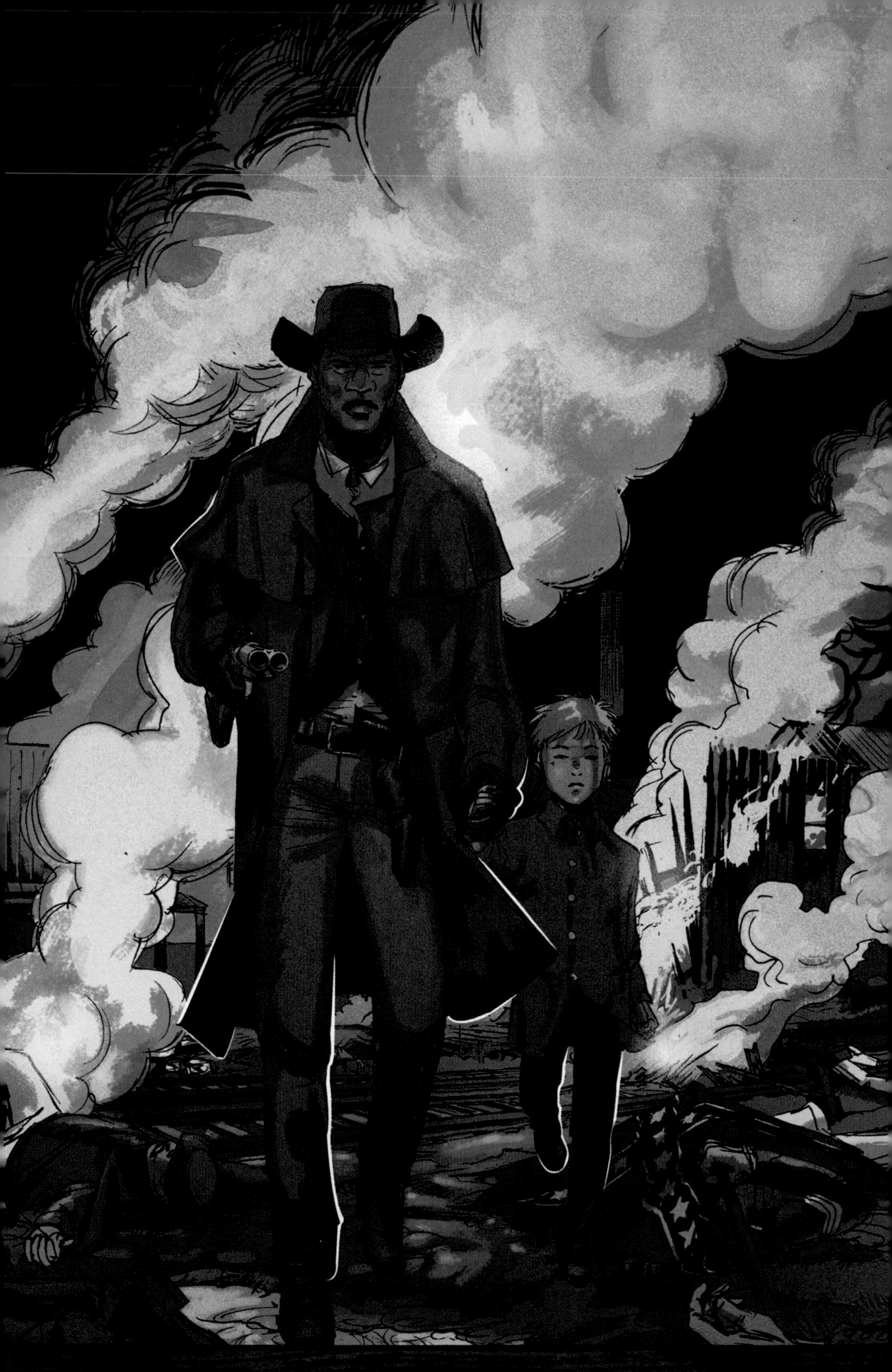

COVER 3: **ROBERT ADLER** COLORS BY: **ANDRES LOZANO**

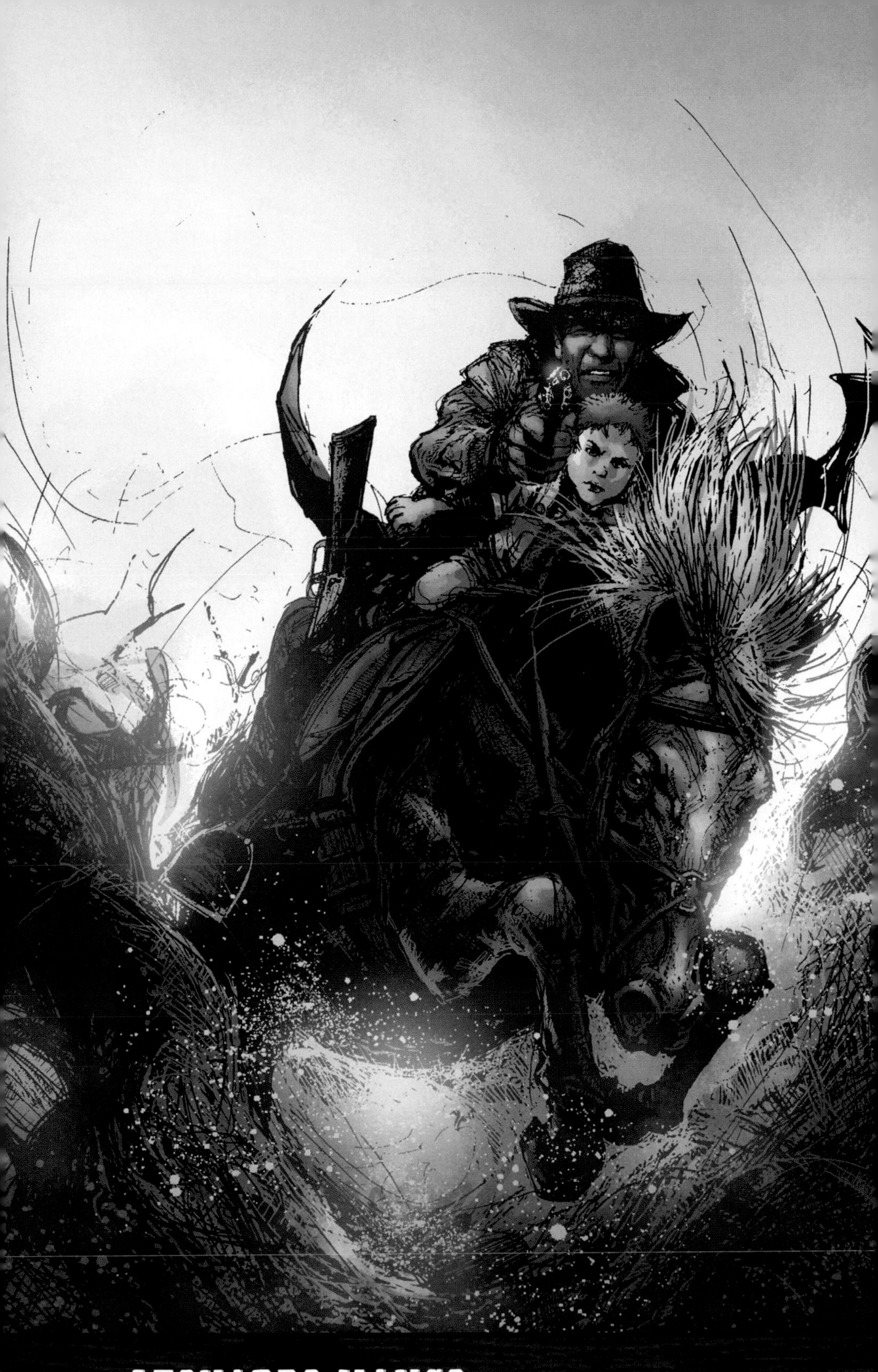

COVER 4: LEONARDO MANCO COLORS BY: MATTHEW WILSON

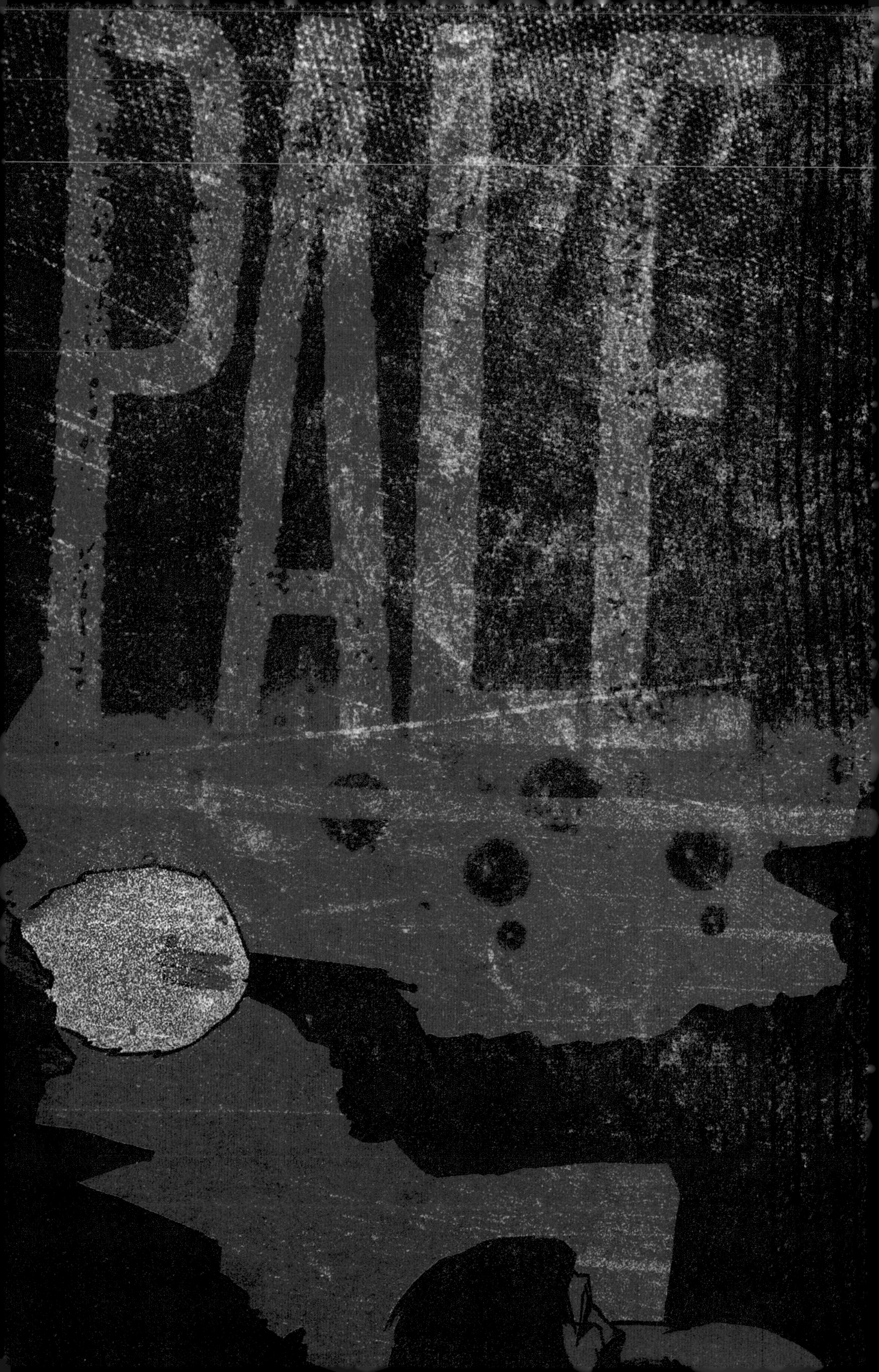

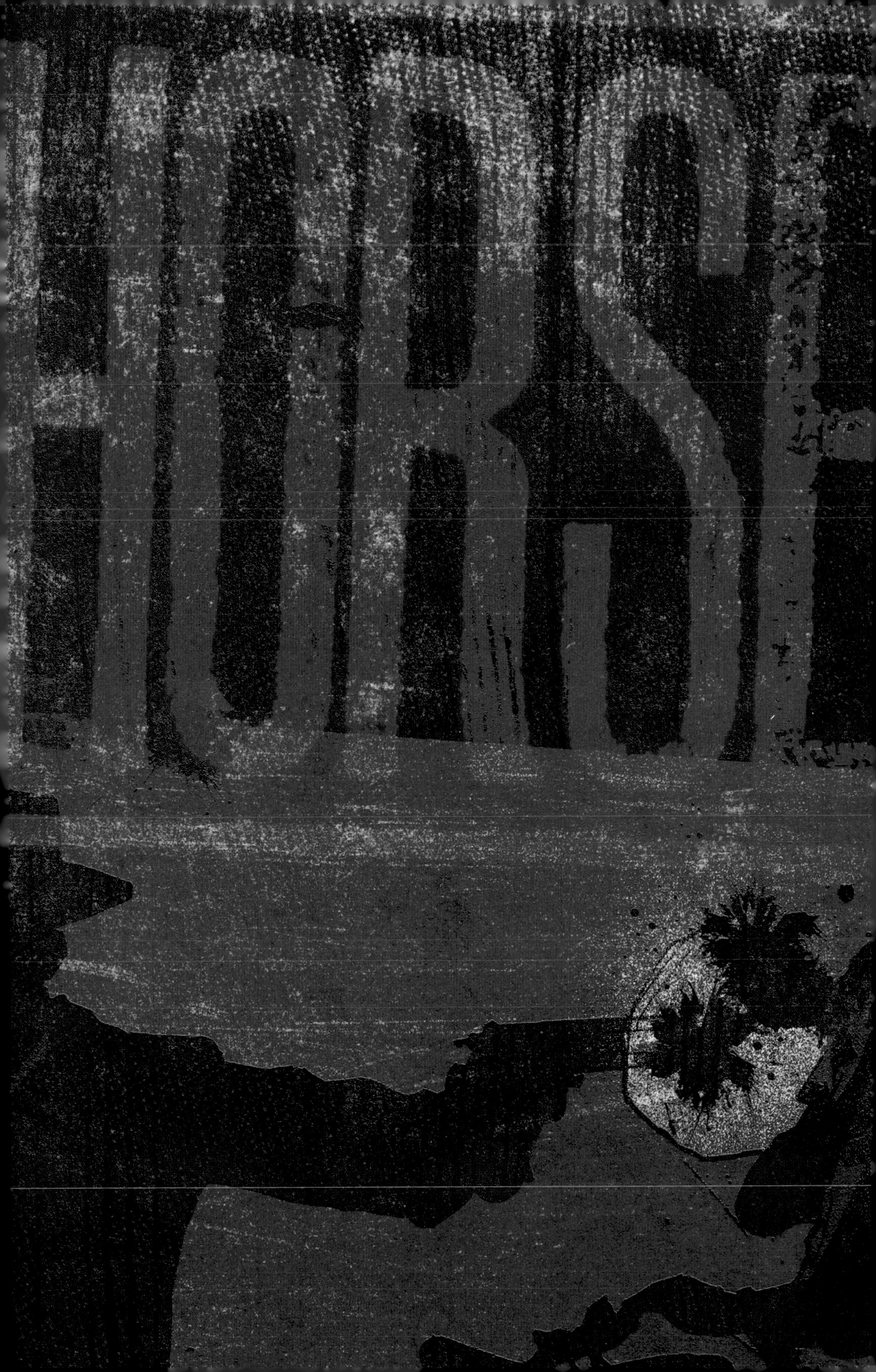

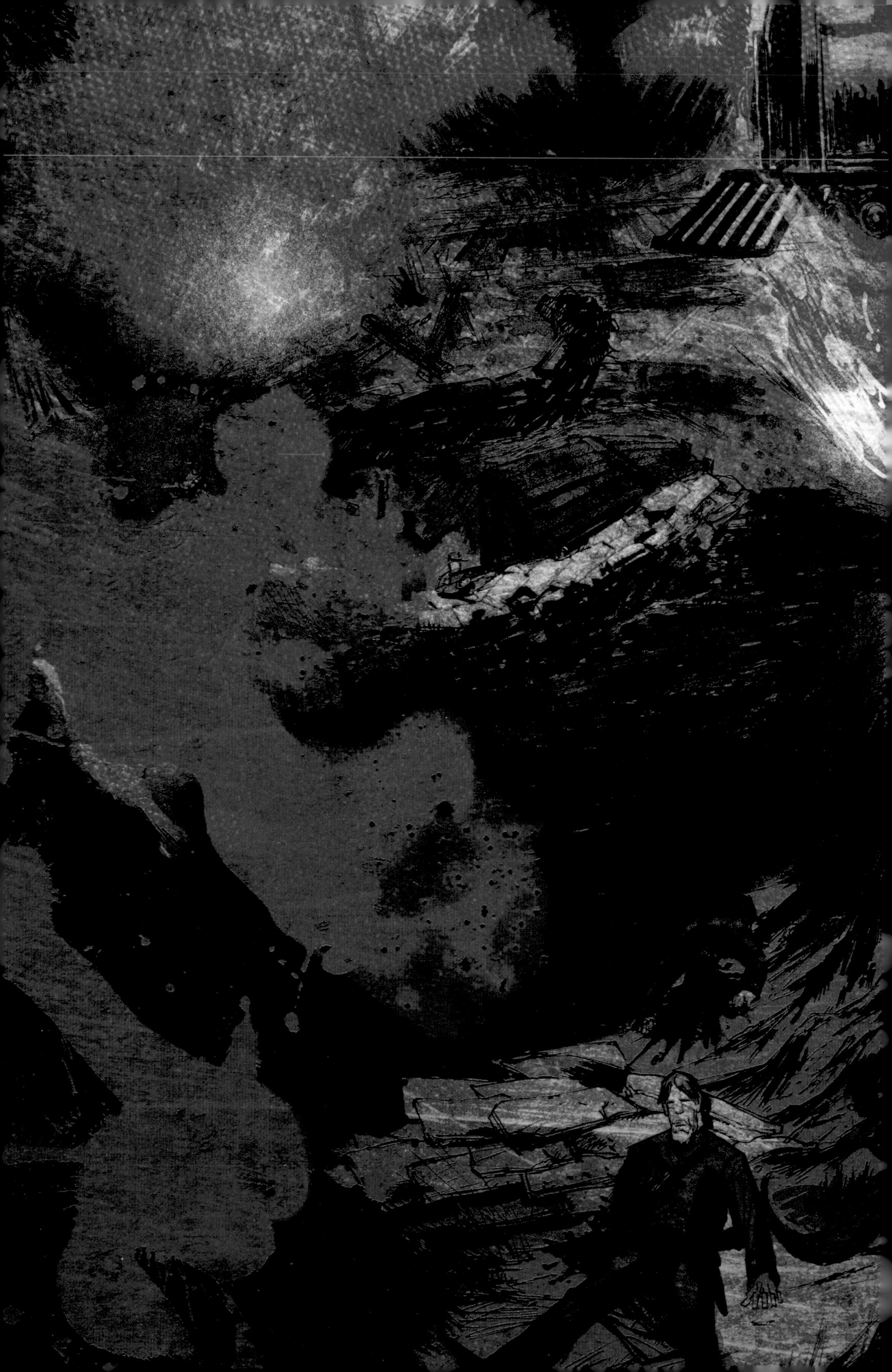